The Contemporary British Novel

Second Edition

York

RELATED TITLES FROM CONTINUUM:

British Fiction Today edited by Philip Tew and Rod Mengham

The *Continuum Contemporaries* series. For full details see
www.continuumbooks.com

THE CONTEMPORARY BRITISH NOVEL

Philip Tew

Continuum International Publishing Group

The Tower Building
11 York Road
London SE1 7NX

80 Maiden Lane
Suite 704
New York, NY 10038

First published 2004 by Continuum
Second edition published 2007

British Library Cataloguing-in-Publication Data
A catalogue record for this book is available from the British Library.

ISBN: 082649319X
9780826493194 (hardback)
0826493203
9780826493200 (paperback)

Library of Congress Cataloging-in-Publication Data
A catalog record for this book is available from the Library of Congress.

Typeset by YHT Ltd, London
Printed and bound in Great Britain by Cromwell Press Ltd, Trowbridge, Wiltshire

for
Bartha Ágnes

Acknowledgements

Others have contributed variously toward my efforts in preparing and completing this book, particularly in terms of responses to my academic papers, useful suggestions both in seminars and informal discussions and the recommendation of creative and critical texts. I must acknowledge Dr Richard J. Lane, with whom I planned a joint study in this field, which finally did not occur because of the exigencies of life in the late capitalist economy. His intellectual input and influence upon me have been immense, and his support seminal in the development of my career. Tristan Palmer at Athlone Press recognized potential in the original proposal, and after corporate mergers I commend the editorial staff at Continuum who 'inherited' the book, most especially Anthony Haynes for his timely enthusiasm for the project. The University of Central England awarded me sabbatical leave during its preparation, which allowed me to undertake much of the final research required, most especially since I had to delve into many areas and texts that I had not initially expected to cover.

Other individuals will recognize their own part, and I remain grateful for their willingness to offer various amounts of their time and effort in support of my efforts, perhaps two of the most precious of all 'commodities'. In this context I must mention:

Dr Tamas Benyei, University of Debrecen, Hungary; Steve Barfield; Dr Gavin Budge, UCE; the late Nigel 'Buzz' Burrell; Jonathan Coe; Jim Crace; Dr Bob Eaglestone, Royal Holloway, University of London; Eyvor Fogarty; Professor Andrew Gibson, Royal Holloway, University of London; Clifford Harper; Professor Dominic Head, Nottingham University; Suzy Joinson, British Council; David Kovacs; Dr Rod Mengham, Jesus College, University of Cambridge; Dr Ian Paterson, Queens' College, University of Cambridge; Dr David Roberts, UCE; Will Self; Professor Philip Smallwood, UCE; George Alister Tew; J. E. Tew; L. A. Tew; Barry Tomalin; Dr Lynn Wells, University of Regina,

Canada; Dr Wendy Wheeler, London Metropolitan University; Dr Glyn White, University of Central Lancashire; and Dr Philip Wright. Additionally credit is due to the staff of the Humanities Two, British Library; my postgraduate students at Debrecen, Szeged and UCE, particularly David, Nicola and Wasfi; fellow participants in various conferences and events organized by the British Council, ESSE, London Network for Modern Fiction Studies, NEMLA and numerous friends and acquaintances.

Regarding the second edition thanks to Jonathan Coe and Matt Thorne for suggestions as to suitable texts, and Gavin Budge for his invaluable help checking references when I was without a library while staying at Lake Balaton. Salutations to the organizers of the Novi Sad International Literary Festival 2006 who invited me to deliver a lecture on the post-9/11 traumatological novel that forms part of my additional sixth chapter. I am also indebted both to Sophie Cox for sterling work on the manuscript proofs and once again all of the London editorial team at Continuum for their highly professional efforts in support of my additions and revisions. My especial gratitude to my Serbian publisher, Jovan Zivlok, and translator Natasha Praticū.

Contents

Preface

Primary Intentions

This book features an area of increasing interest, several new phases of British literary fiction published since the mid-1970s. However, it is neither primarily a literary survey, nor is it a literary or critical introductory reader, but emphasizes textual, thematic and theoretical readings. The literary and critical texts featured, by the nature of such selection, are a partial, but suggestive view. They will not satisfy everyone, but I hope the arrangement is coherent and possesses its own kind of logic, unfolded in the text itself. The critical introduction and various chapters respond to key points (or debates) in literary and cultural criticism, attempting to both illustrate and offer a model of current aesthetic and cultural themes so as to extend our understanding of the novel beyond the 'textualizing' tendencies of post-structuralist and postmodernist exegesis that have dominated the literary field over the past twenty years. The fictions, texts and critical sources are selected to exemplify an idea of a transitional, changing textual culture, but one that is eventful and based within a complex historical reality in transition. The two transformations are in part related, as I hope to suggest, but not necessarily in parallel, that is they are not linked causally in a reductive manner.

The notion of a 'field' in this context is well established in the work of theorists such as Pierre Bourdieu and the post-structuralist, Pierre Macherey. Even Macherey introducing *The Object of Literature* (1990), in 'What is literature thinking about', situates texts historically; when he cannot contemplate 'Leaving aside genre distinctions and the evaluative criteria that conventionally divide the "literary" from what is not recognized as such' (7), his motivation is to dismiss narrow 'thematic' criticism in favour of recuperating from creative and critical texts: 'a form of thought which is neither philosophical nor literary because it is both and to evoke it in the same way that the structure of

successive "movements" can be evocative. It is dispersed and concentrated, diluted and condensed in texts whose fabrics and margins
were woven by the speculative issues that historically conditioned their
production and their reception' (9).

Importantly my present study contextualizes key thematic issues
ideologically and historically; not by offering a textual survey since for
many reasons, including the volume of textual production, such a
procedure would be methodologically fraught, if not invalid. Since all
critical interventions are by nature always far from straightforward and
are not undertaken within either given (a priori) or even stable conditions, one cannot simply assume the validity of one's critical procedure. Any unmediated description would be fraught. And because
recent criticism was driven by certain textualizing obsessions, which in
my view distort the interpretative, descriptive and analytical processes
required to consider texts, this preface and the critical introduction
offer key methodological suggestions, opposing such critiques that
prioritize the linguistic and the self-referential as a closed system.
However, this is not a reductive objectivizing liberal humanist account
in the Arnoldian-Leavisite manner.

Outline of Chapters

As to specific contents, together my first two chapters analyse what I
regard as key major critical and aesthetic issues that help situate
contemporary British fiction since the mid-1970s within larger critical,
cultural, and literary debates. The basis for this periodization makes up
part of my critical endeavour, which I will not pre-empt. The remaining
chapters feature the themes outlined above, exploring them textually,
critically and conceptually. The critical introduction discusses theoretical and critical strategies in this light; the first chapter contextualizes
the debates concerning the definition of 'Britishness' and the understanding of current contemporary British scene, a globalized locality,
within a larger set of referents including historical conditions.

These initial chapters address the shibboleths of intellectual British
culture, from the traditional to the newly inscribed canons. I address
specifically the commitment to textualizing reality and propounding
the relativism that constitutes a large part of postmodern thought (an
irrealist position philosophically). All knowledge is an incomplete
picture of the world. Nevertheless, I offer a certain internal coherence
of major themes and a theoretical notion of a 'reality principle', whilst
not either assuming a closed rational system or alternatively the kind of
reflexivity of any of the closed styles of reading that preclude implicitly
an appeal to a range of literary-critical practices. This follows Pierre
Bourdieu's notion of the fictional narrative and structure – under-

pinning his exposition of the key sociological basis of Gustave Flaubert's *Sentimental Education* discussed in the 'Prologue' to *The Rules of Art: Genesis and Structure of the Literary Field* (1992) – that leads to an 'analysis of the book [that] ought to allow us to take advantage of the properties of literary discourse, such as its capacity to reveal while veiling, or to produce a de-realizing "reality effect" ' (4).

Chapter Two, 'The Fall and Rise of the Middle Classes', addresses the middle-class identifications of the majority of post-war literary critics and many writers, using this to demonstrate the need for a vocabulary within which one can identify the conditions for both placing and contextualizing the contemporary within its own coherent terms. An interrogation of the reflexivity of the traditional middle classes has become an aesthetic consciousness for the British novel, part of the review of the dimensions of a British culture and an awareness that contributes to the literary and critical inflection of hybridity considered in my fifth chapter, 'Multiplicities and Hybridity'. Chapter Three, 'Spaces and Styles – Urban Identities', considers the importance of defining urban cultural concerns in the contemporary novel, demonstrating how often contending narratives, in describing the social and literal space, appropriate and define its cultural relevance. If the contemporary novel has done anything consistently since the mid-1970s it has been to radicalize traditional understandings of the late capitalist cityscape and urban environment. In contrast to its abjectification of an increasingly alienated and commodified Thatcherite city, critiqued within a range of novels considered here, new voices have emerged and cartographized the complexity and heterogeneity of urban existence. The fracturing and collapse of Thatcher's vision as recession hit the nation accelerated these nodes of disillusionment. Scenes of suburban and of provincial city life, and particularly of immigrant and working-class cultures, emerged from this malaise that seemed focused most particularly on the capital and its postmodern 'knowingness'. Chapter Four, 'The Past and the Present', considers closely the essential importance and development of mythic thought and historical awareness and reflection that has been so dominant during the period under consideration. Drawing on the work of Ernst Cassirer to demonstrate the intuitive and archetypal thought that such narratives represent, it situates these concepts in key literary texts, where a resistance to varieties of constraining and dogmatic models of interpretation can be negated. Postmodernism, the reductively rational and the dominance of the scientific are diffused through evoking a range of mythopoeic and historical subversions. In fact this emphasis reasserts a characteristic found in modernism and its experimental consciousness, a regressive need, as Michael Bell (1999) explores in 'The Metaphysics of Modernism: Aesthetic Myth and the Myth of the Aesthetic': 'Modernist mythopoeia, rather than the creation of "new" myth, is the recognition that we cannot *but* live mythopoeically, whether consciously or not. Myth is modernity's form of philosophical self-knowledge' (240).

In Chapter Five, 'Multiplicities and Hybridity', drawing on the preceding work, I examine the notion of hybridity that emerged in postcolonial studies, and its complex and adaptive sense of always contending cultures and individualities can bring about a reading of a new Britishness that absorbs much of the old. This consciousness is active in the literary scene, part of a renewed radicalization of the novel, as I hope to demonstrate, and this is perhaps best epitomized by the huge success and popularity of Zadie Smith's *White Teeth* (2000), a newly 'canonical' academic text within less than two years of publication. It perhaps represents the *Lucky Jim* (1954) for our times, very comic, observational, hybrid, complex and decentred as well as supplementing Kingsley Amis's cultural interrogation with both a wider class and a gendered view. Its density and sentimental commitment to its range of characters make it quasi-Dickensian in mood. However, the cultural differences, rather than the generic differences or similarities, between the two texts are most telling, serving almost like two snapshots of a similar place evoking the dimensions of historical and social change. As this chapter demonstrates, this revision of cultural identification emerges from many places and from a range of subjects, deepening the narrative engagement with a hybrid and ever-changing social and historical landscape. Chapter Six, 'The Post-Millennial, 9/11 and the Traumatological', is considered below, but primarily outlines the underlying sense of collective trauma and uncertainty that appears foundational to the early twenty-first-century aesthetic.

Context and Methodology

In criticism one ought to avoid what Bourdieu would describe as the 'space of possibles'. In his introduction to *The Novel Today: Contemporary Writers on Modern Fiction* (1977a) Malcolm Bradbury defines elements of the novel that seem perpetually to be the subject of critical contention, concerning the 'polar distinctions that have long been made – between, on the one hand, the novel's propensity toward realism, social documentation and interrelation with historical events and movements, and on the other with its propensity toward form, fictionality, and reflexive self-examination' (8). We are shifting from an overemphasis on the second cluster of characteristics or propensities. In redressing this balance I must stress that formal and generic elements are not inconsequential and can balance other sociological and 'meta-realist' readings.

Of course like so many textual 'beginnings' this preface is more of an ending, a review of the process undertaken to produce the chapters that follow. One early thought was an incredulity concerning the populist idea among many postgraduate students that one could not 'avow' or describe anything as 'British', as if the terminology itself were tainted by the sins of the past, some cultural guilt of empire. Recent literary-critical practice appears to challenge many cultural norms, but often in a monolithic assumption of a singular, imperial English experience and of the affiliation of the populace to the supposed and assumed cultural norms, which is highly problematic. Some criticism is disturbing. In all seriousness I find it offensive that Bill Ashcroft, Gareth Griffiths and Helen Tiffin in *The Empire Writes Back: Theory and Practice in Post-Colonial Literatures* (2002; 2nd edition) can comment 'Through the literary canon, the body of British texts which all too frequently still acts as a touchstone of taste and value, and through RS-English (Received Standard English), which asserts the English of south-east England as a universal norm, the weight of antiquity continues to dominate cultural production in much of the colonial world' (7). Two responses. First, the bulk of cultural production in the British Isles, the supposedly colonial world – until fairly recently that is – almost entirely excluded the working classes. Second, Ashcroft, Griffiths and Tiffin might note that numerically considered (and again this is significant in class terms and the assumptions they make concerning this First World set of relations) the spoken English of the south-east is not and never has been RS-English, which is a construct and legacy of a very small elite. Such assumptions are very revealing of an implicit further intellectualization of subtle prejudices held by the intellectual class (one that is wider than simply assumptions concerning language and its cultural significance). This is returned to in this study at certain points. In my experience snobbishness and elitism are alive and well in Britain even among the apparently 'radical' element of the intellectual and political classes. Roy Bhaskar charts as a historical response the exclusion of the working classes from the philosophical discourse of modernity in *Reflections on Meta-Reality: Transcendence, Emancipation and Everyday Life* (2002). Neither the reductive materialism of his 'high-modernists' nor his 'post-modernists' in their tendencies toward relativism and linguisticism expressing an increasingly negative reflexivity acquire any purchase on the nuances and differentiations within the subtle experiences of inhabiting a prejudicially socialized identity outside of the 'repressed so-called "minority interests", which are often in the majority of course, throughout the world', of identity politics (35).

Promisingly there has been a shift in the social practices and experiences reflected in fictional output toward a less narrow view of culture. For fiction and culture more generally, I also see as progressive informed postcolonial critiques, notions of radical hybridity, and of a revived class consciousness. Chapter Five considers aspects of a literary hybridization with its changing culture, its charting of the transitions that make up life, and its insistence on the ongoing relevance to 'real' life of prose fiction, however fantastical or grotesque its intentions, formal characteristics or the generic traditions which such writing might evoke. The themes and structure are cultural inscriptions; they acquire sociological density through metaphor, characterization, allegory, interpretative models inherent in the text and so forth.

After all of the above, concerned as it is primarily with the critical, let me add that this book remains an expression of my fascination with the intriguing dynamics of creativity and its aesthetic reflections of cultural realities and transformations. Perhaps fortunately for both readers and academics, this ontological transformation is an ongoing process. Thankfully, even criticism is a living process, part of the elusiveness and immense possibility of the textual, and yet ironically such inscription militates against such realities. Paying attention both to reality and to the text ought to be the crux of the exegetical urge, together with a compulsion to account for something of the narratives we scrutinize in terms of their specific and always complex relations to the world, to that 'meta-reality' that constitutes ontology. Fiction in recent years seems to be edging toward a recovery of this awareness that Bhaskar in *Reflections on Meta-Reality* describes as viewing and dealing with the world from a 'ground-state' merged with intuitiveness (17), from the objective which understands itself – for we are within it and so constituted – as constituted universally through commonality, mediated by specifics and 'the irreducibility of an essential uniqueness' within 'geo-historical trajectories' together all understood dialectically (47). This understanding – informed by his and others' objections to the excesses of postmodern theory – represents a great part of the foundation for my ongoing critical interventions. As I say in 'Reconsidering Literary Interpretation' (2001b),

All thoughts, all theories, are about something. All perceptions are of something. All texts have referents. These exist independently of our perceptions, thoughts and theories. All texts involve such thinking about our thinking about reality. This is so, however diffuse or complex the process becomes in the narrative and its relationship with the life-world. (202)

However, as I concede, I cannot encapsulate here all of the answers to the multiplicity of questions concerning the relationship of literariness and reality. I hope I might disturb current critical shibboleths and contribute to the lively debate over what constitutes the contemporary, the cultural and the fictional. I perceive a profound change in the literary-cultural mood of new writing, but this is not to suggest that the entire past has been abandoned, as with the many Woolfian influences to which I draw attention. Jeanette Winterson, for instance, echoes Woolf's androgyny and complex relation with the real in most of her work, but most explicitly so with the historical setting and adrogynous themes in *Sexing the Cherry* (1989) where the influence of *Orlando* (1928) is strongly evident. And yet there is something determinedly contemporaneous and different in Winterson's narrative, as its focus lies elsewhere than Woolf's among the lower classes so as to revoke their historical invisibility, for as Jordan reflects, one might discover a parallel between the social inscription of a life such as his own compelled toward the heterogeneity of the city streets of London and the hidden lives Greeks record in invisible ink. 'I discovered that my own life was written invisibly, was squashed between the facts [...]' (10).

Millennial Fiction

British fiction of the new millennium appeared to be marked initially by dark and yet whimsical novels, some looking back to the recent past, narratives recalling the 1970s and 1980s as a time of cultural malaise and personal disintegration. The notion of the historical and the transformational was prominent, typified by such novels as Will Self's *Dorian* (2002), and Tim Lott's *Rumours of a Hurricane* (2002). In *Dorian* survivors among the influential, the fashionable and the wealthy who overcame and yet are defined by their self-obsession with their own excesses of the 1980s are confronted by two symbolic 'landmark' deaths in the 1990s, the murder of Gianni Versace in Miami (273), and subsequently the death of his client, Princess Diana, in Paris. Dorian seems undermined by the apparent impossibility of the latter's demise, someone he knew, whereas his aristocratic friend, Henry Wotton, senses in her expiration a mythic potential. The narrative concludes that 'This is one of those public events that confirms that history is nothing more or less than the confused wet dream of humanity yoked to its own adolescent erotic fantasies' (274). In Lott's novel the narrator summarizes the contradictory mood of the late 1970s as the sense of the contemporary was about to change. 'Inflation, decimalization, the three-day week, industrial chaos, oil-price hikes, Irish terrorists [...] the age is replete, like all ages are, with weird multiplicities of denial' (15). In the following Thatcher years Charlie, a working-class Londoner with simple ambitions, is faced with his multiple failings as the world around him transforms. Initially prosperous as a printer, he loses his job, his wife, and his certainties and eventually he dies alone. During this process he undergoes a cultural humiliation and finally 'Charlie cannot come back, for he is no longer there. His stock and his shame have cracked open the unstable matter of what is left of his life, producing fission. Black energy pours out; he is lost, knows nothing' (374).

Although still focused on the intensity of individual existential fear and chaos, both of the above fictions intimate forcefully that a broad historical, cultural and natural evolution occurs constantly before our eyes whether we recognize it or not, for, as B. S. Johnson says in *Aren't You Rather Young to be Writing Your Memoirs?* (1973), 'Whether or not it can be demonstrated that all is chaos, certainly all is change' (17). Moreover, at certain times it appears as if that process of transformation becomes both more accelerated and seemingly chaotic than is usually the case. There emerges an aesthetic economy of exceptionality. Mostly we know this when our illusory sense of ordered sequences is fundamentally disturbed, thwarting what Johnson in *Albert Angelo* (1964) calls 'the process of imposing the pattern, of holding back the chaos' (133).

9/11: The Impact

Naturally enough such imposed patterns do fall apart, sometimes dramatically. Having completed many of the research notes that would later evolve into the first edition of this book, on 11 September 2001 I cycled to the British Library to continue my research, just as without warning Al Qaeda attacked the World Trade Center in New York, an event afterwards referred to as 9/11. Before I entered the building someone told me of the first plane crash and immediately I returned home to watch the rest of this remarkable drama played out on my television screen from the increasing discomfort of my armchair. By the end of that day one knew that the world was in a spin, and that our few remaining certainties were shaken in the ontological equivalent of a child's kaleidoscope. This was generally the judgement of my generation despite having lived through various phases of IRA mainland bombings, thus becoming somewhat inured to public displays of violence and mayhem. And yet to this day online footage of the moment of the impacts upon and the collapse of the World Trade Center buildings still sustains the power to shock and disturb, unless of course one's underlying ideological agenda is fundamentally solipsistic, or exceedingly partial and fundamentally illiberal.

This event was no deconstructive linguistic attack, nor a post-modern decentring, although many were to claim these were tangentially contributory factors. Quite unlike traditional notions of what Ruth Leys in *Trauma: A Genealogy* (2000) calls 'the original trauma-togenic event' (298) which is often considered elusive, 9/11 still seems indelible and available for vivid recollection, as if uncannily and almost fearfully so. As Fred Halliday says in *Two Hours that Shook the World* (2002), 9/11 achieved global impact after 'The explosions were watched, with incredulity and fear, across the world' (24). Britain was no exception. Everyone I knew was compelled to follow the television images of both that disaster and its consequences. We were affected by this unique act that drew its inspiration from a grandiose Situationist sensibility and became what Halliday describes as a truly anarchic '"propaganda of the deed," an iconic destruction against the clear blue sky, and an event that, at one stroke, launches a roller-coaster of grief, fear and uncertainty' (32).

Responses to 9/11

Clearly during that winter the impact of 9/11 on one's psyche was profound, but these events and their aftermath were far too proximate for any sustained effect upon the aesthetic disposition of the contemporary literary British novel, although some novels like Iain Banks's polemical fiction, *Dead Air* (2002), did incorporate certain aspects of the event. However, rather than evoking a mood of foreboding and unease, the novel is more concerned with the involvement of maverick, socialist, radio 'shock-jock', Ken Nott with threatening gangsters. Although a party with which the novel opens ends with news of the collapse of the Twin Towers, these events remain peripheral to the intricacies of the plot. In my subsequent revisions and redrafting of the first edition of this book I decided not to reflect upon 9/11. Rather I would leave it to novelists who could respond creatively, and given that in 2002 there were too few literary responses, truth to be told I was nervous of approaching such a momentous topic polemically and perhaps ill-advisedly.

Now in 2006, this book has been adopted on numerous courses in very many countries, and has been translated into Serbian by Natasha Praticū for publication in 2006 by Svetovi Press in Novi Sad, Serbia. It is now just past the fifth anniversary of 9/11, and the literary *Zeitgeist* appears to have shifted in many subtle ways. The opportunity of a revised edition of my book allows me specifically to explore the literary impact of 9/11 largely in an additional chapter, which argues for a perspectival transformation in much new fiction. For this I adopt the term 'traumatological' to describe an emerging aesthetic of cultural threat and upheaval, a collective economy of repetition and symbolic return similar to that described by Cathy Caruth in *Unclaimed Experience: Trauma, Narrative, and History* (1996): 'History is to be understood as the history of a trauma, it is a history that is experienced as the endless attempt to assume one's survival as one's own' (64). Society finds almost incommensurable the attempt to reconcile both the underlying persistent threat and what Caruth calls the self's 'incomprehensibility of survival' (64). It is in this context that either explicitly or implicitly much recent fiction senses and articulates a sense of a collective wound and injury as part of its essential narrative sensibility, unsurprisingly since as Jeffrey C. Alexander, in 'Toward a Theory of Cultural Trauma', notes 'Cultural trauma occurs when members of a collectivity feel they have been subjected to a horrendous event that leaves indelible marks upon their group consciousness, marking their memories forever and changing their future identity in fundamental and irrevocable ways (1).

Further post-9/11 events have confirmed a new range of uncertainties, somewhat akin to the always underlying consciousness at the height of the Cold War when fear of nuclear extinction shaped our very dreams (to which I can testify from direct personal experience having lived through the Cuban Missile Crisis as a child aware of the threat of these events). As Ana Douglass and Thomas A. Vogler comment in the introduction to their collection, *Witness and Memory: The Discourse of Trauma* (2003), 'It would seem that in our post-9/11 state, we are being conditioned by threats of terror and a pseudo "war" to exist in a similar state of perpetual fear' (48). A troubled fractured aesthetic seems inevitable, as discussed in the additional sixth chapter, 'The Post-millennial, 9/11 and the Traumatological'. Of course its selection of novels is limited by available space, and a traumatological aesthetic can be identified in a range of other novels.

Further Fictional Responses

Among such excluded novels are: Tim Binding's *Man Overboard* (2005) concerned with real-life Second World War hero, pioneering frogman Commander Lionel Crabb, who disappeared allegedly while spying for MI6, investigating the hull of the Soviet warship, whose narrative centre is Crabb's rootless life, traumatized as he is by both the excitement of and his survival during the war; he is curiously both an anachronistic and yet a thoroughly modern image, finally retired from training Russian divers, remembering as he approaches death behind the Iron Curtain the moment when he is shown pictures of first his own grave inscribed by his mother and of second his lover, Pat, sustaining the novel's theme of the trauma of historical loss and dislocation; James Kelman's *You Have to be Careful in the Land of the Free* (2004) considers sardonically America's closed perspective and the ruminations of a US-based Scots former airport security worker, Jeremiah, as he encounters an increasingly 'neo-con', reactionary post-9/11 America; Tim Lott's *The Seymour Tapes* (2005) is concerned with the intrusive nature of contemporary surveillance culture and its exploitation by the intended victim's spouse, the wife of Dr Alex Seymour who apparently provokes the murder of her husband; and Graham Joyce's *The Facts of Life* (2003), the story of Cassie Vine, her mother Martha, and the abutment of the spirit world, Dunkirk and the bombing of their home city, Coventry, decimated by German air raids, but from which a child emerges after Cassie's spiritualist interventions with a newly deceased virginal youth. In several bars prior to returning to Scotland Kelman's narrator, Jeremiah, a gambler and drinker, trawls his alcoholic life and ruminates over life, work, and the loss of his partner and child. He comments on the changing times, 'I have opinions, everybody has opinions, maist people anyway. I speak as one myself, a person. I am aware that some folks are executed or not executed, tortured or not tortured, deported or whatnot. I can only say what I feel and I feel that nowadays there is very little escape, naybody can be outside the system, there is nay room for hermits in the 21st century, the days of the mystical stargazers are so to speak o'er. There are singular liberties to which folks arenay privy in this world but liberty is one thing, security another' (157). Security, his profession, is impinging on freedom, but his commentary upon American culture questions the possibility of freedom in this land in which it is so volubly proclaimed. Through Jeremiah, Kelman intimates his adoption of the quotidian and his rejection of the underlying relativism of the preceding age.

Real life may resemble reality.
Real life is reality.
Not necessarily. It is a debatable point.
Naw it isnay. Real life has to be reality, what the hell else could it be! Even if it is a fucking nightmare, it is still reality. (187)

It is here that the public world and his private life converge, making him a figure of this uncertain new age.

In *Kingdom Come* (2006), J. G. Ballard – who arguably sensed and incorporated into his earlier fiction the traumatological cultural conditions inherent in the crises of the period from the 1970s – proposes the distinct possibility of a regressive future, replicating the conditions of conflict underlying the great religions, these 'Vast systems of psychopathic delusion that murdered millions, launched crusades and

founded empires. A great religion spells danger. Today people are
desperate to believe, but they can only reach God through psycho-
pathology' (104). It may well be that within our readings of the
traumatological we encounter the tenor of a new emergent British
post-millennial, post-9/11 literary culture, or one distinct phase of such
an evolving aesthetic sensibility. Time will tell. Hopefully as one ages,
one learns caution and to expect the unexpected, especially as it
remains difficult to pin down literary and cultural formations as they
happen. It is in such a context that the sixth chapter's analysis of the
post-millennial fictional aesthetic should be situated and understood,
in terms of its provisionality.

CRITICAL INTRODUCTION

Critiquing Contemporary Fiction

KEY THEMES
Countering Postmodernism • Englishness • Identity / Identities • Literariness /
The Nature of Fiction • Literary-cultural relations • Realism and Meta-realism

KEY TEXTS

Amis, Martin *The Information*
Blincoe, Nicholas and Thorne, Matt
  (eds) *All Hail the New Puritans*
Byatt, A. S. *Possession / The
  Biographer's Tale*
Coe, Jonathan *The Dwarves of Death /
  The House of Sleep*

Freud, Esther *Hideous Kinky*
Kelman, James, *et al. Lean Tales*
Kureishi, Hanif *Gabriel's Gift*
Rushdie, Salman *The Satanic Verses*
Self, Will *Dorian: An Imitation*
Self, Will *Junk Mail*

Dominant Cultural Themes

This study focuses upon selected contemporary 'literary' novels,
grouped thematically to address key themes that characterize a 'new
wave' of British writing emerging from the mid-1970s. Essentially I
have chosen texts to exemplify the cultural codes and creative
hybridity characteristic of this period. The dominant cultural themes
are variously: British identity, the explicit notion of a culture in
transition, late-capitalist or 'Thatcherized' urban spaces, the use of the
mythopoeic and hybridity as renewing literary responses to such conditions, and finally a 'traumatological' uncertainty. All of the following
chapters are concerned with complex identities and their cultural
significations. As Kevin Davey writes in *English Imaginaries: Six Studies
in Anglo-British Modernity* (1999)

> An identity is an unstable, aspirational point of identification, an
> attempt to position oneself, or construct a group – in relation to
> others – through ever-changing representations of a shared or
> distinguished culture, history, memory or set of utopic longings.
> [...] Notions of identity, authenticity, essence, where they do
> gain a footing, have to be created, buttressed, recreated. (7)

At least broadly, fiction articulates such aspects of culture, both authorially, but also through character, thematically and in terms of plot detail, drawing together a series of intersecting, overlapping relations. Without displacing or negating Davey's representational interpretation, it seems wise to recollect that such identities are historically situated in quotidian cultural practice, arguably more stubbornly concrete than 'creation' and 'recreation' might suggest. Although Davey concludes that for the young 'Anglo-British' national identity is increasingly less important (18), certainly his own analysis itself and those of the 'critical intellectuals' he alludes to working from the 1980s onward (16) demonstrate that creatively and culturally both the nature and the deconstruction of the overarching Britishness that concealed a heterogeneous reality (6) is nevertheless compelling and ongoing. The periodization and choices of texts in this present study exemplify something of the relationship of these key themes to the literary-critical field, and by presenting such sources as an ensemble it is hoped together they will reflect a contemporary culture that is aware that both the national and the intellectual landscape undergoes constant transformation.

Literature can reflect both literally and symbolically elements of the past that signify quite how the culture becomes transitional, where even recent post-war co-ordinates are becoming more rapidly outdated, increasingly anachronistic, and yet persistent. Jonathan Coe in *The Dwarves of Death* (1990) describes a run-down old car which might well serve as a symbol for the national condition. 'Chester drove a 1973 Marina, orange. The sidelights didn't work and the heating was broken and there was something wrong with third gear, and yet somehow (like its owner) it inspired trust in spite of appearances. You knew that one day it was going to let you down, badly let you down, but perversely you continued to rely on it' (4). For those that do not remember, the Marina was a badly styled model from British Leyland, launched in the 1970s when this nationalized industry seemed to exemplify the past certainties of the post-war settlement and its subsequent failures for which the trades unions and skilled working class were held to be responsible. Coe's observation reflects a growing creative recognition that during the 1970s and into the 1980s Britain had transformed itself and was not simply a continuation of post-war conditions. Davey comments 'After many centuries, the Anglo-British are beginning to recognise their diasporic and contingent nature. As they acknowledge that their strategies of inclusion may no longer be effective for a range of regional and national identities, and that their imaginary exclusion and abjection of black and European Others is no longer sustainable, boundaries which were based on former identifications and differentiations are dissolving' (10). This present study in part questions both the literary and critical effects, and, the critical assumptions related to such changing conditions. For instance, many critics still define fiction primarily in terms of the legacies of empire, a view I will interrogate both textually and historically.

John Brannigan writes in *Orwell to the Present: Literature in England 1945–2000* (2003) of Salman Rushdie's novel *The Satanic Verses* (1988) that

> like much contemporary fiction of the city, [it] presents a mal-
> leable, ineffable and infinitely imaginable city, available to be
> troped and tropicalized over and over again. London is a centre
> only in its capacity for drawing into itself the stories and images of
> its diverse, migrant population, and in giving expression to the
> effects of diaspora, dislocation, cultural hybridity and diffusion.
> (198)

Dominic Head comments in more general terms in *The Cambridge Introduction to Modern British Fiction, 1950–2000* (2002) 'The election of Margaret Thatcher as Prime Minister in 1979 signalled the definite end of post-war consensus. The policies of Thatcherism attacked con-sensus politics on every front' (30). Literature responded, as one might expect, variously to the emergent conditions, and yet significantly the critical notions of form and evaluation remain, for instance under-pinning Ian Jack's appeal to such implicit categories in his 'Introduction' to *Granta 81: Best of Young British Novelists 2003* (2003b) where he assumes an intuitive sense of literariness. 'The "literary novel" isn't an easy thing to define; you know it when you see it' (11).

The Nature of (Contemporary) Fiction

Importantly, the exact nature of the literariness of texts appears more elusive, given the kind of blurring of genres suggested by Martin Amis in *The Information* (1995) when the narrator attempts to relate them in a classical tradition to the seasons. The narrator thinks of this appeal to apparent certainties and reflects, 'We keep waiting for something to go wrong with the seasons. Something has already gone wrong with the genres. They have all bled into one another. Decorum is no longer observed' (53). In fact, it seems to me that both literariness and generic distinction in fictional narrative are aspects essentially expressive of the creative and cultural struggles Pierre Bourdieu describes in *The Field of Cultural Production: Essays on Art and Lit-erature* (1993) since like all aesthetic acts that function according to an economy of belief, 'The work of art is an object which exists as such only by virtue of the (collective) belief which knows and acknowledges it as a work of art' (35). Moreover, as Bourdieu adds much later 'The artistic field is a *universe of* belief. Cultural production distinguishes itself from the production of the most common objects in that it must produce not only the object in its materiality, but also the value of the object, that is, the recognition of artistic legitimacy' (164). Jack (2003b) in fact engages upon such a process in his introduction, and by soliciting and selecting 'the most interesting, original writers' (11) in what he describes as the 'artistically ambitious work of fiction' (11). Hence he sustains certain distinctions and beliefs. I engage upon a similar process of selection, but engage with the texts thematically so as to demonstrate at least at some level that among recurrent cultural and creative elements one may identify common authorial practices. Importantly an obvious truth alluded to in Jack's apparently off-hand remark above is his assumption that we engage with fiction perceptually, and as Matt Thorne comments in his joint 'Introduction: The Pledge' written with Nicholas Blincoe in the style of a dialogue for the collection *All Hail the New Puritans* (2001a) 'I think we've moved through the excitement of seeing old genres subverted, reinvented and modernised. The challenge now is working out what from this intellectual exercise remains useful to us. We can still write from experience; it is just that our experience has been enriched by modern culture's constantly changing hall of mirrors' (xi). This study is concerned with the experiential, the kind that Thorne outlines both in terms of fiction, but also in terms of criticism itself. It seeks to move beyond postmodernism's obsessions with a textualizing critique. Significantly, Blincoe's contribution to this collection, 'Short Guide to Games Theory' (2001b), integrates both the aleatory and ludic in a world of conventions and practices, in the sociological and legal context of 'nerds' and the mundane. The introduction to the *New Puritans* collection rejects experimentation (viii), questions the priority and emphasis in the literary field of genre, calling for a rupturing of genre expectations (x) and additionally demands writing from experience (xi). Although not strictly antithetical to 'postmodernism' its stated ambitions call for both the recognizable and contemporary 'ethics' (xvi) which signify a movement from heterogeneity and a deconstructive decentring toward apprehensible meaning. As I will explore in parallel to fictional trajectories, criticism is finally moving in a similar direction.

The 'New Puritan' evocation of the experiential and of texts 'as fragments of time' (xiv), and its insistence on contemporaneity is instructive. To engage with a text including fictional ones offers multiple experiences, and not all of them textual. That I can physically hold and view a text to consider its implications (as the reader will be able to do with the text produced from the manuscript I am revising currently on a computer screen) is itself testament to these other ontological aspects beyond its formal ones to which the text relates in complex ways. To textualize this sense is neither to reduce the realm of the sign nor simply to concede the primacy of the reflexive and the postmodern. Dora Chance, the narrator of Angela Carter's *Wise Children* (1991), writes after seeing a film version of *A Midsummer Night's Dream* in which she acted. 'I understood the thing I'd never grasped back in those days, when I was young, before I lived in history. When I was young, I'd wanted to be ephemeral, I'd wanted the moment, to live in just the glorious moment, the rush of blood, the applause. Pluck the day. Eat the peach. Tomorrow never comes. But, oh yes, tomorrow *does* come all right, and when it comes it lasts a bloody long time, I can tell you' (125). The ephemeral may be elusive, but like the celluloid record of the past that persists and shocks Dora, so does the literary often in surprising interpretative ways. As I will elaborate in my critique texts are implicated in the nature of language utterances that persist (in either a material fashion or perhaps even in their survival in the human memory) at least in part in an ongoing referential fashion. Unfortunately for many academics this seems to have become a controversial position.

In recent British writing a modulation of history and reworking of mythic structures has synthesized a creative response that both accedes to literary-critical experiments, to prior traditions, and yet allows a mode of referentiality that inscribes something of what Cassirer describes in *The Philosophy of Symbolic Forms, Volume 4: The Metaphysics of Symbolic Forms*[1] (1996) as the response to outer experience. Firstly there is required a synthesis of 'uncritical, undifferentiated acceptance of the expressive function. It is taken to be the very expression of "reality," that is "mythic" reality' (122) with a recognition that

> Language does not merely contain signs or designations for a being; rather, language is a form of being itself. The meaning which the miracle of language has is not that it refers to a being, but that it *is* a being. We may not, however, here interpret this being as a kind of thing; rather, we must take it as determinative of things. (82)

Yet Cassirer mediates this by talking of

> the intellectual bond that ties language to the figurative arts and creates a kind of 'union' between them. This union is only imperfectly recognized if we begin with the expressive function

alone, if we grasp only the lyrical, expressive aspect of language and art. The true foundation, the legitimation, of this union is found only if we understand both language and art as basic ways of objectification, of raising consciousness to the level of seeing objects. This raising is in the end possible only when the 'discursive' thinking in language and the 'intuitive' activity of artistic seeing and creating interact so as to weave the cloak of 'reality.' (83–4)

This may represent a cultural response to both an overburdening rationality and the deconstructive ambitions of the postmodern age. As Cassirer indicates, in *The Philosophy of Symbolic Forms, Volume 2: Mythical Thought*[2] (1955b), myth suggests its own precedence, to and underpinning of, discursive thought (69), and hence at least fictionally it may sustain myth's original concept of a materiality less subject both to causality (69) and to emphasizing uniqueness and an intuitiveness of action as opposed to post-enlightenment rationalizing constraints on materialism (48–9). The novelistic turn to myth and an apparently non-teleological historiography is rooted in these characteristics far more than any ersatz metafictional or postmodern consciousness, as I will describe in my fourth and fifth chapters. Such creativity based on the mythopoeic combines the experiential, the emotional and the primordial, elements characterizing this new wave of fiction. Both the postmodern dismissal of universalizing traditional critiques and its declaration of indeterminacy as profound is seductive, but as Georges Bataille reminds us in beginning *the unfinished system of nonknowledge* (2001): 'It is a banality to claim that there is a fundamental difficulty in human communication. And it is not hard to recognize in advance that this difficulty is partially irreducible' (5). Although postmodernism depends upon emphasizing a reflexive, closed system of language reference and a crisis of knowledge, as most novelists know at least intuitively, meaning and external reference both persist. Angus Wilson in 'The View from the 1950s' (1961) makes a salient point concerning notions of specific historical forces representing any particular moral or social crisis that is any more fundamental than those in the past, a false foregrounding of immediacy and contemporaneity.

It seems sometimes to have been assumed by the disciples of Leavis, as indeed by many of the New Critics in the United States, that to read a work of literature critically it is necessary only to ask one question – does this work add to the health of society? The question, of course, is based upon the idea that society is sick and needs a cure. I was trained as a historian, and too often it seems to me that this analysis has a false historical foundation, that society is not more sick than it ever has been, only sick in a different way. (137)

It is in this light that both in this introduction and in my first chapter I will attempt a periodization and description of the multiplicity of views and creative responses within contemporary British novels that may be traced to certain common features of a cultural nature influencing literary responses to the real and objective conditions alongside aesthetic ones. This interfusion is often very much part of the texts themselves.

In tracing this intuitive, creative sense of the objectifiably real identified by Cassirer, I draw upon key sources to emphasize this manner of reading culture and narrative beyond that of simply identifying the postmodern. In *Radical Realism: Direct Knowing in Science and Philosophy* (1992) Edward Pols argues that the act of knowing is intrinsically both experiential and rational (2), stating that

> My positive purpose is to draw attention to the experiential engagement of our rationality with reality and, in doing so, to show that the function of language in the life of rationality is not what the consensus claims it to be. To anticipate: although language is essential to our construction of theories and doctrines, it does not function constructively, or constitutively, in other cognitive transactions and so does not make a direct rational-experiential engagement with reality impossible. (17)

The notions underpinning his critique are central to a paradigm shift in the range of theoretical sources and frameworks used in the past few years in the humanities and social sciences in particular. This study assumes that as monolithic intellectual structures post-structuralism and postmodernism are being undermined and that this requires us to engage in a new phase of critical reflections, particularly in the novel since it continues to offer a symbolic, narrative and ideological vocabulary by which many people either understand or engage in cultural shifts.

One objection to any such sociological periodization or cartography of the conditions against which the literary field might be judged, such as the one I embark upon in Chapter One, is to declare them rationalizations superimposed on an ontological void. However, this would be to ignore wilfully an essential function of narrative. Novels both rationalize and engage dialectically with our historical presence, playing their part, however provisionally at times, in our understanding of and reflection upon our lives. Of course they help constitute cultural awareness. In doing these things some marker points, consistencies and even ongoing common disruptions may create a sufficient density of literal and symbolic effects that together can be addressed critically as interrelated. All critics engage in this practice. To pretend otherwise, however cleverly, is simply counter-factual and self-deceiving. I am clear that one needs to seek to avoid conflating the '*internal perspective*' and '*external perspective*' from the real world of the text against which Peter Lamarque cautions in *Fictional Points of View* (1996) (32), but as he insists any textual 'autonomy' does not cut the text off from the 'real' world (21). Later, he remarks

> Because literary works derive their identity from the institution of literature, the boundary between what is in 'the work itself' and what is brought to it from 'outside' cannot be coherently drawn. Needless to say, though, we should not conclude from this that no boundary exists between *relevant* and *irrelevant* considerations (what can be said or thought) in the appreciation of literary works or that citing elements in the text of the work is not an important means of support for literary interpretation. (217)

I situate literature more sociologically, and do not separate literary interpretative commentary from the political quite so comprehensively, but I do agree wholeheartedly with Lamarque's reminder that literary criticism must be viewed as possessing limits and must include an appropriately informed view of the literary texts themselves (218–19). This present study does not adopt its critical strategy in any assumptive or facile sense, but does so to resist the more asinine attempts to problematize literary-critical discourse by outlawing the terminology of periodization and placement (as if by doing so one entered into a colonial reaffirmation of imperial discourses).

J. G. Ballard comments, in conversation with Will Self in *Junk Mail* (1995), upon the persistence of 'The literary culture which dominated English life since the mid-Victorian period and survived intact until the Second World War' (335) and implicitly its effect in a country where 'the class system has always served a political function as an instrument or expression of political control. Everybody is segregated – *hoi polloi* at one end of the lifeboat and toffs sitting around the captain as he holds the tiller – and this prevents anyone from rocking the boat and sending us to the bottom' (340). Ballard's observation is equally true of the literary and critical cultures, and I will return to this context to re-read variously Britain's determination of its culture, the influence of class in reading the novel critically, its effect upon literary judgements, and the consequences for the novel itself. This may be one more reason for the academic resistance to Ballard's work that is described by Roger Luckhurst in '*The Angle Between Two Walls': The*

Fiction of J. G. Ballard (1997) for whom 'Ballard renders visible the space *between* frames, exposes the hidden assumptions behind the secure categorizations of literature and literary judgement. These, operating dualistically (science fiction/mainstream, popular/serious, autobiography/fiction, and so on) all tend to find their mechanisms troubled when confronting a Ballard text' (xiii). This is increasingly true of much of contemporary British fiction.

In *Phenomenological Hermeneutics and the Study of Literature* (1987) Mario J. Valdés raises a range of issues that help contain the critical excesses in addressing the frequently ontological or metaphysical bias of new fiction after the mid-1970s. Valdés' points – ones to which I will return – in summary are:

- the nature of text allows a combination of a fixed and/or variable identity;
- despite a plurality of readership there exists a common ground of reading experience; and,
- any concept of response and reception ought to be mediated not by assumptive singularity, but through an extension aesthetically of a concept of intersubjectivity given an acknowledgement of 'The proposition that a shared meaning of a text is a reality in the world of action in which we live' (ix).

Valdés explains at length:

Because of the relational nature of human inquiry we must look for authority in the consensus of the linguistic and cultural community. And it is because the purpose of writing criticism is to participate in the community that the critic is answerable to the community for his commentary as a factor in readers' redescription of their world. Therefore I consider the deconstructionist who advocates the giddy irresponsibility of a 'joy ride' to be just as misguided as the historicist who reaches for an elusive absolute truth. (4)

Structuralism of all kinds – and postmodernism in its implicit use of a fragmentation of discoursal reference in a fundamentally structural fashion – has an implicit reference to the kinds of relation to reality principle explored by Valdés. Such a reality principle is not a simple matter of correspondence or concretion, and text cannot efface the part played by such modes of reality in discourse, structure and narrative. 'Both structuralists and relational philosophers would agree that the state of affairs we refer to as reality has its existence bound not in things themselves but in the relationships that we construct and then perceive between them. Thus all structures are man's attempts to extend his domain' (18). However, this can be mediated by such structures being themselves dependent upon first the kind of 'alethic' realism Bhaskar (2002) describes as being finally and fully 'ontological (and intransitive, that is characteristically independent of human beliefs)' (200), and second intersubjectivity as an implicit transcendence.

Another difficulty for reading texts critically in the current academic climate, given their verbal nature, is that linguistic reference both in criticism and in fiction has been largely and quite correctly declared elusive. However, the effect of this emphasis has been to downplay the first element in what Christopher Norris describes in *Deconstruction: Theory and Practice* (1982) as the paradox of language with its 'rigorous' quality as opposed to what he determines can be its 'unreliability' as a source of knowledge (xi). By diminishing this rigorousness, any appeal to any certainty (or its approximation) appears to have been outlawed by a whole generation of critical voices, and this has had a consequential effect on the readings of literary text, as will become evident. These are not issues restricted to the critic. Many novelists are increasingly responding to postmodernism and challenging its self-determining features, and in fact have baulked at its restrictive interpretative code. One such fictionalization of these issues appears centrally in A. S. Byatt's award-winning *Possession* (1990). The novel's central characters are literary scholars researching an affair between two Victorian late Romantic poets, Randolph Henry Ash and Christabel LaMotte, following the discovery by Roland Michell, a self-effacing research assistant, of previously undiscovered letters between the two in the Reading Room of the London Library. The referential and knowing quality is enhanced further by the novel's dedication to Isobel Armstrong, a noted British scholar in the field of Victorian studies. Ash refers to a plot driving the two lovers that Roland reflects idly might also be read as being an aspect to be found in his incipient affair with Maud, the LaMotte scholar. A plot within a plot seems reflexive as of course Byatt intends it to be, but the effect is not a fulsome affirmation of postmodern reflexivity. Byatt subverts the structural conceit by expressing other reservations repeatedly through the modern characters' various exegetical engagements with texts and lived parallels, often very explicitly. Roland ponders

> it is probable that there is an element of superstitious dread in any
> self-referring, self-reflexive, inturned postmodernist mirror-game
> or plot-coil that recognises that it has got out of hand, that
> connections proliferate apparently at random, that is to say, with
> equal verisimilitude, apparently in response to some ferocious

ordering principle, not controlled by conscious intention, which would of course, being a good postmodernist intention, *require* the aleatory or the multivalent or the 'free', but structuring, but controlling, but driving, to some – to what – end? (421–2)

As Lynn Wells says in *Allegories of Telling: Self-Referential Narrative in Contemporary British Fiction* (2003)

Roland and Maud must confront the radical instability and historicity of all systems of signification, including their own identities, while being haunted by the desire for a coherent sense of themselves as individuals and as social beings. In the process of comparing themselves to their nineteenth-century counterparts, they confirm their impressions that their own culture, for all its advances, has actually regressed by creating an atmosphere of paralyzing skepticism with regard to intellectual curiosity, artistic endeavour, and interpersonal relations. (104)

Such a sense of the thwarting of enquiry is far from unique to Byatt, as we will discover, and her crucial reflection above indicates something enigmatic that is sensed intuitively beyond narrative and identity and that extends beyond the knowingness with which Byatt whimsically and repeatedly engages. Moreover, as Byatt indicates in her fiction, even in any apparently postmodern conditions of this sphere of supposed uncertainty of reference and language in real world criticism, and by the latter's very medium, the quest for an account of the kinds of ways of interpreting textuality cited above persists. This may constitute another under-acknowledged paradox, a product of contemporary critical hubris. Matthew Arnold in *Culture and Anarchy* (1869; rev. 1875) sees in genuine aesthetic understanding a 'sense for the flux of things, for the inevitable transitoriness of all human institutions' (83). For Arnold this paradox informs art in a collective not simply an individual sense.

David Lodge reflects upon the nature of fiction, ponders the contingency of the aesthetic, and sees parallels between narrative and the nature of cognition itself in *Thinks* ... (2001). The Head of English at an imaginary campus university has to clarify for a new writer-in-residence, Helen Reed, an apparently incongruous comment by his autistic son, explaining that the latter cannot distinguish between characters in soaps and real people (22). When she herself quotes enigmatically the opening of Henry James's *The Wings of the Dove* to a cognitive scientist, Ralph Messenger, offering it as exemplifying both objective and subjective perspectives, he objects. ' "Well, it's effectively done, I grant you," says Ralph. "But it's literary fiction, not science. James can claim to know what's going on in Kate Whats-hername's head because he put it there, he invented her. Out of his own experience and folk psychology"' (43). And yet later he comes to perceive a creative, objective synthesis in narrative fiction and its criticism. As Lodge's protagonist Ralph Messenger insists repeatedly even consciousness and its embodied responses are 'puzzlers'.

Critical reading is central to this present study. Despite the currently fashionable fluidity or apparent heterogeneity of the textual that problematizes grounding one's critical comments, given that one must start somewhere, I will hazard a generalization. There exists some common ground in sketching out in any way any segment of the literary-critical field, since to do so is to assume, at least implicitly, that there is some validity in the very act of responding critically to texts. Critics do not expect their words to fall into an inchoate fragmentariness of utter incomprehension (although some might well deserve such a fate). In fact most critical books progress with this given (a priori) even if they differ as to what aspects to emphasize or what model of understanding is assumed. There is a dispersal of fact and an over-determination of intellectual, epistemic analysis that seizes on difference and heterogeneity against an intuitive ontological sense, a tendency Henri Bergson alerts us to in *An Introduction to Metaphysics* (1913), and a trap of which critics must be cautious. Bergson opposes analysis of ontology, and argues for a subtle use of 'intuition' in reading of our existence and our creative expression, a drawing upon:

> intellectual sympathy by which one places oneself within an object in order to coincide with what is unique in it and conse-quently inexpressible. [...] In its eternally unsatisfied desire to embrace the object around which it is compelled to turn, analysis multiplies without end the number of its points of view in order to complete its always incomplete representation, and ceaselessly varies its symbols that it may perfect the always imperfect trans-lation. It goes on, therefore, to infinity. But intuition, if intuition is possible, is a simple act. (6–7)

Clearly while attempting to be intuitive in my criticism, I cannot rest upon this sense of the text alone, unsupported, left undialectically apprehended. Thus rather than depend upon historical and social practice in criticism as a general justification, I will foreground the implications of my acts of reading and critique as well as my account of texts themselves. However, this foregrounding is not done as a post-modern gesture, for as I detail throughout, I am sceptical of this intellectual tendency or movement, much as A. S. Byatt appears to be through the voice of Phineas G., the narrator of *The Biographer's Tale*

(2000) who echoes Roland of *Possession*, a postgraduate who abandons modern critical theory to explore the 'facts' of an apparently traditional biographer Scholes Destry-Scholes. According to Phineas G. a deconstructive technique is of limited value in understanding human values:

> A semiotic analysis shows only the choice of available sign systems, from the culture in which the signs were made – in Destry-Scholes's case a 1950s pre-structuralist culture. A semiotic analysis is not an instrument designed to discover a singular individual. Indeed, it assumes that there is no such thing. It could be argued (a dreadful phrase I find myself using, still, *in extremis*, when I want to hedge or hide or prevaricate) – it could be argued that Destry-Scholes himself, in evading the identification of his 'characters' for so long, was intending to show that identity, that the self, is a dubious matter, not of the first consequence.
>
> It could be equally argued that he made such a to-do about it because the identity of his people *was* of consequence, because the events he narrated only made sense if the narration concerned these people precisely, and no others. (97)

This is not essentialist, but more to do with a Bergsonian intuition of an ontological rightness and complexity. It is noteworthy that in two significant novels published ten years apart at key moments in the progression and diminishment of the textualizing theories in English studies, *The Biographer's Tale* and *Possession*, Byatt explores very similar ground, feeling it necessary in her fictional discourses to appeal to events and reality beyond the immediacy of the character's world, referring implicitly to critical debates and practices that literary critics ought to find familiar, and thereby to a concept of specificity, in a fictional setting of literary scholarship. Byatt's instinct for the particularity of fiction, of language, and of the assemblage of its effects is a good beginning.

Whatever my critical uncertainties, and there are many, I maintain as a central tenet the need in criticism and fiction for referentiality and a 'reality principle' to locate the imaginary. Texts themselves are part of a larger reality. In part recent movements in criticism returning to such principles mirror contemporary practice in the novel that reasserts the real world aspects of fiction. One of my starting points in assessing the relationship between criticism and fiction is a comment made by Bernard Bergonzi in the preface to *The Situation of the Novel* (1970): 'Even the best literature – and specifically fiction – is full of contradictions and even cowardice, shown by retreats into the generic or the culturally conditioned; a tendency to play the little world of art against the large world of human freedom; or a grateful falling back on the stock response when material gets out of hand. Like people, literature is deeply imperfect' (8). This emphasis is not either as naive or as liberal humanist a position as subsequent critics appear to have indicated in their post-structural and postmodern abandonment of a priority of human value. Whatever else Bergonzi's preface does, it should manage to remind one that fiction and criticism remain very human things which are emotionally and experientially framed; it may also remind us of fiction's propensity, against all the odds given formal and intertextual repetition, for originality. Like Bergonzi I am less interested in any 'comprehensive survey' of fiction or the genre's 'literary mode' and in essence agree that one must see 'the contemporary novel as a product of a particular phase of history, in a particular culture'. As he adds this necessarily leads to 'questions which are regarded as extra-literary' (7). Like him I avoid seeing the novel as simply documentary and reject 'the customary academic notion of the novel as a complex but essentially self-contained form, cut off from the untidiness and discontinuities of the world outside' (7).

Criteria for Textual Selections

What of my selection of texts? The most one can claim is a series of snapshots of cultural and literary currents, or a cartography of some of its salient co-ordinates. Certainly it cannot be inclusive. As Macherey wonders in *The Object of Literature*, we might well ask whether to specify certain texts forms an attempt 'to describe a study which elevates the disparate to the level of principle' (8). My focus on certain writers is not intended to suggest simply a typology of literary response, but more a matter of perceiving within the 'domain of literature', to borrow Macherey's term, an ongoing cultural dominance of theme, subject matter and world-view that characterizes a significant proportion of British 'literary' fiction of the chosen period. As Macherey concedes there exists 'a form of thought that more or less unwittingly produces literature. [...] Literary writings exude thought in the same way that the liver produces bile; it is like an oozing secretion, a flow, or an emanation. All these terms evoke a continuous and gradual process which takes place insidiously at the level of a microscopic chemistry within the subtle parts of the textual organization and the cellular network that makes it up' (232). My process of selection of both the fiction and other sources is one that is justified by the outcome of my ongoing thematic and textual analysis in terms of an effective engagement both of the texts as a whole and of their significance within their broader contexts. All literary-critical projects address (and most often describe) the products and conditions of literary production whatever the view adopted as to the relationship of language–reality–text, and hence engage with something essentially elusive and mutative in an attempt to stabilize or account for such relations. For a critic or theorist simply to declare an inchoate fragmentariness and yet simultaneously to address academically textual specifics or structures seems both paradoxical and to overemphasize the power of critique.

Since the 1970s not only has fiction become more 'multi-cultural' or ethnically diverse in authors and subject matter, for instance from Salman Rushdie through Hanif Kureishi to Zadie Smith and on to Caryl Phillips, the latter becoming a serious and significant British literary figure, but when considered with the emergence of a strongly working class-oriented literature in Scotland after the 1980s because of devolution and the strengths of local publishing opportunities, overall a shift in the focus of British literariness can be traced. This transformation tends to suggest that previously other issues of ideology and partiality of taste may have often been involved in the kinds of texts that were traditionally chosen for publication and academic study, rather than any abstract notion of objective merit, a point to which I return. A corollary of this observation is that this class bias inbuilt into the literary-critical field may well persist in far less obvious ways given that it has been dominant for so long. Again this is a complex issue well beyond the scope of this study, but something any reader might muse upon judging the literary-critical field and many of the assumptions of both novelists and critics. They do need to be questioned. Novels taken together are more than a collection of storybooks. This field is neither produced as a result of neutral nor natural processes. To cite history and critical longevity as offering the only correct or worthwhile arbitration of literary worth – as Martin Amis did at an event at the British Academy in 2002 – is at best questionable and certainly naive. In this light, my intention is to examine what it can be argued is a selection of key or representative texts, ones that offer themes that exemplify issues that are central both to the contemporary literary scene and to cultural mores. The current selection redresses the balance in a number of ways by prioritizing the class and cultural variations of literature in English within mainly local geographic bounds. In the past black or post-colonial fiction and women's fiction were awarded separate consideration as an ideological affirmation, but given that both now constitute a significant contribution to mainstream literary culture, this factor must shape my critique throughout. Hence I intend to integrate such writing rather than marginalize it in my critique and they will not be critiqued as discrete fields. Such an emphasis might help to reshape an aesthetic of Britishness in its broadest sense (this is discussed and exemplified later). Set against any radical impulse is a middle-class occlusion, an ongoing self-obsession that distorts our notion of what constitutes significant literariness. Gradually this aesthetic distortion is in the process of being challenged by writers who reflect a range of experiences and viewpoints that explore other identities than conventional bourgeois ones. This is a process this study wishes variously to detail, acknowledge and enhance. If our society is truly plural and diverse, one primary critical act is the need to question previous hegemonies, not to be drawn too comprehensively into generic and critical structures (and cultures) of the past, with its sense that all is bound into the ongoing circle of 'Eng Lit' and its criticism, while not of course totally neglecting such precedents. 'Black fiction' will be considered throughout, and its critique particularly forms part of 'Multiplicities and Hybridity'.

Considering Periodization

In terms of culture, politics, world affairs, identity politics, and creativity the 1970s represent both a watershed and a period of fundamental change for Britain, one that in retrospect, can be seen to rival and not be simply an extension of the changes brought about by the end of the Second World War. Essentially in the second half of 'Contemporary Britishness: Who, What, Why and When?' I make the case for the shift solidifying around the emergence and election of Thatcher and that this offers a point of transformation in the literary-critical field. Of course, in part the Thatcherite consciousness is marked by a revision of the meaning of the egalitarianism of the 1960s and 1970s, not simply restricted to Thatcherites. Take one fictional example. A similar re-reading of these cultural experiences is undertaken by Esther Freud in *Hideous Kinky* (1992) which semi-autobiographical novel depicts the failings of the previous generation from a child's perspective. The trail to Marrakech proves both exciting and traumatic for the three daughters of a young hippy mother, who is so impractical that the family become hungry and penniless. Although the focus is on the disruption of family and culture, there remains a residue of the political idealism that inspired this generation of dropouts, such as Linda's baby girl being called Mob because of her father's enthusiasm for the anarchism of the collective. Perhaps significantly Linda denies her own mother any knowledge of both the baby and her obliquely radical name (95). Freud indicates through her gentle irony that the baby's father's appeal to the collective is underpinned by an implicit refusal to take such a political position seriously, and by an indifference to the outcome of his act of naming for his daughter. This generation is inscribed by Freud as indifferent to the wider effects of its lifestyle beyond the unfocused enquiry as to their trans-cultural presence in other lives. And, if the political gestures of the hippy generation are undercut by the author and the naive narrator, so too are suppositions concerning its opposition to the commodity and the market. At the heart of the book, when Linda arrives, a central moment is Linda's delivery for the mother of a dress from Biba for which she sent money despite their poverty in Morocco (53). Together such elements signify and symbolize the contradictions of the generation that produces the reaction and cultural shift in the 1970s. Freud grew up as did the children depicted in Morocco, in what she indicates were paradoxical conditions where adults abandon children and fail to nurture them. Thus in this fashion she locates the innate contradictions of the 1960s and 1970s middle-class radical ambitions, much as Malcolm Bradbury does more explicitly and polemically in *The History Man* (1975). Throughout Freud's novel the pull of London and the life left behind reasserts its relevance to and appeal for most of the adults, with various individuals like Linda and the baby returning to their origins, almost bemused by their own otherness in Morocco. One of the novel's major themes is the end of the alternative culture and a cultural shift back toward more traditional responsibilities. This mirrors the political and media agenda that resurfaces periodically. The child's viewpoint allows a distance from what has come before, signifying in the cultural shift almost an image of a *tabula rasa* that can be rewritten or re-inscribed. In its retrospective view of elements taken from Freud's own childhood, the novel also conveys a sense of a new generation defining itself as being distinct in its view of the world, and by her narrative method of retrieving traditional as well as experimental perspectives of narrative. By the time Hanif Kureishi publishes *Gabriel's Gift* (2001) literature has not simply turned away from post-war conditions, but through the perspective of the teenage protagonist, Gabriel, the 1960s of his father's rock ambitions have become ancient history, as is clear whenever they encounter an old friend of his father. 'In the sixties and seventies this man had been a successful fashion and pop photographer. The girls with ironed hair and boys in military jackets he had "immortalized", as he liked to put it, were as distant to Gabriel as Dickens's characters' (2).

As indicated earlier, it is a platitude that ought to be evident to any observer of literary criticism, but one worth repeating, that periodizations of literary and cultural moods are inexact by their very nature, but may be pragmatically necessary and theoretically suggestive. There is no absolute version that offers anything like an empirical or scientific account of any one phase of history, but the change of literary and cultural focus suggested in this study can perhaps best be assessed in terms of it allowing an understanding of the literary dynamics of the British novel. Periodizations, if mediated by a measure of scepticism, remain useful in placing texts and help reflection upon social and literary transformations as dynamic changes. These are often inscribed in the minutiae. In terms of noting such a contemporary transition, Will Self perhaps reflects upon a suggestive detail in *Dorian: An Imitation* (2002), writing of early 1980s London when the need for a change of consciousness was already evident and expressed in the riots of that period. And yet the mainstream culture was slow to adapt.

> Once the pressure built up and the melting-pot boiled over, the Metropolitan Police felt that radical sartorial changes were required. By the middle of the 1990s they were resplendent in Kelvar bulletproof waistcoats, submachine guns dangling across their chests like the ornate breastplates of modern primitives. But in 1981 they were compelled to enter the hail of glass vessels (some half empty, others half full of *parfum de fracas*) wearing knee-length macs and tit-shaped helmets. (50)

In part reacting to voices and movements expressing middle-class discontent that had been brewing in the 1970s, issues that will be outlined in Chapter One, the forces of authority and power responded more generally to new conditions, as did a younger generation of writers. This is not to suggest that this created a textual reflection simply in a mimetic sense, but the ground upon which their views of Britain may be contextualized. Much criticism and some of the preceding fiction can be seen as regressive and conservative, despite the avowal of the opposite by those who wanted their liberal, middle-class culture to be regarded as radicalized. There were some voices calling for change in the literary context in the run-up to the period of literary transformation that is the subject of this study. As early as 1973, just before his untimely suicide, novelist and critic B. S. Johnson summarized his thoughts developed over the previous decade, complaining in his literary manifesto, the 'Introduction' to *Aren't You Rather Young to be Writing Your Memoirs?* (1973): 'I can only assume that just as there seem to be so many writers imitating the act of being nineteenth-century novelists, so there must be large numbers imitating the act of being nineteenth-century readers, too' (15). He demanded change and for Johnson there could be no retreat into aestheticism or simply a formal experimentalism, although there was plenty of evidence of this creeping into the aesthetic of the 1950s to the 1970s. The implications in Johnson's appeal to real life truthfulness may not be the evocation of the mimetic, but more an appeal to transform consciousness. I suspect he might have approved some of the kinds of subsequent literary changes this study critiques. As D. J. Taylor in *A Vain Conceit: British Fiction in the 1980s* (1989) says objecting to Malcolm Bradbury's curious separation of imagination and politics 'The novel *is* politics in that it is an analysis, a reflection, a refraction of prevailing circum-stances' (130–1). Hence the novel, despite Johnson's objections, may still claim perhaps to be one of the most contemporaneous of forms, and writers have engaged with this possibility quite consciously since rejecting the critical crisis, the death of the author syndrome, of the mid-1970s. Richard Sheppard, in *Modernism – Dada – Postmodernism* (2000), outlines a specific example of literature incorporating notions of postmodernity in structuring its textual awareness. He cites Jona-than Coe's *What a Carve Up!* (1994) as offering 'an uncompromisingly social critical message' that uses popular forms to deliver 'a highly incisive attack on Thatcherite postmodernity' but in textual terms to no effect as it concedes in advance its failure to affect a change since 'the signifier has perished but the signified – evil, the system – has not been overcome' (361). My reading stresses that surely Coe's novel is didactically political, reflecting on the recent past to generate a sense of current cultural conditions rather than the text emphasizing its own formal characteristics, some of which are of course utilized ironically. Rod Mengham in his 'Introduction' to *An Introduction to Contemporary Fiction: International Writing in English since 1970* (1999a) says 'Coe imagines the extent to which the shared experience of the Thatcher years is one of cultural psychosis. In the work of Swift, Spark and Coe the individual's sense of relationship to the movement of history is familiarized, rendered intelligible through the medium of inherited stories and myths' (5). I will return in detail to the latter. Certainly the very hybridity of Coe's text reflects cultural conditions, but the novel's moral and ethical centre would seem to indicate something other than a postmodern perspective. *The House of Sleep* (1997) conveys in its depiction of the study of sleep disorders at the Dudden Clinic, named after its director, and the traumatic events of the past the building evokes having been concealed from the outward consciousness of the characters, the suggestion of a troubled and elusive cultural sense. The peregrinations of Terry's filmic obsessions drive him to madness and the fragmentation that haunts contemporary lives. Dudden's despising of 'ordinary mortals' for requiring sleep and showing fragility links him with Thatcher and her manic regime of work celebrated in the media and of which she boasts. Dudden concludes, 'Yes, the real issue was this: that Dr Dudden was right, and everybody else was wrong. *He* could see it, and they couldn't. It was down to a tussle, then, between good and evil. It was Dudden *versus* the rest of the world' (312–13). Thatcherism here is identified with the monomaniacal egotism of modernity, in which contemporary culture is implicated. Thematically postmodernity and fragmentation are allied with the perverse and unsustainable, a narcoleptic sightlessness as the 'Somniloquy' toward the end indicates, Thatcherism implicitly a nightmare from which one needs to awaken.

Challenging Postmodernism

As has already become clear, in interpretative analysis of contemporary fiction one cannot avoid the term postmodernism, but it has itself come to represent an increasingly vexed issue rather than acting as an instrument by which the vexed nature of knowledge can be critiqued, as many postmodern theorists appear to suppose. Critical interpretation of the contemporary novel until recently seemed dominated by the claim that most contemporary fiction at some level represents essentially a postmodern world and offers an 'ontology' despite not accessing any agreed universal reality. Given the currency of this set of beliefs it seems worth pointing out its critical deficiencies that have been neglected by over-enthusiastic theorists and literary critics, and this counter-pointing might help students recognize that the postmodern describes in literary-critical terms what are essentially a range of cultural gestures, and it is in geo-political terms that it has come to serve as ideological tool of both globalization and new-wave post-industrial imperialism. It is this reality that makes the term and a notion of the postcolonial both extremely vexed. The colonial subjects of European empires are enmeshed in a subsequent and overriding economic and geo-political structure that displaced these former loci of authority and privilege, but in a sense maintained effectively a different imperial-colonial relationship. Empire and colonial structures were reconfigured prior to and during the Second World War. The centre has shifted in the main to the US and has adopted a different corporate and military strategy, but persists. Postcolonial is more appropriate a term for the crisis of identity among the privileged middle classes that sustained the empire culturally, economically and intellectually, even providing a critique of its inappropriateness and absorbing its ethnic identities, much as contemporary postcolonial discourse does, while leaving the essential structures untouched. The claim for post-coloniality for certain groups has a further complexity; historically Japan itself had imperial ambitions, as did a range of Islamic states.

In truth the literary term of postmodernism referred initially to diverse creative acts that appear to constitute a mood of cultural and aesthetic experiment. As Sheppard says 'there is a broad consensus that postmodernism as a cultural phenomenon involved two phases. During the first, it was oppositional, anticapitalist, and antiestablishment. But during the second, not least because of the culture industry's increasingly sophisticated ability to assimilate opposition and protest, its status became much more problematic' (351). In critical thought there has emerged increasing scepticism concerning the validity of both a postmodern periodization and the kind of claim typifying postmodern critique that appears radical by undermining grand narratives and universals. To do so it relies upon its philosophical affiliation with post-structuralism where, as Edward Pols describes in *The Acts of Our Being: A Reflection on Agency and Responsibility* (1982), 'the consensus holds that *philosophy*, at least cannot express in language what is extralinguistically the case. What is lost in all this is the naive, but powerful and salubrious, objective of managing to retain *in the very use of language* an awareness of the extralinguistic resonating in it; for of our rational awareness it is only a half-truth to say that it is linguistic' (88). Sheppard recuperates aspects of the post-structuralist stances as both responding to modernism and 'trying to theorize the change that Western capitalism was undergoing in the 1970s and 1980s'. (362) Moreover, as Sheppard notes, in order to legitimize the postmodern one must 'see the essential feature of postmodernism as its *acceptance* of postmodernity with its decentered plurality, ephemerality, fragmentation, discontinuities, indeterminacy and, depending on one's point of view, chaos' (358), Sheppard relates postmodernity to the intensification of a sense of disempowerment while being increasingly confronted by the commodified even in the aesthetic and avant-garde in a world declared as enigmatic (352–3). In a specifically literary context the challenges to the term's appropriateness and efficaciousness are concerned not only with the avowal that such fictions through self-reflexive textual and generic features offer a challenge to universalizing subject positions, but go further in insisting in contrast that a return to material referents may be required if students of literature wish to extend their critique beyond textuality. To do so they must concede Pols's claim in *Radical Realism: Direct Knowing in Science and Philosophy* that the postmodern is deficient because at its basis it depends upon what Pols describes as 'irrealist' and thus 'it claims that what the speaker of commonsense language supposes to be the perceiving of the world is in fact the holding of a bad hypothesis or theory – often called folk theory – about a reality that in point of fact is not perceivable at all' (96).

For some time, as Edmund J. Smyth explains in the introduction to *Postmodernism and Contemporary Fiction* (1991a), it appeared to be adequate simply to gesture to fragmentation and postmodernism as determining features of the contemporary novel, as if by this strategy one were appealing to a different sense of subjectivity (1–2). Smyth challenges this reading and insists with a peculiarly universalizing first person plural 'The liberating feature of radical textuality is the extent which such texts make us confront the ways in which we make sense of our world and how we organize our knowledge of reality. Of course, this interpretative strategy can also apply to what is described as "classic realist" fiction' (11–12). Respectability and commonality implode or collapse. More recently and even more comprehensively, postmodernism is being seen as insufficient for explaining or even describing fragmentation, differentiation and plurality. Brian McHale's definition in *Postmodernist Fiction* (1987), that Smyth critiques, involves distinguishing texts as being determined by an explicit 'epistemological and ontological doubt' and this remains in many ways inadequate. McHale's claim that his book 'does not aspire to contribute to literary theory' seems disingenuous, and to prioritize his wish 'to construct the repertory of motifs and devices, and the systems of relations and differences, shared by a particular class of text' (xi) quite explicitly in opposition to any 'realist' position would seem to preclude a broader understanding of the 'ontological dominant' that he regards as distinguishing a postmodern fiction. His claim that the suffix 'ism' of postmodernism 'announces that the referent here is not merely a chronological division but an organizing system – a poetics, in fact – while at the same time properly identifying what exactly it is that postmodernism is post. Postmodernism is not post modern, whatever that might mean, but post modern*ism*' (5), over-prioritizes the aesthetic aspect of the modernist movement and would seem to undermine the claim not to be indulging in literary theory. The world persists, as do texts within that world; the equivocal relationship between them is not simply a microcosm of a meta-discourse of Enlightenment modernity. Neither that doubt nor Smyth's foregrounding of a performative reflexivity of reading within the text efface a larger reality.

To manipulate textuality is at one level simply to call attention to social and ideological processes (as well as McHale's 'ontological dominant') without necessarily challenging them in any effective sense. Everything McHale describes as characteristic of the modernist text could be applied to texts that he would regard as 'postmodernist' and his notion of a postmodernist text depends on the reflective and structural foregrounding of the 'ontological dominant'. As a 'mode of being' literary texts possess clearly both epistemic and ontological dimensions. McHale acknowledges this, but indulges in an aesthetic contextualization that separates fictiveness from reality, creating a multiplicity of ontological landscapes wherein reality is a collective fiction (36). McHale talks of 'ontologies' as if they might be conflated with multiple subjective viewpoints, and risks what Roy Bhaskar describes in *Dialectic: The Pulse of Freedom* (1993) as 'the "epistemic fallacy"*. As ontology is in fact irreducible to epistemology, this functions merely to cover the generation of an implicit ontology, on which the domain of the real is reduced to the domain of the actual (actualism) which is then anthroprocentrically identified with or in terms of sense-experience or some other human attribute' (4). In *Cultural Theory and Late Modernity* (1995) Johan Fornäs challenges the appropriateness of seeing a distinct periodization or 'new condition' and sees globally 'a radicalization and intensification of modernization rather than its dissolution. [. . .] This new phase is still typically modern. "Postmodernism" might be a relevant term for artistic currents that react against earlier avantgarde movements, but the last decades sometimes labelled "postmodern" should rather be seen as an intensified and accelerating reflexive, ultra-, super- or late phase of modernity' (35). In fact, recent fiction in Britain retains a subtextual appeal to reality and naturalistic social mores, exploring this intensified realm of value and commodification, an extension of these strands of influence upon the Renaissance, the Enlightenment, and Victorian utilitarianism. In *Dorian* Will Self reflects of the supposedly countercultural that evaporates: 'What happened to flagrant queers and uppity blacks and defiant junkies in America was that they got absorbed, then packaged and retailed like everybody and everything else. In America in the 1980s the counter-culture became the over-the-counter culture with sickening alacrity, and Andy Warhol – poor Basil Hallward's name-dropping nemesis – was the acned acme of it all. When the domestic market was brand-saturated they re-exported it all back to Europe, just in case there were any little pockets of resistance that needed mopping up' (91). Not only is postmodernism being commodified, but both its supposed radicality and its uniqueness cannot withstand scrutiny. As Fornäs details postmodern traits which predate this latest cultural phase are present in late modernity (35–7), commenting 'Modernity has from its very start cherished linear goal-orientation as well as polydimensional fragmentation, Enlightenment rationalism and Romanticist anti-rationalism' (36). Furthermore, as Fornäs argues if within 'modernism' a creative consciousness is capable of reflexivity then even in an aesthetic sense this remains intrinsic to modernity and not its dissolution or challenge (38–40). This echoes Marshall Berman's view in *All That Is Sold Melts Into Air: The Experience of Modernity* (1982) where he sees in the development of modernity modernists whose 'ideal was to open oneself to the immense variety and richness of things, materials and ideas that the modern world brought forth' (32), as opposed to his ironic observation that 'Others have embraced a mystique of post-modernism, which strives to cultivate ignorance of modern history and culture, and speaks as if all human feeling, expressiveness, play, sexuality and community have only just been invented – by post-modernists – and were unknown, even inconceivable, before last week' (33). Berman's contrast leads to a most important distinction. If it is to take itself seriously reflexivity risks prioritizing a secondary view of understanding, for as Bhaskar says in *Reflections on Meta-Reality*

> Reflexivity involves an understanding of the self in relation to its context; and the consequences of the failure of post-modernism to sustain adequate contextualisation means that its increasing emphasis on self is ultimately nugatory of any true understanding – for self only makes sense in context, and the consequence and condition of the collapse of any theorisation of the real world is the collapse of any adequate theorisation of its own context. (34–5)

Simply expressed, in the context where the postmodern urge to textualize and so dominate the whole of the literary-critical field is being increasingly challenged, it is well to remember that as George Lakoff and Mark Johnson remind us in *Metaphors We Live By* (1980) 'Ideas don't come out of thin air' (xi). An obvious point, but one we must remember, since this is true of fiction, even of mythic, fantastical and meta-imaginary texts. Texts which are intertextually about other texts are never simply so. They relate to other discourses and to the material conditions of our existence, past, present and anticipated. Linda Hutcheon concedes a similar point regarding irony in *Irony's Edge: The Theory and Politics of Irony* (1994) noting communicative acts as social activities (17) although stressing discursive communities and 'different experiential and discursive contexts' (18). And certain almost platitudinous (and yet ontological) things about narrative remain consistent, even in the contemporary world. Narrative fiction is concerned essentially with the intensity of the living of lives, even the most oblique, the bleakest, or most diffuse or experimental of prose. At times the focus of fiction appears almost to be concerned solely with the self and individual action, but on closer consideration one can recuperate a concern with externality, the self and their immediacy. The paradox is that all such reflections and understandings are retrieved from past action. In 'An Enquiry Concerning Human Understanding' in *Lean Tales* (1985) James Kelman's almost epi-grammatic tale is concerned in part with the impulses that lead to narrative and recollection, constituting an urge to account for concrete actions descriptively, as a method of learning from past errors. This is undercut in ironic fashion, in the banality of ordinariness.

> And I devoted real time to past acts with a view to an active future. The first major item dredged was an horse by the name of

Bronze Arrow which fell in the Last in a novice hurdle race at Wincanton for maidens at starting. I had this thing to Eighty Quid at the renumerative odds of eleven-double-one-to-two against. Approaching the last *Bronze Arrow* is steadily increasing his lead to Fifteen Lengths ... Fallen at the Last number two *Bronze Arrow*. This type of occurrence is most perplexing. One scarcely conceives of the ideal method of tackling such an item. But, regarding Description; the best Description of such an item is Ach, Fuck that for a Game. (105)

The perspective is not finally bathetic and nor is its subject matter truly banal. Kelman's title serves as a reminder that such minutiae – that of the obsessional, the compulsive, and the ill-conceived – are part of the range of being human and therefore of aesthetic responses. Fiction in the contemporary scene rejected the notion of the death of the author – a concept in the British scene very redolent of a middle-class self-obsession and imperial nostalgia and regret – and began to celebrate different exploratory modes of writing and a wide range of identities. As Kelman indicates in his ending replete with a sense of incompletion, the act of fictionalizing may be elusive in its exactitude and correspondence, it may remain mimetically limited, but it is eventful, that is it is related to a range of things and actions, a barometer of the quotidian and the emotional. Of course narrative and generic methods fluctuate and change. As Smyth writes in 'The Nouveau Roman: Modernity and Postmodernity' (1991b) the experimental mode like the nouveau roman is engaged in an attempt 'to introduce narrative forms which would more accurately mirror the intelligibility of the world: the problematic nature of reality had to be more suitably translated' (56). Whatever its disruptions and 'misreadings' in terms of its generic narrative precursors, like all such narrative interventions the nouveau roman has an underlying appeal to that concrete reality that, as Gilles Deleuze says in his preface to *Essays Critical and Clinical* (1993), exists precariously in terms of literature and narrative since 'The limit is not outside language, it is the outside of language. It is made up of visions and auditions that are not of language, but which language alone makes possible. [...] These visions, these auditions are not a private matter but form the figures of a history and a geography that are ceaselessly reinvented' (lv).

Critical Orientations

What some critics appear to have forgotten in their supposed 'ontological' reformulations of culture is that there remain limits to reflection upon the novel form. As a critic one can respond perhaps most appropriately by focusing upon a text and its context, some of the latter evident from the text itself and other influences comprehended through a task of reconstructive effort. Unless one accepts a critical relativism, the appropriateness of any textual reading must be assessed according to its relevance and efficaciousness in allowing the reader to more fully understand key aspects of a text. In terms of authors, movements and periods, patterning and interpreting a range of texts and affiliated materials is the task of the academic critic. For this task the plot and rhetorical aspects are insufficient, but not irrelevant. This placement involves responding both to narrative reflections and to a broader cultural milieu. Kelman's story reminds us that the text is an amalgam of a range of perspectives, including those culturally recognized (hence his title) and ones in the main neglected by traditional prose narratives and academic criticism, such as the corner betting shop experience, and obsessions with gaming or gambling that recur in his fiction. Also the game and the playful are at the heart of the environment: racing, wagers and loss. This can be read as indicating that for Kelman in these motifs he finds something apart from the postmodern; for ordinary folk these experiences indicate that the ludic and the aleatory are ultimately modes of capitalism, instruments of oppression rather than postmodern, metaphysical conceits with the power to liberate consciousness and affect one's life. For Kelman they only appear to offer mediations of oppression, simply to be revealed as illusory. Mostly the gambler fails and loses. It is not abstract, but a real loss, and a negation of any effective 'enquiry concerning human understanding' given its compulsive, coercive structures. As Cassirer says in *The Logic of the Humanities* (1961) 'For all form demands a determinate mass and is bound to its sheer thereness. Life cannot produce form purely from itself, as naked, freely streaming activity; it must concentrate and focus, as it were, on a fixed point in order to take part in [the world of] form' (23). According to Lakoff and Johnson 'The fact that the myths of subjectivism and objectivism have stood for so long in Western culture indicates that each serves some important function' (226). In order to make any ongoing sense of the world one requires both consciousness (self-evidently) and the factuality of independently existing things and events; and although as Lakoff and Johnson postulate 'Objectivity still involves rising above individual bias, whether in matters of knowledge or value' (227), this ought to be mediated by Pols's observation:

The thing attended to is ontologically independent of the act of attending. Propositions and theories are not really exceptions. Although they do indeed owe their form, or at least part of it, to something formative in ourselves, we do not, by virtue of attending to them, contribute yet another form that hides the one we have already endowed them with. (37)

Ultimately underlying my critique of contemporary fiction is a wider ambition, to contribute toward a project parallel (or contributory) to that envisaged by Bhaskar in *Dialectic: The Pulse of Freedom* thus:

> Nor do I think the objects of science exhaust reality. On the contrary, they afford only a particular angle or slant on reality, picked out precisely for its explanatory scope and power. More-over, alongside ethical naturalism I am committed to moral rea-lism and I would like to envisage an adjacent position in aesthetics, indeed viewing it as a branch of practical philosophy, the art of living well. (15)

The literary-critical field can become progressive in this manner and is surely capable of contributing to this process. My sense of the con-sciousness in the novel since the mid-1970s is that there has been an attempt to reconcile and integrate the two traditions which as Doris Sommer relates in 'Irresistible Romance: Foundational Fictions of Latin America' (1990) are contrasted critically. 'Anglo-American cri-ticism traditionally opposed novel to romance in terms that now appear to be inverted. Novel was the domestic genre of surface detail and intricate personal relationships, while romance was the genre of boldly symbolic events' (82–3). New critiques of literature responsive to meta-real rather than the generic conditions of the text (while of course not obscuring these) are now demanded by changing cultural conditions, and certainly by the practice of contemporary fiction as the following chapters attempt to demonstrate.

Notes

1   Hereafter referred to as *The Metaphysics of Symbolic Forms*.
2   Hereafter referred to as *Mythical Thought*.

Further Reading

Bataille, Georges *the unfinished system of nonknowledge* [see bibliography].
A difficult and yet rewarding philosophical account of the irrational, of laughter and of the intuitive supplementarity that allows us to comprehend the world. It would prove useful for any advanced student confident enough to apply its conceptual observations to literary and cultural contexts.

Bhaskar, Roy *Dialectic: The Pulse of Freedom* [see bibliography].
This extremely difficult and detailed account of a theoretical view of reality underpinned by a complex view of dialectical materialism breaks new ground, but is only for the most advanced readers. It remains most useful in countering postmodern, deconstructionist readings.

Bhaskar, Roy *Reflections on Meta-Reality: Transcendence, Emancipation and Everyday Life* [see bibliography].
This complex philosophical work introduces many highly theorized aspects of the concept meta-realism in a philosophical context; since it is arcane and determinedly philosophical it can only be recommended for the most determined of postgraduate students.

Cassirer, Ernst *The Logic of the Humanities / The Philosophy of Symbolic Forms, Volume 2: Mythical Thought / The Philosophy of Symbolic Forms, Volume 4: The Metaphysics of Symbolic Forms* [see bibliography].
These works represent a philosophically inclined and rigorous critique outlining mythical, symbolic and humanistic ways of comprehending man's relationships; not therefore for the faint-hearted or tentative reader, but many excellent conceptual ideas can be gleaned.

Crudy, Catherine (1996) *Salman Rushdie*, Manchester: Manchester University Press.
A good clear introduction to the author's earlier, seminal work, based on sound research and readings of the texts.

Diedrick, James (1995; rev. 2004) *Understanding Martin Amis*, Columbia: University of South Carolina Press.
A good comprehensive critical introduction to Amis's work, accessible for students of all levels, and informed by close readings.

Jeffers, Jennifer M. (2002) 'The white bed of desire in A. S. Byatt's *Possession*', *Critique: Studies in Contemporary Fiction*, 43 (2), 135–47.
This considers the complex signification of reading, of white and whiteness as a metaphor of desire and the *tabula rasa* of creative urges in Byatt's novel; it will prove rewarding to students if read closely.

O'Connor, Erin (2002) 'Reading *The Biographer's Tale*', *Victorian Studies*, 44 (3), 379–87.
This essay interprets Byatt's novel as an anti-romance that serves as a critique of the history and nature of biography, and its place in literary scholarship and academia; intriguing and useful.

Pols, Edward *Radical Realism: Direct Knowing in Science and Philosophy* [see bibliography].
This work is a ground-breaking and challenging philosophical rejection of linguistic anti-realism which accounts for the 'epiphanic' or intuitive qualities of language which is nevertheless still situated within a complex realism; hence another text only for the more advanced student, probably at postgraduate level.

Storry, Mike and Peter Childs (eds) *British Cultural Identities* [see bibliography].
This is a sound introductory essay collection that introduces many key historical and cultural contexts relevant to late twentieth-century British identities; useful as background material.

Tew, Philip (2003) 'A New Sense of Reality? A New Sense of the Text? Exploring the Literary-Critical Field and Meta-Realism', in Klaus Stierstorfer (ed.) *After Postmodernism*, de Gruyter: Berlin and New York, 29–50.
A critical essay that introduces and defines meta-realism in terms of its literary and critical contexts; although theoretical, it will reward students committed to critically complex readings.

CHAPTER ONE

Contemporary Britishness: Who, What, Why and When?

KEY THEMES
1970s Middle-class Crisis • Class Conflicts • End of the Post-war
Consensus • Englishness • Britishness • Multicultural Britain • New
Generation Novelists from the 1970s • Post-war Transitions and Changes •
Thatcherism

KEY TEXTS
Ballard, J. G. *High-Rise*
Carter, Angela *The Sadeian Woman:*
  An Exercise in Cultural History
Drabble, Margaret *The Middle*
  Ground / *The Millstone* / *The*
  Needle's Eye
Kureishi, Hanif *The Buddha of*
  Suburbia

Murdoch, Iris 'Against Dryness' / *The*
  Nice and the Good / *Under the Net*
Phillips, Caryl *The Nature of Blood*
Selvon, Samuel *The Lonely*
  Londoners
Wilson, Angus 'Evil in the English
  Novel' / *Anglo-Saxon Attitudes*

Changing Britain

Caryl Phillips's *The Nature of Blood* (1997) concerns identity, cultural affiliation and the curious dependency of identity on human interaction. The novel juxtaposes the persecutions of Jews both in the Holocaust and in fifteenth-century Venice with that of the fictional protagonist in *Othello*, suggesting both the power and the inadequacy of literature. John Thieme's interpretation in *Postcolonial Con-Texts: Writing Back to the Canon* (2001) is that 'In his representation of Venice, far from creating an extra-social site in which distance apparently intervenes between the pastoral world of play and the social realities of Renaissance England, Shakespeare clearly constructs a locus for investigating his own society's anxieties about alterity' (156). Phillips's novel inverts that cultural focus in part, directing it upon the outsider who enters and is mediated by another culture, from which one might draw clear parallels with the contemporary British scene. He succeeds in establishing such human relationships as paradigmatic in understanding the nature of history and culture. Overall the novel charts traumatic and sweeping forces exploring their effects upon human relationships and individuals. No grand narrative emerges, no sense of overcoming on a larger scale. A key characteristic is a feeling of numbness and bafflement as determining the subject's ability not only to comprehend, but in any kind of engagement with the universe. This sensibility is a common thread in most literary fiction written from the mid-1970s, drawing upon previous phases of experimentalism. Such a sensibility can be found thematically, in characterizations, symbolically, metaphorically or at the level of plot, and so conjoins a whole variety of types of writing, making genre distinctions often misleading. There is a difference in this underlying awareness quite distinct from modernity's crisis of convention, or postmodernism's inchoate subjectivity, its lack of faith in individuality as a sustaining narrative and self-awareness. Often drawing on combinations of the historical, the mythic, the poetic and the spatial, such fiction avows a 'meta-reality', an interfusion in the experiential of a metaphysical, a material, and an aesthetic sense of ontology. In this sense it draws from modernism, postmodern metafiction, and upon postcolonial sensibility and even traditional narratives. Novels may parody grand narratives like those of Salman Rushdie, alternatively decentre and yet position fantasy in disruptions of the mundane, historicize the mythic like Angela Carter, or perhaps mythologize history like Graham Swift, but such narrative is characterized by its own hybridity, a historical consciousness and, unlike perceptions of metafiction in the American tradition, an avowal of identity formation. In his conversation with Self in *Junk Mail*, J. G. Ballard describes a desire to fragment the conventional structures and ongoing traditions of the British novel, by exploring a sense of disruption and challenge. 'A lot of English fiction is too rooted. The writers are too comfortable, one feels. They are like people returning again and again to the same restaurant, they are comfortable with the flavours on offer, and the dishes on offer' (333). Ballard's use of other worlds, a synthesis of science fiction and fantasy elements into those of a more apparently conventional narrative, has been influential. An evolving British aesthetic is concerned variously with a familiarity of location, a disrupted conventionality, and a sense of otherworldliness.

In Phillips's novel the interchanging structure, the text's historical consciousness, the ethnic identity of its author, its notion of identities in a necessary flux, the reintegration of narratives of trauma as possessing a quotidian dynamic and permeation all mark it as a fiction that is characteristic of this aesthetic awareness emergent in the past twenty years and it also expresses British cultural concerns in their widest sense. Hence, the novel reflects a change in emphasis that has come to permeate a contemporary British consciousness and fictional perspectives, it relates not only the instability of the self, but of the self's very dependence upon the framing of others that makes the self always already vulnerable. Unlike the modernists and those in Britain who rejected their experimentation after 1945, for this new generation there is neither an interiorization of the aesthetic nor a fully fledged recuperation of individualistic naturalism. Phillips writes of protagonist Eva, a Holocaust survivor, about to quit a post-conflict dispersal camp: 'I wait for a few moments and then move across to the mirror. A stranger's face, with large puffy eyes. I do not want this anguished expression. How can this stranger be me? I look like them, ugly and ravaged. I begin to laugh at this mask. I smear lipstick around my mouth. A jagged slash, red like blood. Tomorrow they will release me into an empty world with only Gerry for company. Gerry has never seen my true face. Oh Gerry, my heart is broken' (48). In part knowledge of contemporary history must prevent the reader from intimating any sentimentality in this otherwise clichéd claim. As is well recognized, the novel form allows such individuation within broader human experiences to explore metaphoric and metonymic possibilities, but an even more complex reflection occurs in this text as a whole, its structures reflected in this passage. Amidst this crisis of the emotive and somatic self, in its image of defamiliarization and alienation, Phillips inscribes thematically and structurally the fragmentation of identity and its persistence. This is resonant as it encapsulates a literary transformation in British fiction that had been in process for a time about the nature of its legitimate cultural identities. Determining the dynamic and focus of this metamorphosis is a complex and an elusive process because it charts a broader cultural transformation, and because specifying the range of cultural reference has become itself a ground of dispute.

It would be tempting in terms of its content to see Phillips's novel as maintaining the issues of the post-war context, pointing out that it reconsiders the Holocaust as a major event that defined a new aesthetic sensibility and incapacity for expression, and that this has parallels with the slave trade, thereby simply historicizing its motifs. This is to misread the text and the dynamics of a changing intellectual culture that has moved fiction beyond, as we shall see, the territory with which post-war critics had become comfortable. To deal with contemporary British fiction, and to situate Phillips appropriately, requires understanding that writers from the mid-1970s onward have been responding not only to traditions of representation, but more fundamentally to a shift in Britain's intellectual and geographic culture.

Broadly, this involves seeing society as intersubjective, as combining changing, often transitional identities and subjectivities. Such literary texts reconfigure the moral and narrative definitions of literary engagement that reflect changes within Britain itself, as the counter-cultural forces of the 1960s diminished, the globalized economy abandoned the welfarism of the post-war settlement and redefined the role of the state. Certainly national culture perhaps seemed both less entrenched and less monolithic. Contemporary fiction, as with its antecedents, seems to relate insistently to its intersections with a broader culture and upon its own cultural influence. This is expressed variously, but British novels are constantly re-contextualizing this tradition, often questioning explicitly rather than implicitly the parameters of nationhood.

Fiction can synthesize shifting cultural identities with a sense of historical change. One striking example is Hanif Kureishi's *The Buddha of Suburbia* (1990), in that it evokes and reconfigures a Dickensian dialectic of location, identity and English *Bildungsroman*, deconstructing these elements very much in the manner of J. D. Salinger's seminal and laconic novel *The Catcher in the Rye* (1951) toward which Kureishi's opening gestures. 'My name is Karim Amir, and I am an Englishman born and bred, almost. I am often considered to be a funny kind of Englishman, a new breed as it were, having emerged from two old histories. But I don't care – Englishman I am (though not proud of it), from the South London suburbs and going somewhere. Perhaps it is the odd mixture of continents and blood, of here and there, of belonging and not, that makes me restless and easily bored. Or perhaps it was being brought up in the suburbs that did it' (3). Karim declares a grudging adolescent notion of his personal and his national identities that both intersect variously with the implied identities of others, but equivocally so. Despite such ironic and interrogative possibilities, as the entirety of the novel makes evident, cultural specifics do emerge and are further negotiated by Karim. His initial words offer priorities that recur in the narrative, those of personal experience, of a very specific location (suburban and subsequently central London in the main), a broader international context (through origin and travel), a complex of ethnicity and class issues, and of course the very English language with which he articulates. It ends at the point of apparent dissonance as Thatcher is about to be elected in a 'bitter, fractured country [that] was in turmoil' (259). It is within this broadly British historical context that includes Englishness – that is within cultural, theoretical, literary, class, gender, ethnic, geographic, political, economic, and social co-ordinates that can together constitute variations of Britishness – that this study considers a range of significant locally published Anglophone fictional prose from the period with which Kureishi ends his novel just preceding Thatcher's election. In these contexts I argue there are recurrent literary themes which address the overall cultural and historical trends that define the nature of the literary culture since the mid-1970s, and in many ways contribute to Britain's broader culture.

So where does the change of novelistic bias or concerns, perceived above in Phillips's work, become significant, thematically, structurally, culturally and chronologically? The following periodization is intended to underpin a fuller understanding of the processes of a literary-cultural contextualization and of course support my selection of texts as aesthetically and historically appropriate. D. J. Taylor describes a 'new eclecticism' that characterizes the novel of the period, commenting nevertheless 'To locate a new eclecticism in English writing is not, perhaps, to suggest a sea change, and it is not even to say that it is a prerogative of new, younger writers. Novelists as various as J. G. Ballard and Angela Carter have always pursued this approach' (115). For Self writing in 'The Seer of Shepperton' in *Sore Sites* (2000): 'Ballard has always defined himself as a chronicler of "inner space" and attempted to imagine what the parameters of the human psyche will be like in the not-so-distant future. The irony is that the works he has produced have turned out to be far more accurate predictions of the character of evolving modern life, than those written with that intention' (14). Another starting point lies in certain headline literary facts that serve to indicate something of a specific shift in the cultural milieu. In 1978 Iris Murdoch won the Booker Prize with *The Sea, the Sea* (1978); William Golding soon followed with *Rites of Passage* (1980), both very much part of an older generation of writers and traditionally 'English' in an accepted intellectual, middle-class sense. By 1981 Salman Rushdie had won the Booker with *Midnight's Children* (1981) and by the end of the 1980s Kazuo Ishiguro followed with *The Remains of the Day* (1989). Certainly most commentators are coming to recognize that at this juncture something appeared to be happening in the world of the British novel, not only a shift of generations, but also a change in its focus and cultural emphasis. This is something more than simply a question of the subject matter of fiction of this period – although that has its relevance and will be considered in the ensuing chapters – but a kind of literary sea change, a response to a full range of forces. According to Sheppard's overview of the post-war period, there are two phases to its intellectual culture that runs adjacent to British literary culture, the latter responding to the former at least in part:

Just as philosophers, psychoanalysts, and scientists of the 1930s tended, when trying to come to terms with the perceived cultural crisis, to respond to it in terms of optimism and pessimism, so analysts of postmodernism have often divided that phenomenon into two phases. On this account, the first phase (extending from the mid-1950s to the mid-1970s) involved countercultural opposition and celebratory affirmation [...]. But the second phase, which is frequently connected to the political disillusion of the mid-1970s, is thought, especially by Marxist critics who take their cue from Jameson, to be the expression of 'the experience of defeat,' to have lost its critical edge, and so to affirm late-capitalist postmodernity. (359–60)

Moreover, as Andrej Gąsiorek indicates in *Post-War British Fiction: Realism and After* (1995) second-wave feminism had already taken off transatlantically and the mood of unifying optimism had shifted away from a belief in 'feminist fiction' as such (136). There was also a sense of impending collapse, but in *High-Rise* (1975) Ballard perceives something more fundamental than bourgeois and professional cultural mores which are disrupted by an elemental force, something atavistic and unconscious overcoming the veneer of liberal humanist respectability, of civilization. Architect, Anthony Royle, whom his friend Dr Robert Laing kills eventually, initially reacts against the breakdown of order and social structure.

Later, however, the collapse of the high-rise began to strengthen his will to win through. The testing of the building he had helped to design was a testing of himself. Above all, he became aware that a new social order was beginning to emerge around him. Royle was certain that a rigid hierarchy of some kind was the key to the elusive success of these huge buildings. (69–70)

The building is of course a symbol of late-capitalist modernity. Ballard's book can be read quasi-allegorically, conveying the theme of transition and change, of the innate and growing tensions in British culture, its intellectual and professional classes instinctively reaching for a new kind of 'hierarchy'. His thematic impulse predates his more experimental formal work, but the lack of epistemic and social cohesion centres his sense of a contemporary culture undergoing change, *High-Rise* suggestively ending with Laing's morphine habit and his perverse vision of a 'new world'.

Initially this chapter responds to what was one of the major errors – and this is not put too strongly – of literary-critical studies in recent times, which is the *ad hoc*, often unacknowledged attempts to negate

'Britishness' as if the term were too vexed and problematic a cultural concept, as if its adoption were implicitly racist or colonial. In this assumption that a nationalism and an ethnocentrism is inseparable from the term and thus makes it unacceptable, there is a naive assumption that boundaries are bound simply by the historical conservatism of power structures. For many critics and commentators this very issue of Britishness appears to present an insurmountable problem, as if they require that it remain fixed in an imperial context, as an eternal point of opposition and as a negative point of reference, effectively short-circuiting any debate on the potential for a renewed national, intellectual identity. In this context it seems both odd and suggestive that Bill Buford – an outsider arguably with an intellectual investment in this notion of fragmentation that he surveys in a 'participant observation' equivalent of the Whitmanesque – in his 1993 'Editorial' in *Granta 43: Best of Young British Novelists 2* feels it necessary and is confident in dismissing 'the word British, a grey, unsatisfactory, bad-weather kind of word, a piece of linguistic compromise' (15), declaring himself not to know of anyone British who might raise a defence of this national marker, when of course its figuration has always represented a plurality and is no different from that declared in many other geographic-ethnic locators as sufficient and self-evident. The problem is that the underlying, ongoing historical reality of such a plurality is inconvenient both for nationalists and for intellectuals. And naturally, which the glib Buford ought as an American to understand intuitively from cultural norms, all words as points of reference are compromises and generalizations, including any reference to the United States, a country (nation or empire) that produced a hybrid and yet exacting novelistic form that as Bernard Bergonzi notes became a major influence on young intellectuals in Britain from the 1950s to the 1970s. Britishness seems to evoke intellectual opposition that is unmerited and politicized given that the basis for such objections is a narrowing of Britishness to its middle-class, imperial roots (most often from within that class which curiously serves as a self-avowal of such class origins as a universalized national experience), ignoring the term's diversity in a regional and class sense, to which progressively one can add gender and ethnicity. The frequent critical conflation of Englishness with Britain may not be excusable, but it is surely more understandable in that it in part is rooted in the simple demographic reality that the population of England is larger than all of the other regions combined by a factor of around five times (the English represent 81.5 per cent of the total British population), is half the land mass and certainly could be argued to be culturally dominant simply because of the focus of the political, commercial and intellectual classes upon London and Oxbridge experiences and net-works. Of course this tends to distort the intellectual and political apprehensions of Britishness, and the novel has not been immune to such partial accounts.

Neither through wilfulness nor arbitrariness this book considers critically a *British* fiction during the period following the mid-1970s, seeing a cultural transformation accelerating after 1979. Of course, simply to establish the bounds of what constitutes both a significant periodization and the appropriate conditions of the *contemporary* fiction that can be defined as British requires establishing a range of theoretical and terminological principles. Primarily after a lengthy attack by neo-liberal critics, the terms themselves – British and con-temporary – seem overdue for revalidation, but not in any traditionalist sense. In the introduction to *Other Britain, Other British: Contemporary Multicultural Fiction* (1995a) A. Robert Lee perceives in the social process that constitutes Britishness 'the changing of the demographic guard' and sees the nation 'as less some canonical order than, post-empire for sure, an ever more arriving multi-culture' (1). He queries:

> How one, how many *is* Britain? Are those who speak of threa-tened heritage, the loss of an 'agreed' way of life, simply prone to Little Englander entrenchment, nostalgia, a kind of self-validating and all too selective memory? Are those, conversely, who call for post-coloniality, an overdue recognition of ethnic and cultural diversity within a changed (and still changing) Britain, guilty of special pleading, some 'liberal' ethos born only of minority interests? (1)

Lee recognizes that those distorting the newness of Britain are as historically closed as those purveying crisis. Issues of a pluralized eth-nicity have extended an ongoing social and cultural dispute as to the direction, focus, representation, rewards, voicing and so forth of Brit-ishness in all its forms. To see the post-war settlement – arguably a historically unrepresentative 'blip' produced by unprecedented wartime spending and command economy structure even in liberal-capitalist economies – as either continuing or disrupting any settled social order is to diminish the conflicts of the working classes, the Victorian underclass, the servant class, the regions, the migrant labour of Scots, Irish, Welsh, Chinese, blacks and others within an emergent British-ness, as well as the politically unrepresented (and under-represented) including women. One risks confusing large-scale class blocs as representing a history of class and allowing a new multiplicity to negate a tradition that has persisted in plural, confused and complex forms. Dickens, for instance, inscribes a vibrant servant class, a resistant underclass, refers to migrant elements of the labour force and the *nouveau riche* of an emergent professional, propertied class. Arguably he problematizes the notion of identity, as with Copperfield and with Pip to name but a few of his uncertain and mutative characters. Moreover, in terms of more recent conditions it is not the case as Dominic Head concludes in *The Cambridge Introduction to Modern British Fiction, 1950 to 2000* (2002), that the end of 'gritty working-class realism' is superseded by a Britain where 'the rise of the under-class from the 1980s onwards denotes a new kind of social division' (9), whereas a periodic disruption of class boundaries and their remapping is recurrent, recursive and more fully represents the establishment's marginalization and fragmentation of opposition, an Arnoldian pro-jection of external disorder onto self-empowerment and identification. In the Victorian aesthetic cultural disorder may have been exhibited mostly in the comic and grotesque rather than as a central literary trope, but ideas of chaos, indeterminacy and negation long predate the current historical period.

Historicizing the Contemporary Aesthetic

To establish a broader historical context from literary texts, responding to many issues that have both acquired currency in the literary-critical field and obscured such influences, is not to end any substantial creative or critical-cultural consensus, since recent received wisdoms are remarkably vulnerable. First the assumption that some kind of homogeneous culture preceded wartime conditions is not only dis-missive of oppositional forces and pre-existing heterogeneities, but in part potentially racist, since it implies that preceding differences were somehow less obvious and therefore not as critically challenging as those constituted by ethnic (rather than class) variations characteriz-ing the period of post-war transition. Further it prioritizes the con-temporary period over the past. Hence, one necessary task of this chapter is to look backward beyond the mid-1970s to the ideological, historical and aesthetic conditions of the post-war period that many critics still persist in perceiving as – perhaps simply adopting a cultural assumption – defining the contemporary literary scene almost sixty years after the end of hostilities, offering a straitjacket into which all post-war fiction is constrained. The sheer dimensions of this con-tinuing historical congruity defy common sense and certainly any dialectical notion of change. It also is ideologically charged, implicitly reconstituting British intellectual identity as being consonant with Britain before its financial, populist and cultural shift. It may be, as Head claims, 'that the novel in Britain from 1950 to 2000 yields a special insight into the most important areas of social and cultural history' (1), but surely it must be remembered that the world after the mid-1970s is as significantly different from the preceding twenty-five post-war years, as the 1920s of flappers and boom and bust global crisis would have been from the world of Pooter and his proto-Yuppie son, Lupin, essentially a world of the late Victorians. Gąsiorek remarks that 'The "death of the novel" thesis was frequently put forward in the first two to three decades of the post-war period' (6), a revealing observation since this implicitly places another subsequent change critically and creatively around the mid- to late 1970s.

So what is the general critical overview, given that such judgements remain provisional? Essentially many critics appear to believe that British fiction writers, particularly the Movement, reject both the elitist experimentation of modernism, and the foreignness of the *nouveau roman* and continental (particularly French) philosophy. Some critics concede that later novels embrace a 'fabulist' style, moving toward postmodernism. Historically both phases are seen as fairly uncomplicated responses to post-war crisis and the end of empire. So goes the typical critique. There are objections. As Davey comments 'The marginalisation of aesthetic high modernism in Britain, and the replacement of Europe by America as the homeland of modernity and the avant garde, and hence the vector for utopic longings in the immediate postwar years, is a crucial part of the historical context' (3). Moreover, as Samuel Selvon perceives in *The Lonely Londoners* (1966) something more complex is articulated in the common cause of poverty and dispossession, within which conditions he can chart his vision of the social bemusement of the post-war context, as if Britain were in a state of profound collective shock:

> It have a kind of communal feeling with the Working Class and the spades, because when you poor things does level out, it don't have much up and down. A lot of men get kill in war and leave widow behind, and it have bags of these old geezers who does be pottering about the Harrow Road like if they lost, a look in their eye as if the war happen unexpected and they still can't realise what happen to old Brit'n. (58)

Partly, though, it would appear to be because of a crisis of identity not simply in terms of Empire and its decline, but such a refusal of the communitarian base of people's lives that Selvon's narrator observes: 'People in this world don't know how other people does affect their lives' (59). More comfortably situated in aspirational or middle-class settings during the period of 'Welfarism' than either Selvon's black immigrant or working-class communities, the Movement after the Second World War reintegrated a version of naturalism interlaced with more contemporaneous themes and relationships and parodied modernism. In this period there was also an unease about social change and the challenges to the middle classes. Gąsiorek identifies the fears of writers such as Evelyn Waugh and Elizabeth Bowen concerning the new Labour government and its welfare policies (2). Welfarism and more accessible education is one of the open targets for Kingsley Amis's supposedly 'progressive' *Lucky Jim*, alongside its satirizing and parody of bluestocking Bloomsbury artistic notions. Gąsiorek sees this conservatism as part of the artistic divide:

> The dichotomy bedevilling British fiction relied as much on political as on aesthetic grounds. Indeed, what passed for purely aesthetic judgement was frequently underpinned by covert political assumptions. To defend realism in the 1950s was to be aligned not only with 'good old English tradition' (empiricism, common sense, social comedy along the lines of Fielding and Dickens) but also with a broad commitment to liberal humanism. (4)

Angus Wilson describes the dynamics of the post-war period in 'Evil in the English Novel' (1967), a piece that exaggerates the changes in the aesthetic vision of Britain, and reacts to progressive social changes to which he appears inimical:

> Too many present-day English novelists have sought refuge in new class citadels, now that the old middle-class one, whether of country or provincial town has gone. We have lower-middle-class provincial life exalted as having some kind of ethical value which would stand for good; we have the idea of the urban working class, as in Alan Sillitoe's work, as somehow having a kind of nobility. These are new citadels desperately to be defended. All this, however interesting sociologically, seems to me opposed to the development, destructive of the growth to maturity, of the English novel. There is still an attempt to create absolutes out of right and wrong, and out of manners, though they be manners that have been neglected – those of the working class, and of the lower middle classes. There is once more an attempt to build up a citadel that will protect us from a changing world. (21)

Wilson is in a sense engaging in sniping at shifts of power within the middle classes, a set of relations that are the focus of *Lucky Jim*. This was a novel of great influence upon the intellectual class as it remodelled itself and, though rejecting Bloomsbury values, Amis explicitly builds his own middle-class citadel of comfortable rebellion, rejecting an over-aestheticization of the modernist tradition while curiously rewarding the apparent social misfit with the benefits of a consumerist, expansionary economy. The result is a minor shift, but certainly no egalitarian document, for as Head comments 'Writers like Amis [...] never mounted a serious challenge to class distinction or privilege' (52).

If the years that follow the mid-1970s can be regarded as a very different period from the post-war years, what constitutes this difference? First, the earlier period is characterized by a profound economic crisis and a consequent crisis of relationships with its colonies, all of which undercut recovery and the notions of optimism only partially fostered by the Festival of Britain. This overall situation is initiated by Britain's major ally, and this trajectory is maintained when America refused to side with Britain and France in the Suez crisis. Britain's post-war insularity was in greater part due to the unexpectedly sudden end to the war and an anti-imperial American policy explored by Alec Cairncross in *Years of Recovery: British Economic Policy* (1985). After the bombing of Japan, war ended in a way that precluded forward planning by the British Government (3) and brought an equally unexpectedly abrupt cessation of Lend-Lease which had been a reciprocal arrangement since 1942 and the lynchpin of the home and imperial economy (5). Essentially America bankrupts Britain and forces political change. The economic impetus for the UK winding down imperial possessions is clear. 'In 1913 her net overseas assets were comparable in magnitude with the net value of her domestic stock of fixed assets other than dwellings. By 1945 net overseas assets were a minus quantity' (7), especially given a huge commitment to overseas spending on the military (10). 'The total amount made available from capital for war purposes between 1939 and 1945 was £10,000 million – more than two years' output of the entire labour force' (12). As John Callaghan explores in 'In Search of Eldorado: Labour's Colonial Economic Policy' (1993), this allowed Labour to react to economic exigencies and initiate a post-imperial phase with limited opposition, and after the convertibility crisis of 1947 and the devaluation crisis of 1949 (116) to champion colonial 'economic development' (115). Callaghan supports the view that this was a consequence of long-term American policy, with Roosevelt setting a pre-war agenda of a timetable for colonial independence from the European powers (121) and 'The economic neglect of the European colonies was one of Roosevelt's favourite themes during the war' (122). Clearly this policy was not altruistic. Callaghan makes clear this constitutes part of US policy of opposition to the British Empire as a closed economic bloc and similar opposition toward European imperialism generally (124–9).

The conditions in Britain did not continue to be entirely negative, and the management of the home economy strengthened the position of the working classes and increased both their economic and their cultural significance. As Cairncross makes evident the benefits of the Welfare State (17–18) were combined with 'Full employment of a kind never before experienced in peacetime [which] was maintained almost throughout [1945–51]' (18). It is clear that only a certain kind of cultural condition shapes the responses and cultural descriptions of the intellectual middle classes, who extend their sense of an imperial and investments crisis as if it represented both the conditions of the whole nation and a representative creative output. Although reacting to the trauma and exhaustion of the war, together with the shock of the public revelations of the Holocaust, Alex Comfort in *The Novel & Our Time* (1948) describes an alienated society that in its implicit elitist fear of its debasement and loss, together with its rejection of popular culture (31–2), seems unconsciously to prioritize the establishment's loss of empire as the condition of the nation:

> It is a society of onlookers, congested but lonely, technically advanced but utterly insecure, subject to a complicated mechanism of order but individually irresponsible because there is no communal sanction for or against any course of action, largely devoid of artistic expression but inundated with every kind of *kitsch*, and persisting mechanically in routines of a morality and a social pattern which has been switched off and partly dismantled but continues to run for a while with the momentum it received during earlier periods. In this order art and scientific achievement are the only fixed points, the only part of the structure which will influence future civilizations. (12)

Comfort assumes that the novel offers a range of characteristic literary forms derived from common experience and thought, ignoring its narrow base of authorship and reflected experience (9). He makes a range of astonishing claims, including that the bulk of American novels were loss-making (28–9), and that society had become complex in some (untheorized and unspecified) unparalleled fashion (35), and arguing the necessity artistically of a 'fixed point' (35–6). The reductive view from a range of critics of these aesthetic and social conditions persistently described post-war conditions as representing something so fundamental that when synthesized with new-wave feminism they were seen as creating a cultural force that was seen to constitute an ongoing continuum persisting until the present time without further ruptures, adaptations and all of the transformations that mark out any account of a cultural and socio-historical process. For Malcolm

Bradbury, in the introduction to *The Novel Today: Contemporary Writers on Modern Fiction* this defines a post-war optimism that was to fade in the 1960s, but also supplied a generation of writers who for him continued to define British literary contemporaneity:

> By this time, it seemed, much of the impetus of the modern movement had been exhausted; the postwar years saw the revival of the liberal and realist novel. The writers who emerged after 1945 are, of course, very much *our* novelists, and their development is very much related to our development, our contemporary history. After 1945 the novel showed every sign of reasserting its realistic potential, its moral and social concern, its sense of life as progress (10).

This constrained view persists in understanding contemporary fiction simply as a further phase of either those historical forces or the generation unleashed by the collapse of empire.

To confront such over-simplifications of the once apparently radical and now utterly conventionally minded account of a post-war continuum in general and literary conditions, one must be able to place the transition leading to 1979 in terms of subsequent radical transformation of the political, as well as cultural and creative contexts. Why is the mid-1970s a watershed that led to the rise of the Thatcherite world? It seems consistent with the kind of general aesthetic shift noted by many; as Bradbury insists:

> We live in an age in which fiction has conspicuously grown more provisional, more anxious, more self-questioning, than it was a few years ago. Looking about us at the novel now, it must seem that many questions about the nature of fictionality and about its constituent parts – the role of plot and story, the nature of character, the relationship between realism and fantasy and fabulation – have come to the forefront of attention. Indeed, ideas about what the novel is, and what it might be, have shifted so markedly in recent years that we might well judge that a serious aesthetic shift is taking place; that, in fact, there are signs of a distinctive new era of style. (8)

Bradbury sees formal, reflexive issues of style. For Buford it is implicitly a generational change: 'At the end of the seventies, there were only two novelists whom anyone was making a fuss over: Ian McEwan and Martin Amis. [...] The novel belonged not to the young author [...] but to another older generation' (11). As he indicates by the end of the seventies new writers, producing a new wave of novels, responded to a different view of the world, incorporating in their critical understanding new technologies, new customs, punk disruption of the 'peace and love' generation of activists and optimists, to new economic realities and of course to another new phase of Britishness.

Socio-economic Aspects and Class Conflicts

Additionally there are a number of obvious economic and social justifications for such a periodization. Firstly new young, emerging writers had not been defined by the war either personally or experientially. Those with such memories were settling into their middle age. In a period obsessed with youth and its supposed transformative potential, a whole generation had grown up in relative affluence and peace, despite the cold war. The period was also marked by fundamental, significant socio-historic and ideological shifts. As will be seen, the financial crises of the 1970s had fundamental effects culminating in the so-called 'Winter of Discontent' and the election of Margaret Thatcher, who challenges and ruptures the post-war consensus, as Steven Connor points out in *The English Novel in History 1950–1995* (1996):

> A fundamental contradiction within British society which was to become fully visible only with the breakdown of the postwar social consensus after 1979. This was the conflict between the centralist ideals of the Welfare State, producing attitudes that were often protective, constraining and inward-looking, and the more explosive forces of economic growth, which shook apart many of the structures of British society, not least in making it increasingly clear that Britain was dependent upon and vulnerable to the pressures of a newly globalised economy. The irony, it was to transpire in the late 1970s, was that, without the latter, the former could not in fact survive. (47)

As well as evident globalization, this period also heralded the end of the Cold War, a period of increasing détente, but also of an intermittent if not ongoing British involvement in warfare including a last colonial fling with the Falklands, the Gulf War, the bombing of Iraq and Yugoslavia, and the War Against Terrorism with the US campaign in Afghanistan, and the war against and defeat of Saddam Hussein's Iraqi regime. The horrors of mass mutually assured destruction were replaced by the kinds of strategic geo-political campaigns more akin to the traditional 'Victorian' notions of a balance of powers and interventionism.

Politically the 1970s saw major conflicts and transformations that prepared the so-called Thatcherite revolution. Such recognition of a shift in cultural dynamics has long been observed and needs to be integrated more comprehensively in terms of aesthetic, cultural and fictional trends. As David Lovatt outlines in *Unemployment and Class*

Conflict in Britain During the 1970s (1980) there were conscious attempts to limit union power from the early 1970s even though wage rates were not as high proportionately as those in Europe and there was a decline of workers' earnings and rises in prices in the UK economy after the 1976 financial crisis (53) with a concomitant move by the managerial and investing middle classes to increase profits and decrease labour costs from 1975 (56–7). The commonly recognized marker points of class become less distinct due to the rhetorical 'equalitarianism' not reflected in facts, events or conditions but nevertheless often expressed as a new reality by the mass media. Thatcherism, the popular tenets of youth culture and also the more migrant labour force affected the stability of, or perception of, any continuity within communities. The traditional working class appeared to shrink, but arguably simply mutated and British class structures remained conflictual.

However, divisions continued to increase. Lovatt analyses a number of other changes which contributed to the appearance of classlessness whilst in fact configuring an extremely divided society, when interpreted in class and economic terms. In contrast to high unemployment from the mid-1970s among the working classes (43), Lovatt emphasizes that 'A "new middle class" has developed composed of those who occupy positions both in and outside bureaucratic hierarchies' (13), and despite higher rates of social mobility its long-term effects are limited (14). The 1970s had been characterized by the collapse of consensus concerning public economic behaviour, EC entry, and changing attitudes to employment (xiii–xiv), but there was no real danger to the state, so much so that Keith Middlemas in *Power, Competition and the State: Volume 3 The End of the Postwar Era: Britain Since 1974* (1991) comments on the very 'inappropriateness of the 1974 catch-phrase "Who governs Britain?"' (xiv). Of course this is relevant to fiction precisely because in Britain intellectuals including writers and critics saw a crisis of order that was in truth more of a crisis of sustaining middle-class identity and privilege. As Middlemas outlines, such a response is a projection of fears of a world economic crisis, after the end of the period of the post-war settlement in the 1970s, that various governments were unable to handle (3, 8–9, 40). This discontent of the emerging and traditional middle classes, and their innate conservatism, has its clear parallels within the novel. What the Movement and much of prose fiction from the 1970s shared with naturalism (and arguably even some modernist texts) was a focus on a chiefly subjective experience as if the world were comically confusing or epistemically restrictive. Although reflecting on an economic and social shift, whilst incorporating a feminist agenda, Margaret Drabble without any explicit irony also incorporates the smug self-obsessions of the middle class in the mid-seventies such as the oil crisis, entry into the EC, and the growing demands of the populace all of which disturb their self-image. A classic example of this is her notion of the rational, even-handed reflections over strikes and trades unions undertaken by Simon Camish, a working-class barrister specializing in employment legislation, in *The Needle's Eye* (1972). In *Culture in Britain since 1945* (1991) Arthur Marwick overemphasizes Drabble's commitment to social democracy and 'left-of-centre political attitudes', but he is correct that her notion of 'the loss of faith in social progress based on consensus' is revealing (178). However, like many of Drabble's works including those in which Marwick detects radicality, *The Needle's Eye* as a text stands outside of the experience of the ordinary people, and the theme of class affiliation is framed and judged through the rational and apparently objective voice of Drabble's narrative which mirrors that of the professional and administrative class that is the centre of its values. As D. J. Taylor writes in *A Vain Conceit* of Drabble's characterization in *The Millstone*, an early novel:

> This is all faintly redolent of Beatrice Webb: an attempt at ega-
> litarianism undermined by conscious snootiness and an uncon-
> scious assumption that society ought to be meritocratic. [...]
> The tone is very much *de haut en bas*. It is parlour socialism, if you
> like, a vague, concerned leftist stance always pulled up short by a
> sort of gut liberalism. (51)

In *The Situation of the Novel* Bergonzi quotes from a BBC recording undertaken in 1967, 'Novelists of the Sixties', a statement by Drabble: 'I don't want to write an experimental novel to be read by people in fifty years, who will say, ah, well, yes, she foresaw what was coming. I'm just not interested. I'd rather be at the end of a dying tradition, which I admire, than at the beginning of a tradition which I deplore' (65). In fact, despite topographical appearances – a view of which constitutes the social dynamics of its reflection of Drabble's world-view – much in her fiction remains fundamentally unreflective, despite its constant narrative and character-centered ruminations. Reflecting on his use of clichés and courtroom strategies, Simon reflects

> Perhaps it was true that he was biased. There was a connection, a
> comparison, somewhere, that he was on the verge of grasping. It
> was true that he aligned himself often irrationally on the side of
> the employee, even in such absurd cases as this ridiculous twenty-
> four-hour strike that was going on at the moment at Caxton's: a
> strike against the management, it was, but motivated by the fact

that other firms, through strikes, were likely to fail to produce the necessary parts. (218)

Drabble's position is effectively a closet Leavisite one. As Francis Mulhern says in 'English Reading' (1990): '*Scrutiny*'s stand against Marxism is a legend; and, notwithstanding social compassion and episodic political sympathy, Leavis and his collaborators rebuffed any suggestion that the industrial working class had the capacity to sustain or develop "humane culture"' (257).

Set against the reflections of the educated class, Drabble contrasts this not with the labyrinthine and arcane logic of trades union strategies, but rather a vision of mumbling and inarticulate working-class strikers, peripheral and marginal figures as she suggests all such characters seem destined to remain. If Simon is simply indicative or symbolic of the social transformations which were coming into play, at a subtextual level Drabble shares that de-radicalization not simply aesthetically. Drabble's view is not neutral and appropriates change to a hegemonic experience, those of the middle classes. The only genuine plurality is an avowal of women's experience within those narrow confines. By the time Drabble publishes *The Middle Ground* (1980) with its revealing title, a journalist, Kate Armstrong, explores her world set among marital affairs and North London dinner parties, where a woman lecturer quotes for social edification *The Prelude* at length and Kate writes

> Her pieces on middle-class manipulation of the health service, on rows about underprivileged gifted children and the preponderance of black children in ESN schools [which] were classics of their kind, and warmly welcomed, for in those days people were still ready and willing to hear the humane, sensible left-wing view, the so-called 'progressive' view. She and Ted came from backgrounds not dissimilar [...] both in their own way seeking the egalitarian millennium, which would bring security, opportunity and prosperity to all, while awarding its faithful and elect (such as themselves). (43)

Although Drabble critiques such humanitarian ambitions she never separates the narrative focus from its affiliated world-view. As the novel opens Kate reviews her morning post (that Drabble literally lists), consisting of appeals for credit, invitations to talk and write on feminism, and an invitation to 'appear in a fur coat in an advertisement for fake fur, in aid of wild-life conservation' (3). Drabble describes Kate's encounter with working-class women like nurse 'Denise Ball, née Scooter, who had remembered Kate and the old days well, and who had confided to Kate, on Kate's preliminary reconnoitre, that her husband Terry had turned out a right bastard in many ways' (182). Denise cannot articulate her complaints to a powerful, male interviewer. Setting aside the agenda of the text, the working-class characters remain ciphers, most particularly the men, all bit players on Drabble's stage. The novel concludes with Kate anticipating her social whirl in an echo of *Mrs Dalloway* (1925). As she dresses for a party she ponders the possible social permutations and potential gaffes of her set. 'Anything is possible, it is all undecided. Everything or nothing. It is all in the future. Excitement fills her, excitement, joy, anticipation, apprehension. Something will happen. The water glints in the distance. It is unplanned, unpredicted. Nothing binds her, nothing holds her. It is the unknown, and there is no way of stopping it. It waits, unseen, and she will meet it, it will meet her' (248). This peculiar rendition of manifest destiny might be argued to be feminist, or an understanding of a fragmented reality, but its provisionality seems more of a celebration of upwardly mobile privilege, an evocation of middle-class social significance.

In contrast to Drabble's assumption of middle-clas radicality, whether of a complacent or effective kind is a matter of judgement, by the end of the 1970s a new breed of novelists could respond aesthetically to the concrete and profound cultural changes, some offering a more radical view opposing the previous generation's nostalgic longing for a sense of an overarching order. Lee explores in 'Changing the Script: Sex, Lies and Videotapes in Hanif Kureishi, David Dabydeen and Mike Phillips' (1995b) the dominant characteristic of much of the pre-1979 British fiction which for him is its expression of a comfortably familiar (for the intellectual reading class of the period) middle-class Englishness, found in such writers as Drabble herself, despite her gestures to multicultural London, alongside Kingsley Amis, Malcolm Bradbury, Anita Brookner, Iris Murdoch, William Golding, David Lodge, Fay Weldon, and Angus Wilson (74), expressing an apparently 'liberal' view of the informed self (rooted in a version of Leavisite Arnoldianism). Lee cites its limitations:

> The upshot may well be an 'Englishness' ostensibly given over to society, class manners, the changing regimes of marriage, family or gender, or even, in a larger sense, the politics of end-of-empire. But it all remains, somehow, a selective and 'our' Englishness/Britishness, one overwhelmingly of white middle-England [...] (74–5)

Lee asks in his introduction to *Other Britain, Other British: Contemporary Multicultural Fiction* 'Have the post-war years, in fact, not seen a transition from an old coloniality (empire-derived, "immigrant") to a new coloniality (internal, indigenous), or, again, does neither wholly meet the case?' (2).

The literary field prior to the mid-1970s offers a sense of a number of crises that centre and in a curious fashion limit the fictional world-view of many writers. Themes include the loss of authority, and a larger sense of a lack of focus of the middle, the imperial, the intellectual, and the political classes as well as that of the rest of the 'establishment'. These are not in the main radicalizing impulses. Much of this under-lying unease surfaces in the 1970s, as if responding to changes in social, political and intellectual conditions, and it is not a consciousness without social and political targets. The rise of so-called 'Middle Class Campaigns' in the political agenda of Britain in the 1970s is well-charted territory – such as in Roger King and Neill Nugent's *Respectable Rebels: Middle Class Campaigns in Britain in the 1970s* (1979) – but the cultural impact of a general wish to negate the potential of the working classes is less often applied to the literature of the period, and to the dynamics of the literary-critical field. It pro-duced a kind of literary neo-Arnoldianism (much disguised according to critical readings, an account I find unconvincing, for there is little subtlety here), reflecting what is regarded as an ongoing sense of 'light' and 'disinterestedness' in its hardly radical acceptance of the global conditions that had brought imperial ambition and hegemony to its knees, allowed a radicalization of non-European campaigns for inde-pendence, and promoted a global migration of labour following the demands of capital (rather than vice versa). As Roger King explains in 'The Middle Class in Revolt?' (1979) a common feature of such middle-class views is always to be underpinned by the claim to be 'non-political' (14) and this is applicable to many literary critics and nove-lists. This consciousness and a growing Thatcherite confidence brought to the surface long-held antipathies to other classes (13–18). As Neill Nugent argues in 'The National Association for Freedom' (1979) such groups invented the concept of 'the enemy within' to be found among active radicals and working-class activists (89) although as he insists this was always based on a dubious and self-promoting critique.

> The philosophers of the new right who seek to articulate a coherent ideology for 'middle-class' groups based on the doctrine of a more competitive and individualistic society can hardly complain if the working classes take them at their word and compete for a greater share of goods and resources. [...] The logic of the argument is that there is no moral justification for any particular distribution of rewards provided they have been

produced in a 'free economy' which in turn is believed to ensure
the maximisation of individual liberty. (81)

He details groups such as the National Association for Freedom, vigorous in their championing of individual freedom and attacks on trades
unions, creating huge conflict and civil unrest as with the Grunwick
dispute (89–90). As Nugent indicates there is a strange contradiction,
one that we can argue is derived from views that express in cultural
terms self-election and a degraded Arnoldian elitism. 'The message from
NAFF [the National Association for Freedom] thus rings loud and clear:
the best society is the least governed society – except, significantly, in
the areas of law enforcement, defence and alleged abuse of trade union
power' (76). The proposal that certain group values not only represent,
but only such a group can sustain, subjective individualism creates
a crisis of intellectual and creative identity. Its contradictions mean a
contraction of self-awareness and any concept of ethical, rational or
even dialectical truth, so palpable is its blinkered quality.

   Such attacks on subversive forces, while avowing personal economic
liberalism, and free market dynamics were so profound that they
allowed the new Thatcher government to bring about a revision not
only in cultural dynamics, but of the government and economic, legal
and social structures. Some of this was more responsive to external
conditions than their projected machismo would admit. As Middlemas
identifies, the new ideologies of the Thatcherite project were defined
by a rejection linguistically and in policy terms of post-war consensus
(235) with an acceptance of high unemployment as the price of
monetary policy (237) and a rapidity of global influences after the
abolition of exchange controls in October 1979 (241) and less protection of the conditions of the population with large reductions in
public expenditure, PSBR and sale of state assets (241). For Peter
Riddell in *The Thatcher Decade: How Britain Has Changed During the
1980s* (1989) 1979 marks a point one can identify as the cultural and
political 'acceptance' by at least the political class and its allies of 'the
redirection of economic and industrial policy which began in the mid-
1970s and developed a new energy and momentum with the arrival of
the Thatcher Government' (viii). Of course this is in part symbolic,
since as Riddell concludes the logic of Thatcherism and the dynamics
of its policies preceded Thatcher's election and originated in the
Labour Party from 1974 to 1979, and

> The need to bring in the International Monetary Fund in the
> autumn of 1976 may have firmed up some of these developments
> but did not create them. Moreover, the painful process of redu-
> cing inflation after the wage explosion and the first oil price shock

produced only a short-lived reduction in living standards before growth resumed, and at the same time there was a redistribution in favour of the less well-off. The turning-point in macro-economic policy, if not politically, was as much in 1976, as in 1979 or 1981. (16)

Nevertheless, ideologically and culturally the election of the 'Iron Lady' crystallized a mood swing and endorsement of a culturally and economically divided society. Inequality continues. According to *The CIA World Factbook 2001* (which is surely not the most radical of sources) 17 per cent of the British population still lives below the poverty line. These realities are the 'underbelly' of much of the fiction of the period, one which authors either scarcely scratched or in embarrassment concealed to save their blushes. As Middlemas argues the change in political power signifies a sense of profound crisis but responds to ideas of crisis prevalent in the 1970s (and in the post-war conditions). 'I argue that there was a break, but that the change of government in 1979 was itself a consequence of a much deeper clea-vage in the mid-1970s, a crisis for the British government which can be compared to the crisis of the state after 1910' (xiii). Keith Middlemas cites three periods of major cyclical change in the British state which had cultural consequences: the 1840s; the 1910s; and the 1970s, the latter confirming the notion of a profound cultural emphasis after 1979 (xiii). There followed initially not economic success but the major post-war recession of 1979–82 that deepened the crisis and divisions (xiii).

Middle-class Emphases

Many writers from the mid-1970s are concerned with a reconfiguration of middle-class identity, but not necessarily in all cases as a progressive revision, and this very impulse for redefinition ironically has its pro-logue in many of those post-war narratives from which the new gen-eration wishes to distance itself. In fact, both generations share a persistent commitment to an intellectual elitism, feeding into a rejection of populism found in figures as disparate as Sigmund Freud, Theodor Adorno, and F. R. Leavis. In the post-Thatcher generation this will become less explicit, and far more implicit. In the post-war generation there is an often overt and sometimes implicit nostalgia for the myth of the past which leads Iris Murdoch in 1961 to complain in 'Against Dryness: A Polemical Sketch'.

We live in a scientific and anti-metaphysical age in which the dogmas, images and percepts of religion have lost much of their power. We have not recovered from two wars and the experience of Hitler. We are also the heirs of the Enlightenment, Romanticism, and the Liberal Tradition. These are the elements of our dilemma: whose chief feature, in my view, is that we have been left with far too shallow and flimsy an idea of human personality. (23)

In contrast her fictions focus on the very class whose intellectual heritage she would claim to critique, as if any diversity might be recovered from among that class.

Those post-1970s authors who persist with the notion of re-legitimizing any efficaciousness of or priority within a middle-class voice can find themselves almost paradoxically echoing an earlier unease about liberal-intellectual identity and self-image that appeared after the end of the Second World War, a period when the middle classes in particular reacted often with variously bemusement or an underlying hostility to the perceived collapse of empire and the supposed loss of privileges ushered in by what appeared to be fundamental social changes epitomized by the growth of both trades union power and the Welfare State. The subliminal assumption is that there existed some grounds for an intellectual privilege if all else failed. About the latter Murdoch is ambivalent and sees it as

> the reward of 'empiricism in politics'. It has represented to us a set of thoroughly desirable but limited ends, which could be conceived *in non-theoretical* terms; and in pursuing it, in allowing the idea of it to dominate the more naturally theoretical wing of our political scene, we have to a large extent lost our theories. [...] We have suffered a general loss of concepts, the loss of a moral and political vocabulary. (26)

The intellectual conclusion that the (then) contemporaneous represents a diminishment is strong and persistent among post-war writers. Such responses of course include very similar concerns to those that Thatcher would address in her appeal to middle-class conservatism that persisted throughout the post-war period. Whatever doubt as to the role of Britain, the intellectual class continued to appear in and create novels that in the main narrated and critiqued a set of values where liberalism, intellectual observation, and a social interaction are rooted mainly in privileged existences in Westminster, Chelsea and Hampstead and that make the most of these settings, a direct inheritance from Bloomsbury. The reaction to the perceived profundity of social change by this class was to focus on their own social concerns, dismiss the world upheaval and the deep divisions evident in the period between the world wars, and develop an almost neo-Victorian notion of stability. Often the really significant reactions to these transitions are hidden in the fine detail of the texts. For instance,

Angus Wilson cannot resist a throwaway sideswipe at the Welfare State in *Anglo-Saxon Attitudes* (1956) when Dr Rose Lorimer avoids criminal prosecution for a series of poison pen letters. 'The poor lady was certified, and, by some strange freak of the National Health service, confined in an asylum near Whitby. There for many months she gazed upon the hated ground where, at the famous Synod, the true, the Celtic Church had met its defeat' (329). And yet Wilson uses the young, idealistic secretary to one of Gerald's sons and mistress to the other to challenge Englishness from within on grounds of an ill-informed neo-Arnoldianism: ' "We all know about English Philistinism forcing geniuses into rebellion, killing Keats, and all that. But for ordinary civilized people like me it's simply ghastly." She waved her fork at him menacingly. "It's easy enough to make fun of the intelligentsia of Europe, their earnestness and their cafés, but at least they aren't provincial. *Every single* English intellectual is *provincial* and bloody," she ended savagely' (172). Moreover, in a novel about the authenticity of history, as with much of the immediate post-war writing, for Wilson certain social stabilities persist even if they might be under challenge. Gerald is very much centre of his world and does enjoy its privileges, a share of which social capital has been passed on to his children. As Head comments, 'One of the myths of the 1950s is that this was a decade of social stability, courtesy, and traditional family values' (83). Such a view is parodied and yet curiously inculcated, as Head points out, by Wilson in *Anglo-Saxon Attitudes*, where the patrician conservatism of the middle classes and their intellectual culture is made evident. And yet rather than being another 'chronicler of the dissolution of middle-class liberalism' (76) Wilson is far more forthright in marginalizing a whole class through his parody of working-class existence in the Salad family and he satirizes the *arrivistes* that threaten the complacency of the self-appointed intellectually superior inheritors of Edwardianism and Bloomsbury like Professor Gerald Middleton whose antipathy toward historical novelist Clarissa Crane is rooted in his view of a fragmenting notion of history. Social change is a complex process, but the peregrinations of the cultural identity of the academic elite sketched as normative by Wilson convey only something of a crisis of a particular identity. The popularization of cultural form offers another possibly deceiving paradigm. Head is correct in perceiving that to see change in this familiar dream being driven by 1950s youth culture, 1960s promiscuity and 'second-wave' 1970s feminism is to make 'too much of the eventual visible manifestations of longer-term adjustments' (83).

For Gąsiorek '[E. M.] Forster's soul-searching provides important clues to the work of John Fowles and Angus Wilson. Both writers see themselves as social democrats, although they are critical of the political traditions they support' (97). And of Wilson he concludes 'He focuses in particular on what he sees as liberalism's unwarranted confidence in the value of culture and the intrinsic worth of the individual, suggesting that Forsterian humanism frequently conceals gross self-deception and blindness to evil' (97). This is essentially correct, but what Gąsiorek's analyses ought to alert us to is an understanding that middle-class fiction, including Wilson's, most often responds sociologically to its own literary and cultural presence, with a strong notion of an already accepted and established view of middle-class aesthetic and intellectual worth. In what Gąsiorek sees as a reassertion of realism and traditional forms, a turning away from modernism, one must observe that these makings of position represent a form of self-regarding reflexivity, in that they prioritize the response of literature to a literary culture. The parody of social change that such writers inscribe is equally significant. Although Gąsiorek comments, 'For Wilson, Virginia Woolf symbolized modernism's greatest weakness: its neglect of the social dimension' (98), and despite Wilson's later change of heart concerning his lack of aesthetic recognition of Woolf's merits, I feel less convinced by the efficaciousness in contrast to hers of Wilson's 'social dimension' than does Gąsiorek. Furthermore even though, as Gąsiorek points out in terms of *Anglo-Saxon Attitudes*, that often Wilson's controlling mode of gentle parody is more important than the literary pastiche, it is difficult to describe the assumptions upon which his depictions of the working classes are based as a matter of gentle parody, or to claim as Gąsiorek does that 'Wilson combats the waning of a historical consciousness by creating a panoramic canvas' (101). His remains a narrow vision or a sliver of the panoramic (unless of course everything ontological is universal). And other critics tend to narrow the perspective of novels by their critical endeavours. Typically Neil McEwan in *The Survival of the Novel: British Fiction in the Later Twentieth Century* (1981) praises John Fowles's *The French Lieutenant's Woman* (1969): 'The success of Dr Grogan as a character, his blend of intellectual freedom and social conventionality, true to the solidity of life the book creates, vouches for the truth of his humanistic belief; his credibility resists the tricks the technique plays with it. The narrator's new-novelistic interventions come to seem a form of unreliability, which does not, finally, interfere with the character's integrity' (36). McEwan cites somewhat uncritically and out of context Murdoch's assertion 'Real people are destructive of myth' (36). As Cassirer says in *The Metaphysics of Symbolic Forms* 'Wherever specifically human existence and life is apprehended, we already find it wrapped up in the primordial forms of myth. It does not "have" these as objects; rather it *is* in them, has entered into them and is interwoven with them. This holds for the details of myth as well as myth as a whole' (19). Historically modernity is genealogically derived from the mythic and its domain persists in its interstices and within its identity. This is one of the functions of fiction, to play out this relationship.

Such a narrowing is not restricted to a few writers or critics such as McEwan, for in truth a restriction of class perspective is almost endemic among many from the category of 'literary' writers who emerged before 1979, even among those highlighted critically by many as exemplifying a new vision. In *The Nice and the Good* (1968) for all her satirizing of middle-class values, Murdoch negates both working-class and populist existence so much one wonders whether this is meant to reflect or contest 'a far too shallow and flimsy an idea of human personality'. Such a narrowing of perspective reinforces a world-view, and reinforces a class privilege just as implicitly and as effectively as Angela Carter's view of pornography in *The Sadeian Woman: An Exercise in Cultural History* (1979) since 'pornography reinforces the archetypes of her [woman's] negativity and that it does so simply because most pornography remains in the service of the status quo' (17). My feeling is that this has been essentially true of the majority of serious, literary fiction in Britain in the twentieth century until very recently. In terms of novelistic practice, human personality for Murdoch, for instance, seems too often simply a series of middle-class co-ordinates. When John Duncane dumps his mistress, Jessica, Murdoch creates a cardboard cut-out background that defers to bourgeois values.

> John Duncane had been the first great certainty in Jessica's life. She had never known her father, who died when she was an infant. The working-class home of her mother and stepfather had been a place which she endured and from which she ultimately escaped into an art school. But her life as a student now seemed to Jessica to have been substanceless, seeming in retrospect like a rather casual drunken party. She had been to bed with a number of different boys. She had tried out a number of new and fashionable ways of painting. No one had tried to teach her anything. (82–3)

Particularly in terms of class and youth this characterization cannot even be elevated to qualify as parody. Murdoch fails to penetrate such lives. For all her supposed metaphysical ruminations concerning socialism, like so many other writers of this period she is unable to transcend the snobbery of her own position in the social hierarchy. The shooting that opens the novel reveals a fragmentation and perversion among the establishment, but only the most naive would see this as anything but a lack of self-conviction revealing the true underlying conditions of such a class. Lawrence, Woolf and Mansfield all indicate such hidden secrets. Murdoch like so many writers is stuck in a world projecting a sense of contemporary crisis, but one where the intellectual and political class remain secure in their superior vision of the world. In assessing a renewal of personal crisis at the beginning of *Under the Net* (1954) Jake Donaghue concludes of his Irish companion and follower:

> I would be at pains to put my universe in order and set it ticking, when suddenly it would burst again into a mess of the same poor pieces, and Finn and I be on the run. I say my universe, not ours, because I sometimes feel that Finn has very little inner life. I mean no disrespect to him in saying this; some have and some haven't. I connect this too with his truthfulness. Subtle people, like myself, can see too much ever to give a straight answer. Aspects have always been my trouble. And I connect it with his aptness to make objective statements when these are the last things that one wants, like a bright light on one's headache. It may be, though, that Finn misses his inner life, and that that is why he follows me about, as I have a complex one and highly differentiated. Anyhow, I count Finn as an inhabitant of my universe, and cannot conceive that he has one containing me; and this arrangement seems restful; for both of us. (9)

This certainty that Murdoch satirizes gently was certainly a determining feature of the middle classes and their fiction, and at one level centres Murdoch's own narrative responses, but as she senses new conditions represent a need to adapt a renewed and reconfigured sense of the self. As McEwan comments Jake is a 'socially mobile intellectual adventurer hero' (19), but he is entirely an affiliate of the established class nonetheless. The novel becomes more than a reflection of the kinds of middle-class discussions such as that concerning socialism between Jake and Lefty that Murdoch sketches from a somewhat unconvincing platform of critical superiority. Change though is concrete and historical, if conveyed symbolically. By the novel's end Finn returns to Dublin and Jake still finds difficulty in contemplating a more equal or balanced relationship. 'I tried to imagine this; Finn at home and I a visitor. I shook my head. "I couldn't," I said' (279).

It is significant that this social narrowing of narrative focus in many novels represents a vision of British culture and a viable literariness that has been shared by many British literary critics, since generally (with notable exceptions such as Christopher Norris and Alan Sinfield) it passes without notice or analysis; as a consequence in general such critics have failed to contextualize sufficiently the dynamics of the field. This assumption has declined in the contemporary period, and clearly if there exists or one can at least refer relevantly to, for example, a postcolonial phase of Anglophone fiction, or an African literary discourse, or even a British modernism, then the contemporaneity of each type of fiction published and originating in the British Isles can be used as a method of marking out a field of interrelated activities, creative and critical, that represent a market area of literal and cultural capital, and offering a way of understanding the dynamics of such a field of 'possibles' (to use Bourdieu's terminology) and activities. They are sociologically and aesthetically interrelated in some way, even if by their differences or omissions. This is not to claim or even imply any absolute value that cannot be further interrogated (or fragmented). This study does not claim to be a survey of the period, but rather selects certain key texts to demonstrate some of the underdetermined – critically at least – forces at play in the social, literary, critical and political spheres, none of which is sealed or can resist interpenetrative flux. Nor are such fictions simply narratives resistant to material, ideological or life-world influences. Hence the historical changes of the 1970s create the grounds for a new wave of writing, not divorced from previous ones, but sufficiently distinct to merit critical placement and exegetical difference. J. G. Ballard writes in the introduction to the French edition of *Crash* (1974) that it is incorrect to believe that 'The dominant characteristic of the modern mainstream novel is its sense of individual isolation, its mood of introspection and alienation, a state of mind always assumed to be the hallmark of the twentieth-century consciousness' (6), since this characterizes the nineteenth century and for Ballard 'if anything befits the twentieth century it is optimism, the iconography of mass-merchandizing, naivety and a guilt-free enjoyment of the mind's possibilities'. Ballard indicates a transformation in thinking of fiction that will negate any remaining anti-modernist naturalism and pervade the fiction of the period after 1979. It is characterized by a ludic and yet an extrinsic sense of multiple, intersubjective realities.

Changing Perspectives
The apparent essentials upon which writers like Drabble build the appearance of 'radicalizing' reflection are those characteristics and strategies that will fragment and change in the next phase of fiction, not consistently or uniformly, but in multiple and fragmentary perceptions and narrative models explored by a transformative generation of writers drawing on a different range of earlier textual examples from Virginia Woolf and Katherine Mansfield, through Evelyn Waugh, Wilson Harris and B. S. Johnson and on to J. G. Ballard and Muriel

Spark. This disturbance of an immutable subjectivity and a discursive rationality has in itself been over-determined in postmodern accounts. It relies on a notion of a meta-reality that is not intrinsically textual. In the world of *Palace of the Peacock* (1960) Wilson Harris subverts both historical certainties and the primordiality of subjectivity; he combines the nightmarish, mythopoeism and the colonial imaginary. Echoing and subverting both Conrad and earlier colonial ambitions Harris has his protagonist Donne reflect 'We stood on the frontiers of the known world, and on the selfsame threshold of the unknown' (75). It took until the late 1970s before Britain acknowledged its boundaries and ambitions had altered, before the geo-historical changes transformed a multiplicity of the aspects of the nation. Certainly this new phase of writing is increasingly aware of aspects of intersubjectivity in its admission of an ongoing literary dialectic. The very notion of post-coloniality depends upon negating a centring, hegemonic discourse, but its very challenge depends upon interrelated communities of otherness and radicality. Its radical dynamic can only be achieved by an ongoing cultural interrogation. In fictional terms this can be expressed through structure, revision of narrative traditions, a socio-logical awareness, metaphoricity, and so forth. The domain of the self and the self-aware is only one part of a sociological narrative structure. This is why some conservatively inclined writers with a topographical reflection of social change have been misread as progressive and socially challenging. I suggest one should remain deeply suspicious of the literary accounts of the culture by the often complacent intellec-tual elite in the manner of Iris Murdoch, for instance. To reflect upon change in terms of its surface features is insufficient. In contrast, other underlying, radicalizing qualities – however imperfectly understood or conveyed – are the driving force in the works of so many contemporary writers, as we shall see.

Dominic Head finds Bergonzi's critique pessimistic, but he concedes: 'One has to grant, further, that the picture he painted has remained partially true of the post-war novel, notably the preoccupation with parochial themes and topics, and the distrust of experimentation and formal innovation. A focus on the particular, however, need not be taken to signify an inferior form of attention' (6–7). Responding to Bergonzi's objection to the fine distinctions of the English liberal class, Head comments 'The real issue may be the (relatively) undramatic nature of the social life in post-war England, which has not provoked the intense kinds of novelistic discourse that one associates with unstable or extreme political systems' (21). And yet here Head simply echoes Bergonzi's observation over thirty years earlier about the Eng-lish (distinguished in Bergonzi from the Scots and Welsh traditions) and their nation as if this were ongoing cultural and historical continuity. Bergonzi comments:

> It did not undergo the radical transformations that took place in countries which underwent the traumatic experiences of totalitarianism and defeat in war. Ancient traditions and continuities remained undisturbed; there is still a visible stress on the idiosyncratic and the amateur; and a corresponding distaste for the systematic and doctrinaire. In cultural matters we find an unrepentant insularity and an involvement with native elements and traditions, as against the cosmopolitan innovations of the Modern Movement. (58–9)

This is an interesting response by Head in many ways, since firstly Bergonzi's critique is revealing of a number of potential sources of the dynamics of future change, but also because for Head 'the post-war novel' is perceived too much as a cultural and aesthetic whole, unmediated by any major seismic cultural activity. It is not simply a point of Head's later comment that 'Thatcherism, as an international political phenomenon, was a radical and divisive political strategy that stimulated outrage from the novelist, whose broadly liberal sensibilities were deeply offended by the attack on traditional collective values' (45). There persists in this evaluation a dependence on an ideological and critical naivety. The previous decades outlined by Bergonzi had seen a range of radical novelists in the vanguard of attacks on the existing aesthetic where such 'liberal sensibilities' might be regarded as divisive themselves. Bergonzi makes two particularly interesting comments. First, 'That there is a crisis in the English sense of cultural identity is obvious, and what I have called the neurotic stance of much recent literature is one way of responding to it' (71); and additionally 'In American fiction the paradoxes of identity are constantly invoked' (71). He notes the obsession for things French and American in the 1950s and 1960s (64–5), implying their importance in establishing part of the grounds for a more hybrid fictional identity that appears after the mid-1970s. In fact Head's notion that the 'undramatic' nature of those years and their implicit Arnoldian stability would continue after 1979 and Thatcher's emergence runs counter to the true historical conditions. One might consider a range of issues that would constitute the conditions of the nation that Will Hutton in *The State to Come* (1997) describes where 'Inequality is perhaps the single most salient fact in contemporary British society' (6), and where 'the gains of the twentieth century – from the forty-hour week to a public library service – are all under threat' (54–5). Hutton's litany of the excesses of Thatcherism make sober reading, and confirm the dramatic nature of life for a whole range of British people, mostly outside of the middle classes it may be noted. This includes long periods of mass unemployment, the destruction of much of the trade union system and of workers' rights, mass economic migration and intermittent ethnic strife, an ongoing and endemic drug culture and its associated 'black economy', inter-mittent wars and terrorist campaigns, and rising poverty and startling inequalities. In part these are the basis of a post-1970s fictional 'sen-sibility'. Perhaps only a daily fear for life and liberty, or the threat of mass destruction could be more turbulent or traumatic, unless of course all of this was observed from a position of privilege and relative security.

Many of the underlying assumptions that have underpinned aca-demic notions of the post-war and contemporary phases of fiction have been naive; in contesting such readings let us move in subsequent chapters specifically to the grounds underpinning the vibrant literary culture which gained momentum after the election of Thatcher. Ian Haywood details certain salient factors subsequent to the 1970s in *Working-class Fiction from Chartism to 'Trainspotting'* (1997). 'The election of the Tory government in 1979 marked a sea-change in postwar British history, and resulted in a drastic reshaping of the British working class. The new Tory administration under the premier Margaret Thatcher was committed to policies of monetarism, dereg-ulation, privatization of nationalized industries and services, the crushing of trade union power, and virulent anti-Communism' (139). Haywood accounts for many of the dominant features of the Thatcher years: a divided working class; riots in 1981; Thatcher as the most unpopular premier in modern history until the 1982 Falklands War; conservative election victories in 1983, 1987, 1992; and the miners' strike 1984–5 (140). Of course, no period or event is ever discrete or absolute, but this already looks to be a different Britain than the post-war years. And why is all of this important for those interested in contemporary fiction? Well, clearly writers responded to aesthetic and theoretical notions, but also reacted to such changes and uncertainties in the world. This produced a shift in the schema underpinning the world-view, where a belief in the transcendental ego, its identity, the residual Enlightenment and scientific rationalism were shaken and created a crisis in subjectivity. The postcolonial phase itself had not deflected Britain from an age of technology, scientificity, and the white heat of such technological progress for all speculated about in the 1960s that had been derailed by world events and globalization. For the novel this all has consequences. And historic co-ordinates change. Ian McEwan's *Atonement* (2001) places a Second World War narrative firmly as a period piece, one suspects informed intertextually quite explicitly by other cultural representations rather than the collective memory of those who lived through the period, and Robert McLiam Wilson is preparing a novel *The Extremists* (2007) in which clearly from a section published as 'The Dreamed' the realities are the province of the very old and a dream-like recollection of a fragmentary and mythic nature, a 'miraculous' process beginning as the war ended, where like painful recollections the dead as unaged 'returnees' appear unexpectedly. 'It became a secret society, a ghostly mafia, a discreet empire' (316). As time has progressed the newcomers stress through their incredulities the distance achieved culturally and technologically since the war, emphasizing its distance and the cultural transformations that have occurred.

All periodizations are tenuous. Clearly, any such chronological demarcation may be argued to be fraught with conceptual and ideological difficulties, but no more so than any other commensurable definitional generic or movement boundaries. Such difficulties cannot be accounted to be an example of a fragmentation of general meaning or a verification of postmodern aesthetics. This is the kind of reductive assumption that constitutes Bataille's notion of a 'banalization' of critical thinking referred to earlier. Neither can such difficulties debar or undermine a social and literary criticism of fiction since these have become, as I will demonstrate, the essential co-ordinates of creativity, displacing generic obsessions, 'Arnoldian-Leavisite' elitism and the social interactions of the educated classes viewed in individualistic terms. That much I feel I can demonstrate.

Further Reading

Baucom, Ian (1999) *Out of Place: Englishness, Empire, and the Locations of Identity*, Princeton, NJ: Princeton University Press.
This book offers a complex historical positioning of the issue of Englishness, which nevertheless neglects class. Looks at some central figures and contexts concerned with national identity in literary-cultural terms: propounds various notions of migrancy and post-imperial melancholy.

Bergonzi, Bernard. *The Situation of the Novel* [see bibliography].
This study provides a well-argued view of the literary scene before both the 1980s and the theory wars; it is still worth consulting for a view of this earlier period.

Cassirer, Ernst *The Metaphysics of Symbolic Forms* [see bibliography].
Another complex and yet informative study of the symbolic from Cassirer that can be rewarding for advanced postgraduate students.

Ferrebe, Alice (2005) *Masculinity in the Male-Authored Novel 1950–2000: Keeping it Up*, Basingstoke and New York: Palgrave Macmillan.
This book is a good interpretation of literary post-war transitions and changes from a male perspective; suitable for most levels of students, but well-informed by research and theory.

Watson, Tim (2000) 'Maps of Englishness', *Contemporary Literature*, 41 (4) Winter, 726–39.
This essay provides an overview of various books in this area from a variety of perspectives, also discussing literary texts relevant to the issue of national identity; however, at times it is predictable in its stance.

CHAPTER TWO

The Fall and Rise of the Middle Classes

KEY THEMES
Class Conflicts and Politics • Elitism • Middle-class Reflexivity / Self-obsession • New Middle-class Identities • Post-1970 Middle-class Culture • Victorian Values and Legacies

KEY TEXTS

Amis, Kinsgley *Jake's Thing*
Barnes, Julian *Metroland*
Bracewell, Michael *The Conclave*
Brackonbury, Rosalind *The Coelacanth*
Bradbury, Malcolm *The History Man*
Coe, Jonathan *The Rotters' Club*
Diski, Jenny *Nothing Natural*
Drabble, Margaret *The Ice Age* / *The Millstone*
Ellmann, Lucy *Sweet Desserts* / *Varying Degrees of Hopelessness*
Ishiguro, Kazuo *The Remains of the Day*
Johnson, B. S. *See the Old Lady Decently*
Kelman, James *Not Not While the Giro and Other Stories*

Kureishi, Hanif *Gabriel's Gift*
Lodge, David *Changing Places*
Lott, Tim *Rumours of a Hurricane* / *White City Blue*
McEwan, Ian *The Child in Time*
Miller, Miranda *Smiles and the Millennium*
Moorcock, Michael *Mother London*
Murdoch, Iris *The Bell*
Orwell, George 'The Lion and the Unicorn' / 'England, Your England'
Self, Will *Junk Mail*
Storey, Jack Trevor *Live Now, Pay Later*
Weldon, Fay *The Cloning of Joanna May*
Welsh, Irvine *marabou stork nightmares*

Middle-class Crises

Neil McEwan at the end of the 1970s reflects upon the 'death of the novel' and the crisis among the post-war generation of writers. Attempting to reaffirm a continuity of tradition, he counters any need for a new aesthetic. His terms of reference are almost entirely generic and humanistic, conflating ideas of the culture with traditional Englishness, concluding: 'We have seen that relations between contemporary English novelists and their predecessors are more complex and creative (and better equipped for survival) than is recognised by the usual distinction between "experiment" and "tradition"' (163). McEwan's fear of an aesthetic crisis is perhaps rooted, despite his confidence in continuity, in the confrontation between successive generations of intellectuals and writers, and two phases of Britain's culture. Drawing upon autobiographical impulses, Lucy Ellmann in her comic novel, *Sweet Desserts* (1988), retrospectively describes in a chapter called 'Suspended Animation' the arrival of two young American sisters, Fran and Suzy Schwarz, daughters of a transatlantic academic, into the liberal humanist world of Oxford in 1970 through the voice of the younger sister, Suzy (the author's father arrived from America and his two daughters were absorbed into the English middle classes). 'Like the end of childhood that it was, England turned out to be tawdry. Scones, lardy-cakes, Eccles cakes, the rightly famous English reserve, their taste for the mundane, their pride in the postal system, the lingering memories of ration books and their resigned acceptance of unhappy occurrences, did not give me confidence' (41). Stodgy as the images are, the novel as a whole delineates a peculiarly bourgeois environment, the kind of world familiar to McEwan, where he can claim 'postmodern disruptiveness is meaningless when it loses contact with literary convention' (18), without any serious consideration of the ideological and class assumptions tied into those very conventions some sought to overturn. Although the earlier periods described in *Sweet Desserts* counterpoint the life Suzy leads in the 1980s, this moment of arrival is one of a resignation and backwardness that are sustained as an undercurrent to all of the events. Suzy's problem with food represents symbolically not only her problem with her intellectually conservative father, but with the culture she has adopted.

At the end of the decade on the eve of Thatcher's first electoral success, Rosalind Brackenbury reflects on similar dynamics in *The Coelacanth* (1979), a neglected novel of multiple perspectives which epitomizes the transitions facing the novel form, and explores the continuing obsessions of the intellectual class through relationships of and themes inherent in the lives of Margaret and Nicholas, a writer. Unlike their friends, they imagine their world to be as Nicholas describes it 'a microcosm of the whole of England' (35) claiming an irrational romanticism. The first part serves in part as an *hommage* to Virginia Woolf's *To the Lighthouse* (1927), including as it does Brackenbury's middle-class, seaside childhood holiday home setting, an intellectual husband, a scrabble of children on the beach, night terrors for a child, Jacob, and an awareness of a world in transition, even under threat.

Of course, it was closed after summer, the shared house, the house of childhood in which three brothers had grown and played; and the grandmother's hat still hanging in the cupboard waiting to be used, and the dried yellowed plimsolls that would never match, the cracked Quimper vase stained inside by bracken stalks, the mirror that knocked always gently against the wall. (108)

Such details speak of not only a Woolfian literary precedence, but also of the cultural ownership, habits and provenance of the traditional middle class that are a central inheritance of Brackenbury's narrative from Woolf. At the novel's opening the coelacanth of its title, a fish previously thought to have been extinct, an anachronism from a prehistoric past is being tossed back in the sea by horrified children. As a motif the creature suggests one reading of the position of the middle classes in a changing world, and yet Brackenbury's narrative, with its appeal to Woolf and its dissection of the personal crises and nuances of various members of that class, in fact suggests the contrary; it offers an ongoing love affair of the intellectual and educated middle classes with their own social relevance (or challenges to that determination) and with a lost Victorian/Edwardian eminence. Jasia, the vaguely lower middle-class, half-Portugese wife of an old friend of Margaret and Nicholas, says she has not imagined such snobs ever existed and complains 'It's this habit they have of assuming they're right about everything all the time. They impose their view of things, their values' (18). Her husband, Toby, responds by accusing her of snobbery, defending Margaret by pointing out her social graces. As Brackenbury suggests, part of Britain resists change, perpetuating a world of the Dalloways and Ramsays, and implicitly that it is with this social space that the new middle classes compete and yet to which they aspire nostalgically. The working class is simply absent, negated. Nevertheless, much as Woolf herself does at least implicitly in *Between the Acts* (1941), Brackenbury does interrogate the self-consciousness of the traditional middle classes. Toby suggests to Nicholas that their world might be archaic. 'All of us. All of us liberal people. Specialising in useless things. I feel it, you see, in my incapacity' (23). Toby almost rages at the complacency of their kind, of its obsession with art and the traditional novel. And yet Brackenbury predicts there is an almost Darwinian possibility of survival for this apparently endangered species. Toward the end of the novel the image of the coelacanth merges almost mystically with the child about to be born, as if it were swimming in what it senses is a predatory world, and yet continuing undaunted. Bataille comments in *the unfinished system of nonknowledge* that 'Within the liberal world, so-called changes in value retain the fundamental belief in a certain equivalence, consequently in the innocuousness of everything. The new values can be satisfied with a new literary form' (9). An emphasis common in British fiction is an authorial notion of a similar conviction of the innocuousness of liberal attitudes; even where there might appear superficially to be a literary transformation – subject matter, inclusion of new cultural values and fashions, generic shifts, self-consciousness – many writers retain a conceptual world-view based on liberal values and the cultural significance of the middle class. Concomitant to this sin of inclusion is a sin of omission that will be traced, the effective effacement or reduction to parody (at best) of the working classes.

Class Prejudices

A certain strand of fiction concerns itself with these issues, but does so almost entirely in terms of evoking middle-class existence and its turbulences, making of this class 'a microcosm of the whole of England', achieved by displacing most other elements unless ideologically and culturally mediated by that view. This Hanif Kureishi features in terms of social struggles between individuals in *The Black Album* (1995), discussed in the final chapter. In *Junk Mail* Will Self says in 'The Valley of the Corn Dollies', a disquisition first published in 1994 in part concerned with the elusiveness of the term 'culture' with reference to the English, 'Contemporary English culture is both colonizer and colonized [. . .]. Is English culture bigoted or liberal? It is both. Is it hermetic and introverted or expansive and cosmopolitan? It is all of these' (204–5). He adds 'The English obsession with class is in great shape and over the past fifteen years has received a booster course of anabolic steroids in the form of government-inspired promotion of gross economic inequality' (208). As Bart Moore-Gilbert indicates in *Hanif Kureishi* (2001) Kureishi's novel very specifically subverts the modern and contemporary middle-class campus novel, radicalizing it with 'a marked inflection [achieved] by his unrelenting attention to issues of race and ethnicity' (112). Together with its clear consciousness of the issues of class, as Moore-Gilbert suggests the novel both offers an analysis of the challenges to liberal humanism and manages to explore concepts of high culture in a way quite different from the genre traditions developed in Malcolm Bradbury and David Lodge (111–12).

Of course like any reference to a specific 'culture', as a term 'class' may prove vexatious, and there is insufficient space here for a full explanatory definition of the term 'class', but generally I take this term in great part to refer to the 'perceived interests', 'reality of social

relations' and 'reality principle (e.g. effects of oppressive power relations' (291) sketched out as aspects of the ideological order in 'The
Dialectic of Material Interests' by Roy Bhaskar in *Dialectic: The Pulse of
Freedom* (1993). In more specific terms Frank McDonough in 'Class
and Politics' (1997) makes evident the ongoing social and practical
relevance of class and its divisions even in a post-Thatcherite world,
where as a consequence of Thatcher's policies 'The result is an upper
class which has never been more wealthy' (209), noting that this is still
a society where 'though public school pupils account for only 5 per
cent of the total school population, they account for over 50 per cent
of Oxbridge places. A public school/Oxbridge education moulds an
integrated élite' (210). Hence McDonough dismisses the commentators who claim social fragmentation obviates such a perspective, which
sense of class awareness Britons instinctively recognize as persistent
(205). Bourdieu analyses the ongoing aesthetic aspects and inscriptions
of class in *The Field of Cultural Production*, involving: 'the principle of
legitimacy corresponding to 'bourgeois' taste and [. . .] the consecra-
tion bestowed by the dominant fractions of the dominant class' (51);
'the struggle between the dominated class and the dominant class'
(44); and including potentially a 'correspondence between positions
and dispositions' (72). Bourdieu's work makes clear the tenuous connection of bourgeois art with radicality and its tendency to ignore the
process by which the dominant culture – of which it is part – effaces its
own legitimacy and its derivation of 'social value from the power of
social discrimination, and from the specifically cultural rarity conferred
on them by their position in the system of cultural competencies'
(129). Many British novels engage in such 'social discrimination' in the
interests of a narrowly based world-view, and do so either actively or by
acts of omission in terms of a whole gamut of qualities such as subject
matter, characterizations, settings and all the usual suspects. More
recently, writers raise these social concerns more radically as explicit
themes.

By reconstituting fragmentary elements this chapter explores the
ongoing subtle 'emanation' of class concerns in the creative and
political process. Unimpressed by notions of a new classlessness, Asa
Briggs in *A Social History of England* (1991) maintains that under
Thatcher, despite her working-class support, 'the power of "class"
continued to remain strong' (356) and subsequently 'John Major,
promised a "classless" society. Yet differences in property and income
continued to influence social attitudes, life styles and family expectations, even more than they had done before the Thatcher governments' (356). McDonough confirms this assertion, noting that simply
'pronouncing the death of class is premature' (205) and that class is

simply becoming less visible, but no less efficacious in creating privilege
and prejudice (207). This appeal for classlessness which is unsupported
by material facts is referred to by Head in his analysis of Penelope
Lively, but nevertheless he perceives in this shift a complexification of
class that may imply a difficulty in its efficaciousness as a conceptual or
categorical tool (80). The paradoxical claim for a 'classless' British
society has an earlier lineage as a middle-class illusion of both change
and an underlying fear of unruly elements that challenge their cultural
dominance. Elements of both Thatcherism and the obsessions of the
middle classes precede the 1970s. In *Live Now, Pay Later* (1963),
satirizing the expansion of consumerism, Jack Trevor Storey very
specifically parodies both a middle-class claim for a classless society and
the paradoxical insistence of that class on the lack of aesthetic judg-
gement among the working classes (97). The social tensions of his
trilogy's provincial town setting derive from an intellectual and commercial debasing of lower-class experience. As Briggs indicates, a
detailed sense of Britain's class mechanisms may still be retrieved from
George Orwell's critique. Consider his wartime essay series 'The Lion
and the Unicorn: Socialism and the English Genius' (1941), where in
'England Your England' he declares that: 'England is the most class-
ridden country under the sun. It is a land of snobbery and privilege'
(87) and a country where the establishment looks backward to avoid
change. Thatcher radicalized this urge for the past, for Victorian
nostalgia, making an ill-informed and illusory political gesture, but in a
curious sense managed to redeem a regressive deferral to the social
forces of the past, and its inequalities. For Miranda Miller in her
dystopia, *Smiles and the Millennium* (1987), particularly through the
description of Smiles, a shantytown for the dispossessed of London, the
Thatcherite social reality is based upon the emergence of a new
underclass and social dependency. In the contrast to such deprivation,
the lives offered as a result of the theme park empire of the protagonist,
Simon's parents, modelled on the new Thatcherite middle classes in
their anachronistic and Darwinistic rush for wealth, are divisive,
echoing as a populist version of the privileges of the imperial middle
classes. The government uses spectacle and a conscious evocation of
the 'Dunkirk spirit' to efface the gulf between the classes (187). As
Simon's lover, Christy, reflects of his brother Merlin and the parental
home,

> She couldn't see his face but she knew he was at home here, safe,
> with enough space to dream in. The sooner we get him to Smiles
> and he sees what real life is, the better, she thought viciously. He
> was the image of pampered childhood. Then she remembered

he'd suffered quite a lot, for someone of nine. Middle-class suffering was always psychological. (235)

Arguably this sense of angst is what underpins the crises of Martin
Amis's anguished males. As with Keith Talent in London Fields (1989),
who remains a parody of the working class, Amis makes these men
central to a new populist ethos, downplaying the persistent realities of
ownership and power, blurring ideological responsibility and density of
ideological influence. As Frantz Fanon comments in the colonial
context analysed in The Wretched of the Earth (1963): 'The working
classes of the towns, the masses of unemployed, the small artisans and
craftsmen for their part line up behind this nationalist attitude; but in
all justice let it be said, they only follow in the steps of their bourgeoisie' (125). These are recurrent Thatcherite strategies. After
Thatcher's successive electoral victories, for most writers the emotional unity of the nation to which Orwell alludes in wartime seems
something from another age, but perhaps a sense of Orwell's claim for
an 'invisible chain' helps explain the mood of nostalgia and mourning
of the preceding generation of post-war writers. Even after the mid-
1970s other aspects of Orwell's critique remain relevant, including the
innate class divisions, an avoidance of social change and the role of the
intelligensia as 'sub-sections of the middle class' (93) despite the
attempt of that very class to efface its central role and its tendency
noted by Orwell to denigrate the nation and its customs. In Miller's
novel the complicity of the middle classes in the new social divisions
and immiseration is a major theme, and so too is their concomitant
denial of their own relative privilege. As Christy reflects on being
invited to Simon's friends, 'She was mystified that all these middle-class
people were convinced they were poor. Surely it was only the difference
between owning a vast flat and a medium-sized one, between holidays
in India and in Devon, between good wine every evening and an
occasional bottle of plonk?' (208). Few writers of the period address
privilege quite so bluntly and directly. Although as Ballard indicates in
his conversation with Will Self in Junk Mail, a resurgence of class
interests and divisions began to separate the 1970s from the preceding
consensus, indicating regressive elements in the culture. 'When the
class system began to ... well, it didn't disintegrate but it seemed
irrelevant in the sixties, I thought, "How wonderful, this country is
about to join the twentieth century." And then in 1971 – I think
Heath had just got back into power – I heard someone use the phrase
"working class" and I thought, "Oh God, here we go again"' (340).

Resisting Social Change

Like nationality, in Britain class is an elusive or protean concept. Orwell recognizes that Englishness is both difficult to define (76) and will be subject to change, but he does specify certain key characteristics about the nature of the society, including the importance of class in the nation's culture, including its intellectual culture. This is despite his recognition of 'the upward and downward extension of the middle class' and 'the spread of middle-class ideas and habits among the working class' (97) an ongoing social factor that has been exaggerated in its effect in terms of removing difference and privilege. As Orwell makes evident the improvement of living conditions is often a matter of outward appearance where 'The unjust distinctions remain, but the real differences diminish' (98). Orwell's Britain is still divided immensely in terms of wealth (83), its popular culture of 'the common people' (78) exists separately from that of the 'bourgeosie' and more generally is defined by two characteristics: 'One is the lack of artistic ability. [...] And linked up with this, though not very obviously, is the lack of philosophical faculty, the absence in nearly all Englishmen of any need for an ordered system of thought or even for the use of logic' (85). Arguably it is the wish to compensate for this first deficiency that continues to mark out the intellectual and literary middle class, and their celebration of Orwell's second failing expresses itself variously in the guise of the amateur rather than the expert, and in a humanistic liberalism that is implied to be a vehicle of cultural continuity. Bradbury's *The History Man* catches the mood of change that marks out the two intellectual phases of the post-war period. His text can be read as incorporating both of the Orwellian prejudices. The novel is ultimately concerned with the expansion and emergence of a new middle class, epitomized by the protagonist, Howard Kirk, and his wife:

> They came, both of them, from well-conducted and more or less puritanical homes, located socially in that perplexing borderland between working-class anarchism and middle-class conformity. [...] Both of them, Howard and Barbara, had had sights lifted by a grammar school and university education, but they had retained toward that education the same attitude that their parents had held; it was an instrument, a virtuous one, for getting on, doing well, becoming even more respectable. (23)

However radical its stance, the very title of Howard Kirk's first book, *The Defeat of Privacy*, marks it as being concerned primarily with middle-class cultural values. The Kirks represent what Briggs describes as a transition where 'The real break had come during and after the middle years of the 1950s, when, with increased prosperity, educational opportunity and social and physical mobility, society seemed to be more fluid and less willing to accept old ways' (357). As Briggs makes clear Thatcher rejected consensus and challenged the welfare state so that 'The underlying philosophy was economic individualism, even in the name of restored Victorian values' (355). Like Thatcher, Bradbury sets himself up in opposition to the forces that the Kirks represent, and appears in Hitchcockian fashion toward the novel's conclusion, with a brief exchange with his protagonist. Kirk for all the detail of his life remains a parodic figure, an 'Aunt Sally', mocked for his social interventionism and commitment to causes. More substantially in the tradition of 'a middle-class microcosm of the whole of England' that underpins Bradbury's narrative position, Kirk is damned essentially firstly for being uncreative, expressed in his implicit jealousy of and subsequent attack on a literary student, and secondly in a more profound sense for holding views antithetical to Bradbury's liberalism. The grounds for this undermining of theory seem to derive ultimately from the very middle-class liberal values identified by Orwell.

So what inspires such middle-class attacks on this kind of theory and radicalism that appears to be interpreted as being at odds with Britain's underlying liberal position? Traceable in earlier fiction, it surely expresses something of the self-image of the intellectual class, and this legacy may persist. Certainly most aesthetic issues remain political ones. The condition, conflicts and nuances of power among the different echelons of the middle classes much occupied post-war writers. It is true as Head says

> This state of affairs in society as a whole hinges on the larger middle-class group, which thus emerges as the crucial (and culpable) term in the post-industrial equation. The nature of what it means to be 'middle-class' is transformed in the post-war years, generating a crisis of identity no less problematic than that which surrounds working-class experience, and post-war novelists have not left the contradictions of middle-class experience unremarked. (75)

It is important to note that such a transformation might in fact have engendered a climate of progressive change among intellectuals, but this is most often not the case in terms of the majority of the fiction of this period cited critically. Head's analysis also neglects three major elements: a middle-class identity crisis is concerned with a position of relative privilege and hegemonic power; the continuity of privilege in British culture; and the capacity for many key writers to pick obsessively over their own middle-class identities to the exclusion of almost everything else. This capacity explains much of what Mark Currie in *Metafiction* (1995) takes more narrowly as constituting a generic reflexivity which he labels 'Literatureland, the place where texts and acts of interpretation constitute the world of experience which the novelist, knowingly or unknowingly, represents' (3). This has wider ideological signification than simply an avowal of metafictional undercurrents.

For Margaret Drabble in *The Ice Age* (1977) there is a sense that change ought to be immanent and yet the patrician Victorian legacy smothers the nation in tradition and a refusal by the establishment to grasp alternatives. Curiously the new wave of the middle classes is the conduit for these regressive values. Anthony Keating somehow finds a Balkan jail to be preferable to 1970s Britain, a state that the narrative perceives as needing recovery. Anthony ponders on the condition of the nation before his ill-fated foreign journey that ends the novel:

> The room was a room of the past. Nothing in it spoke of a future. Victorian England surrounded him, as it had hung on Clegg's office wall, in the shape of camels and an oasis, and dangled from his office ceiling, in the shape of the crystal chandelier. So that was it, that had been England. Anthony stirred, restlessly. Surely, even as a boy, he and his clever friends had mocked the notion of Empire? Surely they had known all the past was dead, that it was a time for a New Age? But nothing had risen to fill the gap. He and his clever friends had been reared as surely, conditioned as firmly, as those like Humphrey Clegg, who had entered the old progression, learned the old rules, played the old games. [...] But where were the new tricks? They had produced no new images, no new style, merely a cheap strained exhausted imitation of the old one. Nothing had changed. Where was the new bright classless enterprising future of Great Britain? (252–3)

His inclination is that the future must obtain from a spirit of enterprise, the very middle-class identity pervading the early novel. In contrast, B. S. Johnson in *See the Old Lady Decently* (1975) deconstructs the (always) oppressive nature of empire, its genocidal origins, and the potential common cause of the new imperial subjects and the British working classes, but a world where in the General Strike 'There were too many ignorant to make it work; and the ignorant are always for the *status quo*. Insufficient workers obeyed. Had they done so, they could have had them on toast, the soup-kitchen ladies and Etonian bus drivers' (92). Johnson's view is more sceptical and historical, more deconstructive, recalling economic crisis.

We abandoned the phallic gold standard because we could not keep it up, and devalued by thirty-five per cent. We docked sailors' wages, and other civil servants suffered in silence. We abandoned Free Trade and imposed a General Tariff on imports. We were changing, oh so unwillingly, we were totally failing to look ahead, we were so complacent; and as usual we were governed by a devastating coalition of fools and criminals. Oh, brave days, those, they said! (122)

The collective 'we' of course is ironic. Hence, in contrast, in Drabble Keating's apparently innocent reflections adopt a range of middle-class assumptions that Johnson would find ludicrous, but they do encapsulate the tensions in the contemporary world for writers from the middle classes reflecting on their own presence and cultural influence.

One senses in this the intellectual preparation of the grounds that allowed many among the intelligentsia to support Thatcher and her project. Underlying Keating's reflection is a presumption that only the energies of a revitalized middle class can rescue the nation. This social and intellectual presumption has historical roots in terms of capital and power, for as Fanon says 'The European states achieved national unity at a moment when the national middle classes had concentrated most of the wealth in their hands. [...] The middle class was the most dynamic and prosperous of all classes' (75). Considering the dead hand of the past is not simply to dismiss middle-class aspirations. It involves a deep sense of nostalgia and loss. One strategy is to excuse one part of the middle classes by ascribing the sins of the past simply to patriarchy. However, although Drabble intimates that Keating's opinion is really an expression of issues of masculine power, this theme of the dead hand of the past, of a notion of former glories and social stabilities, persists in the age of feminism. It is perhaps considered differently in Ishiguro's *The Remains of the Day* where through the apparently self-effacing narrative of Stevens, the butler to the aristocracy, the narrative demonstrates the arrogance of the upper classes whom Stevens serves and the paradoxical identification with this tradition by the very middle classes who are despised by this elite. In post-war conditions Stevens can be argued to represent those continuing this bourgeois aspiration for supposed traditional values and structures. Before the war Stevens recalls being questioned on detailed political issues by his master, Lord Darlington's dinner guests. They laugh at his inability to answer. ' "And yet," Mr Spencer went on, "we still persist with the notion that the nation's decisions be left in the hands of our good man here and to the few million others like him. Is it any wonder, saddled as we are with our present parliamentary system, that we are unable to find any solution to our many difficulties? Why, you may as well ask a committee of the mothers' union to organize a war campaign'" (196). Lord Darlington may epitomize the aristocracy's fascistic tendencies, but Ishiguro in part creates in his narrative certain key themes recurrent in a range of post-1979 novels.

Apparent Transformations

The post-1970s generation of writers while seeking to reconfigure a legitimate middle-class identity, distancing their cultural identity from the hegemony or elitism of the past, are not immune to assuming the superiority of their critical perceptions to which supposedly 'radical' novelists of the post-war period were prone. In part this resulted paradoxically from centring narrative on bourgeois life incapable of seeing its replication of renewed versions of older partialities. It is important to emphasize that much of this expresses a response to a perceived threat, for the middle classes were shocked at the scale of the Labour victory in 1945 and the apparent decline of Britain's role on the world stage, and that this trauma was to bifurcate and become apparently diffuse, without negating its underlying set of prejudices. Nevertheless, for many authors any attempt to redefine the bourgeois self seems a threat. One senses a shock for the traditionalists by the 1970s. Kingsley Amis responds acerbically in *Jake's Thing* (1978) to therapy, feminism, the activities of the trades unions epitomized by British Leyland (considered far more sympathetically by Coe in *The Rotters' Club*, 2001), and finally women generally with

> their concern with the surface of things, with objects and appearances, with their surroundings and how they looked and sounded in them, with seeming to be better and to be right while getting everything wrong, their automatic assumption of the role of injured party in any clash of wills, their certainty that a view is the more credible and useful for the fact that they hold it, their use of misunderstanding and misrepresentation as weapons of debate, their selective sensitivity to tones of voice, their unawareness of the difference in themselves between sincerity and insincerity, their interest in importance (together with noticeable inability to discriminate in that sphere), their fondness for general conversation and directionless discussion. (285)

It seems difficult to agree with Neil McEwan's position that Amis possesses 'a common sense that guards his work from the pretentiousness afflicting some writers of black comedy in France and America' (97). Exactly whose kind of 'common sense'? Amis shares Murdoch's 'pretentiousness' in assuming that the legitimacy of an intellectual judgement and viewpoint can overcome mediocrity. Amis's uncertainty reflects a major shift in the cultural mood of the 1970s.

As Brackenbury reflects in her characterization of Nicholas and his friends in *The Coelacanth*, certainly many of the earlier pre-1979 novelists and intellectuals seem willing to indicate a lack of agreement even among the middle classes, and further resist the synthesis of any new critique upon which the next generation could both agree and rebuild new versions of authority. Middle-class life, as Brackenbury senses and as Ellmann insists, possesses a sacral quality in the self-imaging of that class, from which most authors emerge, and this is part of their self-mystification. This becomes increasingly the subject for thematic reflexivity. In *How the Dead Live* (2000) Self makes these instinctive discriminations transcend life and permeate the afterlife itself. 'Dulston was as good an area within which to exercise the greyhounds of my contempt as any living suburb of London. Who'd've imagined it – but the late English middle classes were exactly the same pompous pricks they'd been when alive. Still piling up infinitesimal gradations of accent, demeanour and education into staggeringly baroque edifices of class' (206). As seen earlier in this study, in their experience of a real, living Britain when faced with change, bourgeois intellectuals began to apply the notion of everything breaking down and of the fragmentary to the world as a whole rather than the hegemonic system they had lost. These imploding certainties are not those of the population of either Britain or the empire at large, but of certain classes. And yet certainly there is a historic change that is hardly a rupture, more a return to a more uncertain, less planned or controlled social and economic determinism, with its market fluctuations. Michael Moorcock indicates his recognition of these forces in *Mother London* (1988), where journalist Mummery discusses the future of London with Tommy Mee, a recently elected Tory MP who predicts a falling London population engineered by rising property prices as part of the free market ethos. Yet, Moorcock suggests that for the majority the changes more broadly consist of an ending of a particular period of post-war conditions, whose reversal indicates not only change, but a reassertion of the greater diversity and instability of earlier social structures in its loss of the temporarily familiar.

> In the familiar situation, where no action was called for, Mummery felt comfortable. He was convinced he had lived through a Golden Age which had lasted up to the making of 'Let It Be'. Older than most of the others, he had known the true awfulness of 1950s austerity; he had enjoyed a better life than anything he had ever expected; National service had been abolished before his

call-up, the economic revival had arrived in time for him to enjoy it, and he was not going to complain, just because the best of times were passing. (103)

Increasingly in the last half of the twentieth century, the Western middle classes, including its intellectuals, did complain, announcing it was an age of the inchoate, the fragmentary, the unstable and the irrational. As global capitalism expanded, and an eco-crisis deepened, the Age of Reason was subverted and a critical position that offers an 'irrealist textualized pluriverse' began to colonize and challenge the past with its intellectual endeavours, challenging the progress of intellect, reason and science. Arguably apart from the increasing level of pollution and despoliation of natural resources, the material relationship was unchanging (or the rate of flux and change between the human subjects and the material world was fundamentally the same). Curiously, somehow, the crisis of definition and exposition became that of the world as a whole and its ontological presence. This is a fundamental paradox for creativity and fiction in such a period. Either it seeks (ultimately unsuccessfully) to become inward and solely self-referential, or it bifurcates a series of further bifurcations. Culturally, the crisis was that of the historical roots of the middle classes themselves, of the industrial, commercial and intellectual structures and traditions from which their authority derived. Essentially the movement was to fragment the declared tradition and any cultural centring in a crisis of identity and subjectivity. In Fay Weldon's *The Cloning of Joanna May* (1989) this becomes literal, where the forces of science and nature contest that of the ego. 'We would have been perfect people if we could, but our genes were against us. We would have been faithful, kind and true, but fate was against us. We are one woman split five ways, a hundred ways, a million million ways' (265). This symbolizes the concept of the fragmentary subject, determined in ways beyond itself.

Reasserting Continuities
In the 1970s the world appears in a state of flux, and yet at the moment of potentially radicalizing social and intellectual influences, more conservative middle-class forces inspired by global economic conditions create a countervailing consciousness. As feminist, postmodern and postcolonial theories cast doubt over historical and hierarchical stabilities, globalization entrenches a sense of an age of new, heightened uncertainty. There emerges a range of middle-class novelistic attempts to redefine class-consciousness, often in terms of a 'Middle Englishness' whose impulses are understanding and certainty.

As Bataille comments, 'Knowledge limits itself to *what happens* and all knowledge is extinguished if we envision *what does not happen*. We know only objects, or objectified (personal) subjects' (217). Hence the confident affirmation of familiar class co-ordinates inverting in Bataille's terms 'the substitution of the unknown for the known'. This preference explains why ironically there remains a resonance in one of the endings to Ellmann's *Varying Degrees of Hopelessness* (1991). 'Robert returned from America a wiser man, with a tan, and married Isabel. They made a very imperfect couple and lived happily ever after in the country cottage, where Robert wrote books on the sublime and Isabel carried on with her performance art. He never admitted how silly he found her work; she never mentioned how romantic she found his' (181). Imperfection as Ellmann makes clear is no barrier to intellectual and class privilege. Exposing the complacencies and con-tradictions of the middle classes of the 1970s is central to David Lodge's parody of the intricacies of such cultural dynamics in *Changing Places* (1975) where Rummidge University 'had never been an insti-tution of more than middling size and reputation, and it had lately suffered the mortifying fate of most English universities of its type (civic redbrick): having competed strenuously for fifty years with two universities chiefly valued for being old, it was, at the moment of drawing level, rudely overtaken in popularity and prestige by a batch of universities chiefly valued for being new' (14). The almost internecine war of hierarchy and prestige is itself instructive. For Philip Swallow, the amateur of this earlier age, the threat is from below, typified by the intrusive Charles Boon, who is also similarly off to Euphoric State, America.

> The young man had graduated a couple of years previously after a contentious and troublesome undergraduate career at Rummidge. He belonged to a category of students whom Philip referred to privately (showing his age) as 'the Department's Teddy-Boys'. These were clever young men of plebeian origin who, unlike the traditional scholarship boy (such as Philip himself) showed no deference to the social and cultural values of the institution to which they had been admitted, but maintained until the day they graduated a style of ostentatious uncouthness in dress, behaviour and speech. (35)

The American arrival at Rummidge, Morris Zapp, is more shocked by his Head of Department's admission that Swallow lacks both an academic field and a doctorate.

'He doesn't have a PhD,' Hogan said.
'What?'
'They have a different system in England, Morris. The PhD isn't
so important.'
'You mean the jobs are hereditary.' (60)

This very privileging social context persists in Britain's culture and
recurs fictionally. In Lodge's *Nice Work* (1988) Swallow is Dean of Arts
and the novel's protagonist is Robyn Penrose, PhD from Cambridge
and a temporary English Literature Lecturer bloodied in the so-called
'theory wars' that Lodge parodies. The narrative centres around an
exchange scheme, and her weekly visits to an engineering works,
Pringle's, to shadow Vic Wilcox, the Managing Director. The interplay
of class perspectives and their persistence is the major theme of the
text. Even though Robyn may see the novel and the spirit of capitalism
as 'expressions of a secularised Protestant ethic' (39), her own life
charts a new kind secularization, that of a middle-class aesthetic, a
politically liberal anti-Thatcherism, a commitment to progressive
causes, and a comfortable elitism in a house whose deposit is supplied
by her academic father. As the novel ends Robyn watches the students
moving about the lawns to avoid the mowing of a young gardener, by
unspoken agreement. 'There is no overt arrogance on the students'
part, or evident resentment on the young gardener's, just a kind of
mutual, instinctive avoidance of contact. Physically contiguous, they
inhabit separate worlds. It seems a very British way of handling differences of class and race. Remembering her utopian vision of the
campus invaded by the Pringle's workforce, Robyn smiles ruefully to
herself. There is a long way to go' (384). Lodge is a precursor of change
in that he configures culture, using the idea of the condition of England that is implicit in the theme of Victorian literature, as insistently
complex, drawing from strands beyond those of bourgeois self-image.
Just as Swallow is naive during his stay at Euphoric, so is Robyn despite
her notion of feminist commitment and critical edge, escaping the
fallout from her affair with Vic at her parents' South Coast sea-view
house where

> she couldn't help reflecting that although she was only a hundred
> and fifty miles from Rummidge, she might as well have been in
> another country. There was no visible industry here, and no
> visible working class. Black or brown faces were rare, mostly
> belonging to students from the University, or to tourists who
> came in motor coaches to stare at the fine old cathedral set
> serenely among green lawns and venerable trees. (305)

After the need for the immediate post-war settlement faded, and the former imperial centre had absorbed both new waves of migrants and the return of a proportion of the imperial middle classes, what is clear is that Orwell's socialist state did not emerge, and in recent years middle-class intellectuals were faced with a new reality echoing the past, an immense separation of wealth reinstated alongside the ongoing privileges with a new middle-class status reflected in most social indicators. Clearly, the aesthetic problem for many writers after 1979 becomes how to sustain a middle-class world-view that can exist in such changed conditions, one that does not appear to offer simply a replication or reiteration of the prior privileges of that class, and in its questioning of cultural conditions does not seem simply to reiterate the intellectual arrogance of the post-war generation. After the so-called cultural revolution of the 1960s, many intellectuals, including writers, saw themselves, whatever the underlying substance of their texts or lives, as a radicalizing presence. Increasingly they appear to be confronted both by what Will Self describes in 'The Valley of the Corn Dollies' as 'the cultural exhaustion suffered by the English middle class' (Junk Mail, 209), and by the persistence of class divisions, as indicated by the American narrator in Martin Amis's London Fields: 'Class! Yes, it's still here. Terrific staying power, and against all the historical odds. What is it with that old, old crap? The class system just doesn't know when to call it a day' (24). Moreover, given these contexts, what emerges is a cultural effort by the intellectual middle class to separate itself from the Thatcherite project and its perceived Philistine 'Middle England' Englishness with which very few intellectuals identify, except to perceive that it engaged in necessary change, invariably the reduction of power in the hands of the working classes. Rather than admit such levels of complicity, of course one solution for critics and writers is to invalidate the relevance of class, its negation invariably including reference to a heterogeneity and new notion of identity. Traditionalists like Neil McEwan can describe a middle-class intellectual environment of middle-class novels appropriately with reference to the wider plurality of the Victorian novel, but his primary concern is with challenges to traditional forms from experimentalism. Subtextually his descriptive criticism with its appeal to universals and an ongoing fixed moral order represents a refusal to perceive in fiction any ideological and political predispositions. Exactly for whom for instance are Murdoch's characters Michael and Dora in The Bell (1958) so 'convincing and moving' as McEwan claims (44)? The power of art is insufficient in creating the grounds for a philosophy by itself, but is dependent on a world-view. McEwan seems to avoid this necessity in his all too conventional praise of Murdoch, for how can the elision of the bulk of the population of Britain be to take life seriously or to approach it with moral seriousness (54)? This emphasis is not restricted to liberal humanists opposing 'theory', but curiously extends to its proponents. Typically, for a newer and apparently more radical rendition of this kind of view, Claire Pajaczakowska in 'The Ecstatic Solace of Culture: Self, Not-self and Other; a Psychoanalytic View' writes in support of a supposedly new radicalism in 1997 that:

> Over the last decade a new category of politics has emerged. Variously described as postmodern, post-Marxist, or identity politics, it is characterized by its recognition of the necessarily heterogeneous, if not fragmented, basis of alliances or interests. This is in contrast to assuming that there is a unified mass of shared interests or need, which would automatically lead people to identify their political interests. If historical materialism pro- vided a unified and rational theory of the politics of class, there seems to be no equivalent unification of the history of identity politics. In fact the limitations of historical materialism could be seen as the starting point of identity politics. Classical Marxism omits any sustained understanding of gender identity, race or ethnicity, childhood and ageing, as countless critiques have pointed out. (110)

One is reminded of Doris Lessing's parodies of Marxism in *The Golden Notebook* (1962). Both conflate Marx with the most generalizing applications of his theory. As Bhaskar argues variously in *Dialectic: The Pulse of Freedom* 'The most characteristically Marxian form of philo- sophical materialism is practical materialism, asserting the role of human transformative agency, based on a double freedom [...] in the reproduction and transformation of socio-spatial being' (94), 'Marx's emphasis is on causal, not conceptual, necessity' (95), and most importantly 'Marx's epistemological materialism presupposes a *differ- entiated* world' (96). However monolithic historical materialism's sup- posed preference for reading the world, even at its most banal it always represented a method that was directed at deconstructing aspects of class structures and identities. Ultimately, the kind of view typified by Pajaczakowska's assumptions is one-sided, and risks sociological naivety. Such positions confuse critique with social conditions and needs, not admitting the complex hierarchies of a heterogeneous kind that constitute social class, and its related prejudices and subjections.

One fictional response to a fragmentary world is to recover the conditions of youth, exploring rites of passage, and so creating a space of innocence, which avoids ideological culpability. Julian Barnes's *Metroland* (1980) scrutinizes quintessential suburban Englishness; it opens in 1963 with a schoolboy incursion into the National Gallery. Although Toni and Christopher represent the first fully post-war generation, the intellectual emphasis is in fact upon their traditional route from the lower to the intellectual middle classes. So what the narrator-protagonist, Christopher, later describes as his 'deconditioning' (39) by an immersion in high art in fact represents is another depiction of the tensions between the different levels of the middle classes, the very same ones found in Amis's *Lucky Jim*, the new middle classes of the industrial age aspiring to the privilege of the successors of the Bloomsbury upper middle classes who achieved a control of the aesthetic and intellectual structure and proximity to the aristocratic and commercially wealthy. Lost innocence, in the literal sense, and attempts to recover the innocence of childhood determine middle-class existence for the two males at the centre of Ian McEwan's *The Child in Time* (1987). The children's writer, protagonist Stephen Lewis, has presumably entered the world of some sort of creativity. He senses in himself an antagonism shared with other commuters inching through Thatcherite London toward the supposed freedom of the poor.

> Further up, just before Parliament Square, was a group of licensed beggars. They were not permitted anywhere near Parliament or Whitehall or within sight of the square. But a few were taking advantage of the confluence of commuter routes. He saw their bright badges from a couple of hundred yards away. This was their weather and they looked cocky with their freedom. The wage earners had to give way. (8)

This offers a vision of the culture of tension and blame emergent during the Thatcher years. The other dominant cultural dynamic is of exclusion. Ellmann's *Varying Degrees of Hopelessness* is a postmodern pastiche of a postmodern text cleverly debunking the elitism of the study and practice of art history – still renowned, however unfairly, as a notorious sanctuary for the kind of elitism I am analysing in fiction – at the Catafalque, a thinly disguised Courtauld Institute, with a fictional parody of the Surveyor of the Queen's Pictures, Sir Anthony Blunt, in charge of the institution. The proximity to privilege, patronage and a cultural aesthetic narrative could hardly be clearer. The very title of the novel conveys something of the muddle and amateurism that Ellmann sees as underpinning this kind of intellectualization of the national culture. Isabel, one central character among many, is an unworldly 31-year-old virgin addicted to the novels of Babs Cartwheel (in whom one might see an allusion to Barbara Cartland). The unfeasibility of these lives is one of the novel's central points, its being divorced from the world, and the paucity of alternatives for these people. Before the novel disintegrates into a parody of alternative endings, which mock the serio-pomposity of John Fowles's adoption of this strategy in the frame of a neo-traditional novel, the only student with any apparent self-determination, Pol, seduces her tutor, who spontaneously combusts after her departure, after which she inherits his cottage on the Norfolk coast. In Pol Ellmann creates a thoughtless postmodern version of Sally Seaton – from Woolf's *Mrs Dalloway* – the *arriviste* who although a rebel with predatory sexuality is an acceptably attractive and ultimately unchallenging social presence. The intertextual allusions and epigrammatic, parodic style allow Ellmann to sustain a cumulative effect where the whole is certainly much greater than the parts. She turns the pomposity and self-elevation of the middle classes against themselves in a very knowing and self-deprecating fashion. Bataille comments 'If laughter degrades man, sovereignty or the sacred also degrades him' (203). In the attack on romantic fiction that structures the book – with its reference to a heroine, a hero, its use of rivalry and transcending misfortune – Ellmann deflects attention initially from the real subject of scrutiny: the manners of the British middle class. She both mocks and belittles the dependency of the English intellectual class on the narratives and habits of the past – as Lodge does in *Nice Work* – as well as mapping a series of cultural intersections: emotional reserve, social snobbery, property, connections with Royalty and aristocracy, the pathology of perverse desires, which are set against these lower-middle-class aspirations and aesthetic ambition that finally support such structures.

Jenny Diski's *Nothing Natural* (1986) confronts other underlying assumptions inherent in the lifestyle of the intellectual middle class, with its proximity to the upper middle classes. The text is ironically layered so that one becomes interrogative of the very assumptions and practices underpinning the life of Rachel, the protagonist. The novel concerns itself with sado-masochism, and specifically the protagonist's previously unexplored penchant for violent buggery, and with a fear that her apparently Oxbridge lover, Joshua, might be a rapist. Rachel's world appears familiar: the Hampstead existence of a Jewish teacher working at a Home Tutoring Centre, with her dinner parties spent arguing politics; and yet her separation from upper-class male Englishness allows the narrative to critique its privilege. It is another world she knows she ought to despise. As we learn 'Joshua had given up his job as an economist with the Home Office when he had received a legacy decent enough to launch himself in the stock market' (32). The dynamic of their relationship is made concrete in her recollection of their sexual encounters and her attempt to analyse them rationally:

She remembered suddenly how he had smacked her and won-
dered how she would feel if it happened again. She couldn't figure
it out: it was, she had to suppose, aggressive. You smack someone
if you're angry with them, and she recalled his eyes as he made
love to her. Well, if Joshua were a woman-hater he had certainly
made a careful study of his enemy. Her image, if she had thought
about it at all, of 'spankers' was of ex-public school Englishmen,
men who were sexually inadequate, replacing the terror of real sex
with a bottom fetish. Repressed homosexuals punishing Mummy
for being a whore. Chinless wonders, thin, pallid men who
sometimes hit the headlines and make the nation laugh. The
English Disease. (25)

The typically English retreat into clichés is revealing. Here the perverse subjection appears to lie beyond the rationality of the middle
classes, and yet Rachel's mind turns to the Sadean notion of power and
its excesses. Her initial parody of the privileged class in some senses
defers the reality of middle-class complicity in failing to challenge the
ongoing narrative of a national identity masking the truth that
Rachel's very seduction and return for more degradation of her identity
symbolizes the vulnerability of the middle classes to indulge forms and
practices of privileges, however perverse. Despite her work with the
underprivileged it is only with Pete, a boy of mixed race tattooed with
fascist symbols, and with his IQ of 120 that she sees a potential worth
bothering with, but this is frustrated by his death after flinging himself
from a roof of a detention centre. Although Rachel might mock her
own background in her description of her mother: ' "She's a socialist
saint. Academic. Very Hampstead, very worthy. Long since cano-
nized" ' (45), Diski makes clear that Rachel's social instincts are the
same, but her sexual life is like a narrative displacement. 'She couldn't
make last night real in her mind. It dissolved like candyfloss. The
memory of events was there but not as lived experience, not as if they
had actually happened to her, last night. She might have read it, or
seen a movie. It was a recollection of a drama, of a story she had heard,
not part of the fabric of her life' (51). This is not simply an example of
estrangement or the fantasy that Rachel perceives that Joshua offers.
The implicit suggestion is that the events are far more archetypal.
Rachel wants both to be abused, and yet finally to be loved by the
patrician class that creates a narrative of its own empowerment, as
does Joshua in making Rachel voice the demand for her own abuse at
the novel's end.

One central quality of Rachel's self-image and idea of her identity is
that the position she inhabits becomes one of abandonment, by which

she can negate any idea of her own intellectual or social privilege. Her depression is an internalization of this appropriation of the ills of the world, of her insistence on its senselessness, although on a visit to her doctor she realizes others are far worse off in a practical sense. Her malaise leads her into more disempowerment at Friern Barnet mental hospital when the consultant blocks her attempt to discharge herself after a voluntary admission. The power of the state becomes apparent.

> She had put herself into another world and saw her right to choose, even her actual freedom, slip away. [...] Nonetheless liberal, middle-class, western Rachel couldn't quite believe this was happening. She was aware, however, of the rules – at least in general terms. There was a section of the Mental Health Act that allowed a doctor to keep her there against her will if he deemed her a danger to herself or others. (212)

It is only her intellectual and social precocity that saves her. And yet curiously it is an overarching authority that finally rescues her. Finally, the escalating violence of Joshua's attentions brings the intervention of the police called by neighbours, and Joshua's attempt to create a different context, and implicitly a self-justifying vocabulary for their encounters, is finally challenged by Rachel when she re-contextualizes Joshua's attempt to explain her beating:

> 'This is a misunderstanding ... this isn't what it seems ...' he began hoarsely.
> 'I wouldn't say anything if I were you,' the older of the two policemen growled, evidently fighting down his rage, as Rachel, clutching her cotton dressing gown around her, got up carefully from the bed and started to walk shakily towards the bedroom door. She stopped before she reached the two men and turned back to look at Joshua standing helplessly by the bed. Her dark eyes held his, locked them in a long cold stare as she said quietly, 'This *is* what it seems, this is real life.' (239)

This vignette is symptomatic. The perversions of privilege are revealed dramatically, as is the compliance and subjection of the lower middle classes. The insistence on a reality check to end the novel is telling. External to Rachel's self-obsession and Joshua's unmediated perversity is a world of grounded, plural and more broadly based experience. Diski indicates this thematically, but like so many other writers, the eye of the authorial lens continues to focus on the traditional subjects.

A New Emergent Elite

As Diski suggests at least peripherally, other novelists demonstrate that, in portraying a middle-class world, there can exist both a plural and an intelligently critical view of middle-class culture and its place in British society. In Jonathan Coe's *The Rotters' Club*, a novel which of course has the benefit of a greater hindsight than available to those writing during the 1970s, the issues of that period in which it is set are positioned far more comprehensively among the ideological tribulations of the decade. For Coe one predominant theme, central to his intricate and affectionate portrayal of the provincial landscape of 1970s Britain, is the wariness of the different classes of each other, despite their social and workplace proximity. The provincial setting allows a bridging of the gulf often portrayed in depictions of London culture, several families in Birmingham sharing schools and workplaces. All of the classes exist within the city and within the text itself. None is ultimately privileged in a narrative sense, as they all share the pathos of bad judgement, the bad taste of the 1970s, and being faced with a world of contradiction as Theodor Adorno describes it in *Negative Dialectics* (1966).

> It can be recognized only by the contradiction between what things are and what they claim to be. True, vis-à-vis the alleged facts this essence also is conceptual rather than immediate [. . .]. Instead, the conceptuality expresses the fact that, no matter how much blame may attach to the subject's contribution, the conceived world is not its own but a world hostile to the subject. (167)

This separates Coe from what would be an ultimately humanistic response and allows him a plurality of sorts, a cartography of pathos. The intersection of the different social classes is epitomized in an informal and yet uneasy meeting of a few representatives of management with trades union officials from the British Leyland plant in neutral territory, The Bull's Head in King's Norton. By using this apparently humanistic strategy, Coe nevertheless reminds his reader that the mythology of the demonized class war consisted of individual lives and opinions in among the brown-coloured world of 'Ted Heath's egalitarian 1970s' (16). Moreover, Coe comments on the depth and complexity of historical contextualization that is negated when a populist political culture provides the record. Coe in effect recuperates the role of the novel, its need to critique and engage, even in a post-modern environment:

> People forget about the 1970s. They think it was all about wide collars and glam rock, and they get nostalgic about *Fawlty Towers*

and kids' programmes, and they forget the ungodly strangeness of
it, the weird things that were happening all the time. They
remember that the unions had real power in those days but they
forget how people reacted: all those cranks and military types who
talked about forming private armies to restore order and protect
property when the rule of law broke down. They forget about the
Ugandan Asian refugees who arrived at Heathrow in 1972, and
how it made people say that Enoch had been right in the late
sixties when he warned about rivers of blood, how his rhetoric
echoed down the years, right down to a drunken comment Eric
Clapton made on stage at the Birmingham Odeon in 1976. (176)

It is evident from this kind of contextualization that, very unusually for
a post-war British novelist, Coe in his narrative appeals to and integrates a broad public rhetoric, establishing a mixture of ethnic and
class positions, and importantly within the voicing of the text he sets
out a series of middle-class voices – including his own implied narrative
position – where each one exists simply as a contributory viewpoint in
the generality that is the order and disorder of social affairs. The very
provinciality of the setting provides a double effect. In general terms it
emphasizes this balancing of provisionalities, and yet by using Birmingham Coe establishes as a historical moment the atrocity of the
Tavern in the Town pub bombing as part of an IRA campaign that
determined the political obsessions, necessities and discourse of the
ensuing years. Other moments emerge as significant for the cultural
landscape that will follow. The ambivalence of an incipient entrepre-
neurialism that will lead to the 1980s is alluded to with reference to
the NME/Virgin Crisis Tour and Roll-Up Reg's reference to '"This
cunt Branson – he's all right, isn't he?"' (99). Mixed in with romantic
advice Reg confronts Benjamin Trotter, the schoolboy protagonist's
assumptions, warning against categorizing the IRA and the unions as
simply malign forces. If there is any priority in Coe, it is to the instinct
of the working classes and those of the lower middle class when
uninfluenced by its love affair with aesthetic intellectualism. This
theme runs throughout his work, especially *What a Carve Up!*

In *The Conclave* (1992) Michael Bracewell considers various
nuances of class, from the ongoing and yet adaptive elitism to the
obsessive rivalry and interplay of the lower and intellectual middle
classes. The text appears to ironize and critique these failings and self-
obsession, but one drawback is that his narrative concerns itself almost
exclusively with the progress through and the suggested legacies of
Thatcherism, the failing of its cultural idioms of perpetual success. As
with Ellmann, this is a world of the Thatcherite urban experience

where virtually no one from outside of these charmed social strata is even mentioned. It might very tenuously be argued that such texts ironize the inwardness of these classes, but the exclusion is too dismissive and totalizing. In a world of the postmodern the level of narrative plurality is limited. After emerging from the lower middle classes into the elitist and consumerist Thatcherite bubble, protagonist Martin Graham Crispin Knight comes slowly to realize that perpetual success and youth are simply mythic concepts. He has been escaping from his upbringing, an existence confronted with the fact that 'Complexity and dullness, in fact, lived side by side within him' (2). Of the managerial class, Martin reacts against the suburban prosperity of his upbringing close to an environment similar to Hampstead. 'The Heath installed a further sense of paradox in Martin. His niche of middle-class comfort, it seemed, stood side by side with a tract of romantic wilderness. The old asylum, and a shallow quarry which lay to one side of it, increased the mystery of this wilderness' (5). Traumatized by bad school grades and failing to reach Oxbridge Martin studies at Liverpool Polytechnic, a city he finds disrupted and working-class. Martin redeems himself by marrying into the intellectual and moneyed class through Marilyn Fuller, through which theme Bracewell essentially updates the same kinds of social and personal dynamics found in Leonard Woolf's *Wise Virgins* (1914), and Bracewell's protagonist's character offers the mercurial presence of a postmodern Lupin Pooter, linking him surely with an earlier phase of 'yuppie' or middle-class aspirant, although this latter generation aspire to middle-aged confidence and property as opposed to Lupin's aesthetic hedonism, what Bracewell labels as 'New reactionaries'. Significantly, Marilyn – like Virginia Woolf herself – is bankrolled in life by the legacy of a rich aunt so that 'Once more, Martin was aware of the wealth that, since he was a teenager, he had always believed the urban middle classes effortlessly to possess. At home, in Thornby Avenue, such sums were only whispered about' (204). Refreshingly Bracewell is willing to indicate quite explicitly that possessions, cultural capital and actual money are often primarily issues of class and privilege. Much like the latter Victorian period, the new 1980s deregulated economy encourages new identifications, obscuring its expression of global, late-capitalist forces.

A new class of Briton, neither 'upper' nor 'lower' in background, was busily extending the scope of his territory. And it was a curious world this new class inhabited; there was a prevalent attitude, comprised of myriad impressions, amongst its young members, that some comforting spree was getting under way.

Whilst, occasionally, the politics of that era were vehemently criticised by those who were enjoying the illusion of opulence that was being created, the illusion itself was so strong and so persuasive that its boundaries could not be perceived. For this particular class, participating in a self-assured, cosmetic renaissance, all things appeared possible. Their tastes and their ambition flattered, a generation of young consumers was taking up residence in an urban wonderland. (158–9)

Martin finds himself confronted with the re-emergence of another vision of the elite. 'Martin surveyed the restaurant. A party of four, two men and two women, were conversing loudly at a neighbouring table. Their accents were like a caricature of the English upper classes at play; they appeared to be totally at ease, and were wholly oblivious to the noise they were making' (218). Conspicuous, excessive consumption marks the occasion. Martin responds with a nauseous feeling, but cannot extricate himself from this world willingly. His only escape is to fantasize about an aesthetic and cultural vision, a utopian space. From a contrast of this narrowness of vision with the pathetic and uncomprehending quality of Martin's sense of betrayal at the social collapse after Black Monday, Bracewell creates a narrative and therefore moral distance from this class that constantly dramatizes its own excesses, vicissitudes and cultural presence so as to establish a mythic sense, a denial of factuality and consequentiality.

For Martin Knight, the year 1984 – as a legendary date – had always possessed a romantic quality. A signifier of futuristic despair, the year which was just commencing, as cold, short days made him think about mythologies and 'fictions'. As the City began to grow in power and fashionability, and as those media that commented upon popular, or 'meta'-culture became more entrenched in their own vision of urban society, so too did Martin, as a willing consumer of these infatuations, begin to find something invigorating about living in a year that had been marked for oppression and despair. (165)

Otherness becomes simply an objective correlative of one's own cultural centrality that allows Bill Fuller, Marilyn's intellectual and academic father, to declare postmodernity as a belief system beyond communism and socialism, a world shattering ethics (183, 185). Nevertheless, as stated above, one notable feature of the novel is the almost total effacement of working-class life, and although it might be seen finally as an ironic gesture on Bracewell's part, perhaps finally this total absence cannot be excused or seen as transcendent. It remains part of the partial culture that it critiques. Nevertheless, Bracewell's novel remains the most acute, self-aware and politicized concerning the contemporary middle classes' notion of themselves and of British culture generally.

Contemporary Renditions of Class

Various contemporary authors continue to concern themselves – sometimes peripherally, occasionally implicitly, but mainly explicitly – with issues of a singular class perspective and often do so by reconfiguring the apparently classic British novelistic motifs of smallness, marginality and its realms of domesticity. The world of many such writers is a post-industrial remodelling of the bourgeois world of novelists such as Jane Austen. Often, the cast of characters and concerns assumes the cultural relevance of a narrow class experience, confirming the undercurrents of an individualistic late modernity. Thus it seems so concerned with individuals in their mutual interplay of a particular kind of social manners. In Ellmann's *Sweet Desserts* the world of Suzy in London of the 1980s is narrowed almost pathologically to her concerns: eating problems, relationships, unsuccessfully avoiding DHSS scrutiny of her cohabitation, her study at the round reading room of the British Museum, an arrogant male dispossessing her of her desk in the old reading room and finally motherhood briefly reminiscent of Margaret Drabble's *The Millstone* (1965). Her dependence on benefits is a passing comment. Another world defines her existence. At Hampstead at night she describes a twilight walk, terrified by rumours of psychopaths. 'My aim was good: I came out near Kenwood House, that bastion of decency, and marched out in the lighted street with a great sense of my strength and resilience' (60). Ellmann's prejudice is platonic, a belief in cultural authority and the imperishability of good. For Suzy the world in general outside of the established order, that of 'civilized' values, is threatening. As an outsider, Kenwood becomes a symbol for the evolving and yet ongoing privilege of the class to which she aspires. Finally the substance or feel of Ellmann's literary, postmodern pastiches are revealing. She makes of this world something almost singularly middle-class in its territory, obsessions and objectification, in a contemporary society that perceives in itself a greater plurality and fragmentation. Her view of London seems to confirm McDonough's suspicions. He asks, 'Can it be mere coincidence that British people reserve their most negative comments for accents associated with areas containing large groups of working-class people?' (207). Most middle-class literature fails to extricate itself sufficiently from such prejudices, for even if expressed covertly such views are present. Arguably in Ellmann's text the humour fails to create distance between the narrative and the characterized perspective. The only significant intrusion – for that is how it seems *in situ* in the text – by a member of a different social background ('the lower orders' one is tempted to say) is a vignette of a patronizing AA serviceman who is reduced to a sexist stereotype, complaining of old hags and insisting that she smile. 'I was free! I drove around for half an hour to revive the battery, and to recover from the AA man. And was it AA policy to ignore the old bangers of old hags?' (89). Similarly, in *Varying Degrees of Hopelessness*, the only working-class character is a taxi driver that Pol seduces for a one-night stand. This solitary moment of presence is telling, but in its very paucity it remains problematic, since typically for such middle-class narrative orientation, and despite some cutting satire, like the novels of the preceding generation, few of these novelists allow the majority 'other' of society into their social narrative. Ellmann may be making an oblique critical point through this absence or negation, but much as her work is admirable in many ways her practice separates her insufficiently from the class and intellectual traditions to which she is not only responding, but in which she must surely be considered as being immersed. Among major exceptions are novelists such as Coe, Diski and Michael Moorcock. In contrast to Ellmann's cabby, in Moorcock's *Mother London* a cabby driving two of the major characters, Mary and Leon, to Kensal Green Cemetery offers them his Cockney erudition. ' "I like to drive at night. That's when the city's bones show. It helps you." The taxi-driver drew up outside the great Doric gates and removed his pipe from his mouth. "All Greek Revival here, see. Portland Stone." His curly grey hair, horn-rimmed glasses and soft, tanned square face emphasised a broken nose' (120). Absences in texts must be as significant as that which is present, familiar ground in postmodern and postcolonial theory. This is so especially in terms of assessing their contributions to cultural and literary discourses. And the lack of presence of working-class characters of any real merit may be a significant feature. The discourse of the middle classes concerning themselves needs closer scrutiny as to its fuller social and ideological significance. It can be one of the most recursive, regressive and resistant of narratives. As one character, David Mummery, the son of a Speedway rider, says to an old friend in the chapter 'The Yours Truly 1980' in *Mother London*, which counters this narrowness by the diversity and ambition of its urban cartography: ' "The further away from common reality you go, the better things look. Money does that, Leon. The middle classes, no matter where they started from, really hate to hear bad news. They'll discount it or discredit it in any way they can. Being middle-class is accepting the conspiracy of lies" ' (394–5). This 'conspiracy' is an uncomfortable and mostly unacknowledged factor within the literary field that most academics refuse to address sufficiently.

Authors may explore a sense of localized community in an increasingly disjointed world, but mostly through a middle-class prism, often with undercurrent hankerings for Bloomsbury. Nevertheless, rather than being subsumed by the crisis of an increasingly complex culture, the characters and narrators in a range of contemporary writers – almost too numerous to mention, but including Martin Amis, Jonathan Coe, Jenny Diski, Esther Freud, Alison Kennedy, Will Self, and Iain Sinclair – very specifically interrogate the crises of identity of their own class, its enculturation and the species of peculiarly liminal urban ontological existence that they at least imagine that they particularly have to endure. Mostly they assume a degenerative crisis or a world suffused with banality to which their own existences are opposed and therefore assumed to have radical potential. This is the 'trick' (or strategy of self-effacement concerning the ills of the world) derived in part from the so-called 'Angry Young Men', although there are subtle differences, including subtextually a more Nietzschean mode of negativity and a touch of 'Bloomsbury' elitism. Significantly by the end of *Metroland* the middle-aged protagonist finds himself swathed in the very same suburban lower-middle-class light that he so detested in his youth. In fact that such lives are culturally central is important in the sense of what its very persistence can reveal about our depictions of culture and its failings, and of the very limits of its aesthetic field of vision. The concerns of a writer do not emerge from a vacuum, but possess historical, literary, critical and sociological contexts and precursors. To understand these issues, it is not sufficient to explore the topography of either the texts or simply the surface of the contexts from which they emerge. To obtain a more comprehensive view one requires a critical interrogation, using the kinds of overall concepts that can be theorized via the social and historical contextualizations of writers such as Herbert Marcuse, Pierre Bourdieu and the critical theory alluded to in the critical introduction that counters an underlying irrealism and linguistic philosophy in aesthetic and intellectual culture. In this context this present chapter offers an attempt to redeem even the identities that are narrativized by these texts, but does so by perceiving in them an ideological impulse in characterization, plotting and so forth. As for character in these texts, one must admit that those present and mostly assumed as being normative are middle-class presences, and those most often either elided or marginalized are the working-class ones. This is a quasi-empirical reality, as any intelligent reader might find out unaided by criticism. As the bedrock of such writing, a particular class affiliation is a constant, whatever the strength of the fictional motifs signifying an awareness of the dimensions of gender, regionality, internal migration and multi-accented social forces. All of this leaves a final question as to whether this tendency I have charted represents a failure to adapt, or an insistence on the part of a certain class to be involved centrally in determining an aesthetic and intellectual hegemony based on a relative uniformity of self-reflection and self-representation. And finally the conditions of this kind of consciousness are beginning to be addressed directly in fiction in terms of a set of overarching assumptions and social contexts. Hanif Kureishi in *Gabriel's Gift* addresses this class assumption underlying the intellectual and imperial classes bluntly, when Gabriel's troubles are compared implicitly to those of school-friend Zak, whose parents are in the chattering, publishing classes and are affluently and ideologically 'slumming' among the 'ordinary people'. 'Zak had never been poor. He didn't know what it was like. The established middle class had different fears from everyone else. They would never be desperate for money; they would never go down for good' (32). This very much confirms and contextualizes Moore-Gilbert's observation where he distinguishes Kureishi's style from that of Rushdie, noting that 'the attachment to realism also derives from Kureishi's desire to engage with pressing social issues and bring these to a wide audience' (29). I would conjecture that a differently class-based concept of cultural awareness and hybridity distinguishes him more comprehensively, an awareness that constitutes the stylistic difference.

In fact, Kureishi's edgy urban males emerge as part of a wider picture of an ever-transforming mode of writing. Limitation of space has not allowed me to chart fully how much the voice of working-class and lower-middle-class existence has mutated by being articulated from within, expressing its own experiences in such a way as to acquire poignancy and dignity especially in its frequent images of immiseration, which perspectives elevate the apparent banality of ordinary lives defined by debt, class prejudice and the vicissitudes of what is regarded culturally as inevitably a non-inscribable existence. The lack of understanding between the professional, intellectual class and those outside of the hegemonic frame becomes part of the voice of the reflections of the accused in the rape trial in Welsh's *marabou stork nightmares: a novel* (1995b), conveying the implicit male prejudice in the system of law and legal representation that mediates certain acts despite an antipathy between the barrister Conrad Donaldson, QC and those he represents and their families. The final acts of retributive violence blurred into Roy Strang's consciousness, distorted by the effects of the influence of the drugs, create an ambivalent, ambiguous poeticism. Whatever the moral effect, Welsh inscribes the parameters and yearnings of lives outside of the normal pre-contemporary fictional frame. Other writers remind one of the cultural effacement to situate their understanding of its effects. In Tim Lott's *Rumours of a Hurricane* (2002) the protagonist, Charlie, is effaced, as he finds when he breaks into his newly Thatcherite ex-wife's house. 'Any remnant of Charlie's marriage to Maureen seems to have been comprehensively erased. There is none of their old furniture, pictures, ornaments, nothing. He is a non-person. He has been erased' (372). Far from elegizing the working class with Charlie's death, Lott in *White City Blue* (1999) charts the different kind of sense of effacement and constantly renewed inferiority faced by the newly educated class of people like estate agent Frankie Blue with his lower second 'degree in Politics and Philosophy from the University of West Middlesex, or if you prefer its original nomenclature – my friend Nodge always *insists* on it – Staines Technical College' (1). Very different kinds of writing, texts from James Kelman's *Not Not While the Giro and Other Stories* (1983), to Tim Lott's novels, published around the turn of the century, demonstrate the development and continuity of such kinds of aesthetic response and consciousness. In a passage which encapsulates and challenges the inscription culturally of notions of ignorance and thuggery upon the working class, Lott reflects within even the male working-class culture of supporting football (Queens Park Rangers in Frankie's case) the increasing effect of a hybridization, a topic to which I return in the literary context more broadly in Chapter Five.

> Tony looks very sophisticated, even though he's just a yob, same as the rest of us. More of a yob, actually, because I'm not a yob at all, come to think of it, and neither is Nodge or Colin. Most soccer fans around here stopped being yobs years ago. They read Irvine Welsh and listen to Classic FM, then clock in for work at the print shop or the carpet warehouse. Nothing fits the world any more. Me with my degree, Tony with his thousand pound suits, Nodge and his unreadable books. A cab driver with his nose in Rohinton Mistry, for fuck's sake. It's all hybriod, atomized. (25)

Such changes in cultural practices and co-ordinates are surely something critics must recognize and factor into both the critical and the literary model upon which they reflect. The 'hyper-intellectualization' of theory of late has perhaps masked deficiencies in the literary-critical field in this area.

Further Reading

Brook, Susan (2003) 'Engendering Rebellion: The Angry Young Man, Class and Masculinity', in Daniel Lea and Berthold Schoene (eds) *Posting the Male: Masculinities in
Post-war and Contemporary British Literature*, Amsterdam and New York: Rodopi,
19–34.
This chapter considers novels of the 1950s and beyond with an apparent class perspective, questioning the radicality of so-called Angry Young men.

Ferrebe, Alice *Masculinity in the Male-Authored Novel 1950–2000: Keeping it Up* [see
Further Reading in Chapter One].

Tew, Philip (2006) 'Jenny Diski's Millennial Imagination 1997–2004', in Philip Tew and
Rod Mengham (eds) *British Fiction Today: Critical Essays*, London: Continuum, 67–
77.
This essay analysing Diski's major texts before and after 2000: *Skating to Antarctica*
(1997), *Only Human: A Divine Comedy* (2000) and *After These Things* (2004); it offers a
detailed reading of her work that will reward the student who perseveres, although Tew's
analysis adopts a somewhat theoretical orientation.

Thurschwell, Pamela (2006) 'Genre, Repetition and History in Jonathan Coe', in Philip
Tew and Rod Mengham (eds) *British Fiction Today: Critical Essays*, London: Continuum, 28–39.
This chapter is an interesting and accessible account of Coe's major works, suitable for
most levels of students.

Wells, Lynn (2006) 'The Ethical Otherworld: Ian McEwan's Fiction', in Philip Tew and
Rod Mengham (eds) *British Fiction Today: Critical Essays*, London: Continuum, 117–
27
This is a theoretically sound and interesting reading of McEwan's work that will reward
all students, intelligently analysing the ethical aspects of a number of his key fictions.

CHAPTER THREE

Spaces and Styles – Urban Identities

KEY THEMES
Caledonian Urban Spaces • London • New Urban Detective Fiction • Post-modern City • Provincial City • Spatial Codes • Thatcherism and the City • Urban Youth Culture

KEY TEXTS

Ackroyd, Peter *London: The Biography*

Amis, Martin *Money: A Suicide Note / London Fields*

Barnes, Julian *Metroland*

Bracewell, Michael *The Conclave / The Crypto-Amnesia Club / Missing Margate*

Coe, Jonathan *The Rotters' Club / What a Carve Up!*

Davies, Pete *The Last Election*

Drabble, Margaret *The Middle Ground*

Elms, Robert *In Search of the Crack*

Johnson, B. S. *Christie Malry's Own Double-Entry / Aren't You Rather Young to be Writing Your Memoirs?*

Kelman, James *The Bus Conductor Hines*

Kennedy, A. L. *Night Geometry and the Garscadden Trains*

Kureishi, Hanif *The Buddha of Suburbia / The Black Album*

Litt, Toby *Corpsing*

McEwan, Ian *The Child In Time*

Millar, Martin *Lux the Poet / Milk, Sulphate and Alby Starvation / Ruby and the Stone Age Diet*

Nye, Simon *Men Behaving Badly*

Self, Will *How the Dead Live / Junk Mail / The Sweet Smell of Psychosis / Tough, Tough Toys for Tough, Tough Boys*

Smith, Joan *Don't Leave Me This Way / A Masculine Ending / Why Aren't They Screaming*

Thomson, Rupert *Dreams of Leaving*

Weldon, Fay *The Cloning of Joanna May*

Welsh, Irvine *Trainspotting*

Social Codes and the City

Beyond the modernist vision of an alienated anonymity threatening the subject within the industrial city,[1] lies Henri Lefebvre's vision in *The Production of Space* (1974) where 'Capitalism and neocapitalism have produced abstract space, which includes the "world of commodities", its "logic" and its worldwide strategies, as well as the power of money and that of the political state' (53) threatening the urban. These tensions derive from the very contradictions of space which affect contemporary narrative, especially as many writers seem aware that as Lefebvre notes 'social space can in no way be compared to a blank page upon which a specific message has been inscribed [...]. Both natural and urban spaces are, if anything, "over-inscribed": everything therein resembles a rough draft, jumbled and self-contradictory' (142). In terms of the diversity of different fictional accounts of the city, the present chapter cannot hope to be comprehensive since its subject recurs so frequently in so much of recent British writing. Moreover, the city and its spatial over- inscription intersects with other key themes; hence certain writers with texts concerned with the city who convey such a notion of abstracted space will be considered elsewhere, particularly those like Pat Barker re-reading history (being particularly concerned with diachronic, split narratives) and others engaged in contemporary re-workings of both mythic and parabolic world-views. What seems typical is that many evoke an interrogation of urban space similar to Peter Ackroyd's query of a geographically redrawn capital toward the end of *London: The Biography* (2000): 'Is London, then, just a state of mind? The more nebulous its boundaries, and the more protean its identity, has it now become an attitude or a set of predilections?' (750). Contemporary fiction has been concerned too with the abstract quality of provincial urban dynamics, as will be evident with writers such as Michael Bracewell.

Contemporary fiction returns often to the city and urban social practice and spatial realities variously as a location, subject matter, a cultural source, for energy and as a symbol of change. Clearly, conveying creatively the abstract meaning of the spatial involves more than a descriptive act or a mimetic attempt to transcribe our lives. Through urban narrative, drawing on a long tradition of such writing, many post-1970s authors depict often quite explicitly changed social contexts or perceptions. As a site of narrative and culture the city is mobile, existential and yet perversely monumental, combining in contemporary fiction the globalized economy with both the localized dynamics of intersubjectivity and a sense that culture always creates a sense of loss through its very ongoing adaptation, or evolutionary survival. As we shall see these characteristics both emerge in literature after the 1970s and contribute to shaping a shift in narrative consciousness. One can agree with Patrick Parrinder in *Authors and Authority: English and American Criticism 1750–1990* (1991) that in an appropriate criticism the 'author's words must continue to be found worth quoting' (349), and hence I draw from a range of texts –

including those commonly cited alongside some intriguingly neglected narratives – to map the relationship of contemporary creative prose and the city. Another starting point is to concede that the city is not simply a contemporary experience (although it is interesting that to many its characteristics have changed so rapidly they might imagine this to have been the case), and that the city space did not emerge in modernity, but its presence can be regarded as both constituting and being transformed by modernity's secular subject experience, implicated in what Lefebvre describes as the envelopment and commandeering of nature (269). Thereby through such signification 'a language arose for speaking at once of the town and of the country (or of the town in its agrarian setting), at once of the house and the city. This language was a *code of* space' (269). Fiction codifies urban space and such codification reflects ideological dimensions of culture and the aesthetic. This is not a self-referentially linguistic matter, for as Jürgen Habermas insists in *The Philosophical Discourse of Modernity* (1985) 'The meaning of the individual speech act cannot be detached from the lifeworld's complex horizon of meaning; it remains entwined with the intuitively present background knowledge of interaction participants' (350). Hence the city through its social and personal realities provides the grounds for any such 'spatial code', reminding one of the meaningful participation and complexities of social experience, which itself is dialectically influenced by the spatial. Such relations are conditioned and shaped by what Lefebvre refers to as a globalized social order hidden in a spatial order that evolves constantly (289).

The Changing City

The eponymous middle-aged protagonist complains in Kingsley Amis's *Jake's Thing*, 'People's behaviour changes, "society" changes, but not feelings' (264). In his unease about the city and contemporary life, Amis typifies a 1970s view that although the city changes constantly, mirroring the mood exudes middle-class crisis considered in the previous chapter, its mood is unease and often validates a conviction concerning the symptoms of decline. In Drabble's *The Middle Ground* London is multicultural and iconic for a group of middle-aged, middle-class professionals who feel separate from the world of their children. If this is simply the grounds for their distance and confusion from the realm of the city then they might simply be 'Pooteresque', but Kate's encounter with Mujid, an Iraqi student she has inherited from her feminist networking, brings home to her the social shift in the culture of the city that has evolved and challenges the limits of her liberalism. Mujid is mystified as to why divorce is so common, so many women work, and why her children cannot be tutored in French which together with his anti-semitism bring her to the point of wanting to throw him out as a guest, but cannot do so as she regards him as a refugee (74–5) until she feels 'The truth is that she knows herself trapped by her own good nature, and all its defects, now, as never before' (76). Kate universalizes her responses in terms of an entrapment of social expectations, but her city is one of social engagements, intellectual conversation and an uncertain social etiquette. The resolution at Kate's party, with Kate wearing Mujid's gift of Arab slippers, is a liberal mediation with its echoes of the resolution of crisis in the party that ends Woolf's *Mrs Dalloway*. From friend Evelyn's twelfth-floor flat, Kate sees the panorama of the city as if it possesses a common aesthetic drawn from its diversity:

> From the twelfth-floor window London stretched away, St Paul's in the distance, and the towers of the City, and beneath them, nearby, the little network of streets, backyards, cul-de-sacs, canals, warehouses, curves and chimneys, railways, little factories tucked into odd corners; unplanned, higgledy-piggledy, hardly a corner wasted, intricate, enmeshed, patched and pieced together, the old and the new side by side, overlapping, jumbled, always decaying, yet always renewed; London, how could one ever be tired of it? How could one stumble dully through its streets, or waste time sitting in a heap staring at a wall? When there it lay, its old intensity restored, shining with invitation, all its shabby grime lost in perspective, imperceptible from this dizzy height, its connections clear, its pathways revealed. [...] The aerial view of human love, where all connections are made known, where all roads connect? (218)

This romantic transcendence depends upon being removed either literally or socially. The desire it expresses seems tentative and vulnerable. By the 1980s it would seem that even Jake's (and clearly Amis's) universal humanism of a common emotional response was under challenge from concepts of fragmentation and plurality, but as Fay Weldon writes in *The Cloning of Joanna May*: 'Chernobyl went up, making a large world into a small one, by reason of our common fear of radiation' (20). In Drabble's *The Ice Age* Anthony Keating finds London increasingly unpleasant, like a 'sinking ship' (13) and when Alison Murray returns from the Balkans and travels to St Pancras station she responds to its new reality:

> She looked up, at the crazy Gothic façade, at the impressive iron arches. Victorian England had produced them. She had so loved England. A fear and sadness in tune with her own breathed out of

the station's shifting population: old ladies with bags, a black man
with a brush and bin, pallid girls in jeans, an Indian with a tea
trolley, a big fat man with a carrier bag, they all looked around
themselves shiftily, uneasily, eyeing abandoned packages, kicking
dirty blowing plastic bags from their ankles, expecting explosions.
It can't be like this, thought Alison: how can it have got to be like
this? Who has so undermined, so terrified, so threatened and
subdued us? How petty, how perky, how irrelevant, the few signs
of improvement: the Shires Bar, the Buffet signs. (165)

This symptomatic middle-class gloom and negativity that resurfaces in
this earlier fiction will change, but it is not simply because of the
greater success literally and symbolically consequent upon deregulated
global capitalism, but because like B. S. Johnson with his dictum that
change is a constant, later novelists and critics will see such transformations as social and ideological responses, or ontological necessities. Johnson reflects in *Aren't You Rather Young to be Writing Your
Memoirs?*: 'Change is a condition of life. Rather than deplore this, or
hunt the chimæræ of stability or reversal, one should perhaps embrace
change as all there is. Or might be. For change is never for the better
or for the worse; change simply *is*' (917). He recognized that 'present-
day reality is markedly different from say nineteenth-century reality.
Then it was possible to believe in pattern and eternity, but today what
characterises our reality is the probability that chaos is the most likely
explanation; while at the same time recognising that even to seek an
explanation represents a denial of chaos' (17). In this Johnson pre-
figures part of the paradoxical elements of culture that will be labelled
'postmodern'. That the city is protean, narratable and elusive is not
simply a postmodern observation; it has been long recognized narratively, even from well before the modernist re-visioning of personal and
public space (such as the opening to Joseph Conrad's *The Heart of
Darkness* (1902) where Marlowe is moored off the monolithic presence
of imperial London which appears real and symbolic) up to a range of
more recent theoretical spatial observations. In his seminal work *The
Image of the City* (1960) Kevin Lynch describes the city *per se* as
variously something with aesthetic potential, as superseding individual
perception and of complex sequences where 'On different occasions
and different people, the sequences are reversed, interrupted, abandoned, cut across' (1). Until 1979 the representation of the city was far
from singular in the post-war novel; certainly apart from a vision of
metropolitan centres recovering from wartime damage and its economic consequences, there were three strands that are rooted historically: first there is the city as a site for the ebullience or the

threatening disruptions of youth and hedonism; secondly urban living evoked as a symbol of moral or physical decline; and thirdly there are explorations of the potential in terms of a site for social realism. From the 1950s there emerged a variation of writing of the city with more focus upon specifically provincial urban centres and the contradictions of youth. Given this background, one of the purposes of this chapter is to illustrate both the nature of the ideological and literal transformations that writers perceive in city living from the mid-1970s, and any features of that change in the urban experience that have influenced and counter-influenced dialectically the relationship of such narratives reflexively, a changing of the literary culture of the spatial codes.

Versions of London

In Brackenbury's *The Coelacanth* various characters return by different methods and at different times to London toward the end of the narrative. The reappearance of the metropolitan centre as an even partial site of resolution is significant. As described there is only an implication of its density, but its effect is transformative and vivid. In a recognizably traditional fashion the urban contrasts with the openness of the coast and its marginality, the latter offering a space of unresolved opportunity. Margaret finds herself in a London hospital without her husband, about to go into labour, a place that seems conspiratorial and enclosing. Brackenbury reflects several responses toward the urban as the 1970s end. Firstly, London acquires a sense of threat, offering itself an image evoking historical catastrophe and destruction, against which Nicholas maintains a siege mentality as his wife is about to give birth:

> The hospital a fortress, square against pink lit sky. As if all London were on fire. And lights on at all the windows, the new block with its big panes of glass; a cold, lit square remainder. The windows all closed, containing it making a secret. A healthy man's fear. No, one did not like to think. A way in existed, but only for the few, like himself, who belonged, were expected. (134)

The scene is striking, almost painterly, but clearly it depends upon images of initiation, and of limited inclusion for those who can chart its institutions socially. The inference is that the city ought to be read as a space of social practice if it is to retain any kind of rationality. For the protagonist, Martin, in Bracewell's *The Conclave*, the city seems to offer inclusion and ownership, a sense of control, capable of being defined in terms of an individual vocabulary that resists the communitarian or intersubjective.

Martin walked on with the sensation that he was already master
of all that he surveyed. He window-shopped, and studied displays
of Italian crockery. He thought about his imminent job interview,
at a large modern office near the Monument. He had been flattered by the tone of the letter that the corporation had sent him;
he was amazed at the size of the 'graduate trainee' salary which
was being offered. London, he thought, was money in action. The
names of the shops and the offices were like poetry to him. He
glanced down the shadowed side streets as though he was walking
in the country and had just discovered a long, secret avenue that
promised some mysterious beauty. (79)

Martin ignores the hint of the mausoleum, the foundations of war and
violence upon which the new economy is founded. For him the city
offers acquisition and a kind of largesse. And of course the title of
Bracewell's novel is also suggestive of social enclosure. Although in
Brackenbury one has not yet reached a narrative defined by youth,
success, or hedonism, one can make out a second important factor, the
recognition of such impulses that are motivated by a self-awareness
dependent upon a notion of separation, or of being chosen which will
become familiar among certain writers as we shall see. In Martin
Amis's *Money* (1984) John Self selects and pursues perversely success
within an economic system modelled by sexual and competitive urges,
a debasement of a self that the protagonist cannot identify in himself,
but he commodifies and sublimates his instinctual urges through self-
destructive or compulsive practices such as alcoholism and pornography. Although set in 1981 it is a swansong to the pre-AIDS world
bequeathed by the 1970s, one defined by promiscuous sexual commodification and glib relationships. Self returns to London from the
topographical slickness of America to find a nation in chaos but sees it
in terms of his own emptiness. 'The other morning I opened my tabloid
to find that, during my brief absence, the whole of England has been
scalded by tumult and mutiny, by social crack-up in the torched slums.
Unemployment, I learned, was what had got everyone so mad. *I know
how you feel*, I said to myself. *I know how you feel.* I haven't got that
much to do all day myself. I sit here defencelessly, my mind full of
earache and riot. Why? Tell. Inner cities crackle with the money chaos
– but I've *got* money, plenty of it, I'm due to make lots more. What's
missing? What the hell else is there?' (66). Self's lack of empathy and
vision typifies the urban divide in the Thatcherite world, a world
seeking either an existential place, or, if not, some sense of election,
even if this is an act of faith and self-delusion. This is what Self divines
as separating the American experience from the British one,

epitomized by a kind of self-belief including New York with 'the electricity of the place, all the hustle and the razz' (96), 'California, land of my dreams and my longing' (167) and the super confidence of those like Fielding Goodney. It may be illusory, but it appears the basis of the culture itself, with its gestures to a secular election, the religion of *money*. This contrasts with his view of the early 1980s city where 'In the shades of kitchen mists, with eyes of light showing only murk and seams of film and grease, the air hung above and behind me like an old sink full of old washing-up. Blasted, totalled, broken-winded, shot-faced London, doing time under sodden skies' (159). Self's metropolis is perversely neo-Dickensian, evoking literary *and* spatial codes.

A British version of the possibility of Calvinist election permeated the Thatcherite experiment and became the basis of the self-belief of the new generation. At times literally, at others allegorically, this election offers itself as the central motif and metaphor of Rupert Thomson's *Dreams of Leaving* (1987), with the young Moses Highness being plucked from a basket just as his Biblical precursor is pulled from the bullrushes. Brought up in a village that has archetypal inde-terminancy, set in a region called New Egypt, much like a mythic rendition of the rural world by Agatha Christie as an uncertain pro-mised land, policed by the oppressive Inspector Peach (surely in part an ironic name with historical reference since Blair Peach was one early victim – some might say martyr – to heavy-handed police tactics). The perverse version of a promised land is a paradigm for Thatcherism and its 'Middle' England support, its authoritarian controlling under-currents, a tendency parodied in Pete Davies's *The Last Election* (1986). Moses has been adopted and remains curious about his origins, so his quest for identity and belonging almost paradoxically takes him to London, a world of sexuality, all night partying and opportunity, and he moves apparently effortlessly from the dole to entrepreneurship. This is the cartography of the capital that Davies narrates as a chaotic and vicious interface of ignorance, greed and desire. Thomson's world is apparently dichotomous, but these two worlds of the mythic and the fashionably chthonic collide in Moses' experience, but through this juxtaposition Thomson implies the cultural identifications of the provincials who seem, according to their own view of themselves and the city, to fill this metropolis. In a reverse of Moses' quest, they escape their upbringing. Of course these are among the targets of Thomson's observations, since youth and success were among the conjoined myths of the 1980s. The novel ends with a brief vignette of his accidental and brief return in the twenty-first century, Moses 'a good deal larger now than he had been in his youth' (433), revisiting the site of the club, the Bunker. Thomson dismisses the past of Thatcherism and its foregrounding of the ephemeral quality of the social experience. It is as if the past has receded. This is not an inclusive, open vision, but partializes British culture in terms of generational identifications, much as Martin Millar does in a laconic, sub-Bukowskian trilogy of novels set in London's sub-cultures, *Milk, Sulphate and Alby Starvation* (1987), *Lux the Poet* (1988), and *Ruby and the Stone Age Diet* (1989). Their setting is what might be described as rave culture, drug excesses and 'squatocracy'. Millar's emphasis is on the counter-cultural forces of the unemployed. In *Milk, Sulphate and Alby Starvation* the hypochondriac Alby explores this world his paranoia fuelled by a 'hit' arranged by the Milk Marketing Board after he has alerted the public to harmful additives, a world of drugs, pubs and festivals, the inverse of mainstream culture.

> The pub they go to in Brixton is tolerable as pubs go, frequented by people largely concerned with dyeing their hair the correct shade and getting through life without starving to death before the next giro arrives from the social security, the social security are well known enemies of society populated by senior officers who take physical pleasure in watching people starve, yes, we've sent your money they will say over the phone when in reality they have lost the papers relating to your claim, have no idea where they are and really couldn't give a fuck. (118)

Millar reflects the end of a divided Thatcherite society, one that will lead to the Poll Tax Riots with a sense of rebellion and disorder that mirrors that in the riots at the beginning of the 1980s. As does Davies in *The Last Election*, Millar reflects these anarchic, anti-authoritarian forces in *Lux the Poet* where the unemployed Pearl, involved in a film project, stumbles across a riot:

> Down by Stockwell there is a thick mass of people, young blacks from the council estates and young whites from the local squats, all throwing stones and bottles and petrol bombs and sometimes whole ignited garbage cans at a force of policemen who are retreating, outnumbered.
>
> A girl beside Pearl throws a petrol bomb and it spills over the top of the policeman's riot shield to burn round his helmet and some other policemen beat out the flames and this creates a gap in the ranks and more and more stones and bricks start pounding down onto them.
>
> 'Sugar and washing up liquid,' says the girl to Pearl. 'It's no good just putting petrol in, you have to make it flare up and stick to the skin.' (57)

The riot symbolizes the conflicts in British urban culture, but ultimately the riot itself becomes the subject matter for freelance journalists, filmmakers and the more official media. The generational
'them and us mentality', on which such concepts of alternative and
youth culture are posited, mirrors another more mainstream kind of
dismissal of the forces beyond those that characters identify as representing themselves. In *Ruby and the Stone Age Diet* the novel opens
with the discovery of 'a corpse, it was the body of a girl who had been
around for a short while, I didn't really know her. She spent her time
with the heroin users up the road' (1). In a narrative of understated
emotional response, of a world lacking judgement, Millar continues to
combine social commentary with aspects of the surreal; Ruby mirrors
her own life with her fictional story, that recurs in the narrative of
Cynthia Werewolf. At a gig toward the end of the novel the reality of
his existence strikes the narrator, a sense of alienation. 'I look around,
and I realise for the first time what a drab room this is. Drab and lifeless
and totally dull. Too dull for anyone to enjoy themselves in' (147). He
intervenes to finish the tale of Cynthia Werewolf, allowing her to leave
the poverty of the sub-cultural 'lowlife' for musical success that contrasts with the failure of his own band. The desire for transcendent
success underpins these lives and hence this alternative culture palls
and as the transient community predictably disintegrates, the protagonist finds 'a job as a library assistant in a college and I am quite well
suited to this, sitting quietly behind a counter stamping books,
watching for students. Without Ruby's support I stop squatting and
start paying rent' (150). As his fantasy world subsides a version of
conventionality reasserts itself. In the trilogy Millar reflects upon a
disparate, fragmentary set of individuals, but its effectiveness is limited
by the very nature of its popular genre form, its understated prose
verging constantly on banality. Nevertheless, its world-view makes it a
significant contribution to the evocation of the Thatcherite city.

   In *The Coelacanth* Nicholas's middle-class consciousness and his sense
of the city does not simply express his alienation, but articulates his
unconscious fear of the challenge of the mass, of the inchoate, and the
public. This is part of the new middle-class sensibility and colours not
just a sense of self and identity, but of environment and urban mores. It
might seem that one can differentiate between the earlier narrative of
Brackenbury and that of Bracewell's later cartography of Thatcherism in
terms of narrative position toward the characters that these texts reflect
upon, if one accounts for the latter as a postmodern text, a term referred
to by one of Martin's acquaintances, Piers: ' "Try to think of postmodernism as a means, as opposed to an end. Stick to it as an aesthetic
theory – romanticism in a suit, if you want" ' (255). Piers becomes

dissatisfied with his own account, and Martin is bemused since 'he could only follow those parts of the argument that he could visualise, as a narrative' (256). Finally, though, both novels are quests for middle-class belonging, and in both the characters resist any diminishment of their sense of cultural centrality, a need not just to belong, but to interpret the spatial and social codes of their culture. Both texts have to confront the characters' sense of their relative impotence.

Considering the 'Postmodern' City

Critically labelling the contemporary city as 'postmodern' may be unproductive given that the term implies so many things in the different disciplines that impact upon urban spaces and, taken in a narrower sense as a cultural and narrative term, its knowing irony is both deceptive and exaggerated. Quite how do the 'postmodern' elements of irony and of the populist and the generic impact on the overall mood of contemporary fiction's account of city life? For McEwan, especially in *The Child in Time*, there emerges more a sense of melancholy loss; in Self one encounters a recurrent interstitial emergence of the transgressive, the perverse and the mutative; and in Amis the British city, notably in *Money* and *London Fields*, weaves visions of the dilapidated and perverse with the apocalyptic, the mono-dimensional and the violently pathological. Primarily, each of these key urban writers is more concerned with re-working the patterns of myth and parable – hence the moral compulsion of each text is thematically foregrounded – rather than a sociological or realist pattern. For McEwan the literal and symbolic loss and failed recovery of innocence are ongoing myths, but in a Thatcherite society very specifically McEwan deploys archetypally an intellectual and the culturally significant figure, one who avoids the logic of an increasingly powerful right-wing establishment. The protagonist, Stephen, cannot accept his urban realities and offsets them with his yearnings, mostly for his own past or for his lost daughter and, as with his first novel, *Lemonade*, he appears to be seeking the kind of illusory fairness and certainty of his colonial childhood in a military family. 'It occurred to Stephen that if he could control events in the way his mother controlled sleep, then he would make his parents King and Queen of the entire world, and they could set right all wrongs they described so wisely. For was not his father stronger than any ogre' (71). Beneath or behind the apparent indifference in McEwan's city there exists a world of observation, as with the supermarket where the child vanishes. 'The anonymity of the city store turned out to be frail, a thin crust beneath which people observed, judged, remembered' (18), but clearly for Stephen this fails him and he retreats from its outer certainties. Stephen's task as part of a government advisory committee preparing *The Authorised Childcare Handbook* is ironic given his loss, and also represents one of the hidden narratives within London that the establishment institute in its obsessive concern for public and civic responsibilities, inspired by a need to control and yet removed from 'the din of Central London' (49) that is implicit and yet which the narrative rarely confronts, considers, or reacts to apart from its retreat into the self-absorption of loss and nostalgia. Self's stories and novels reconsider alternate views of the contemporary city, a meta-reality of the return of the self, an afterlife in the current world, and the minutiae of the illusions of contemporary urban culture and its myths. Lily Bloom, dead protagonist of *How the Dead Live*, reflects on her junkie daughter. 'She's beautiful all right – my Natasha. She ought to be in elbow-length white gloves and writing on her dance card with a silver propelling pencil. Instead she's got the sleeves of a black cashmere cardigan pulled down to her wrists. I wish she'd shoot up in the soles of her feet. Her black hair looks as if it's been cut with pinking shears. Her blues eyes have kohl round them, obscuring blacker circles. She's stoned – of course' (43). In this world of historical events, the city closes in upon itself, with narratives of the alternate world, of cultural fashionability parodied in the restaurant chain opened by spirit guide Phar Lap and more narrowly the daughter's junkie existence leading to an inexorable decline. In Amis's *London Fields* the very characterization synthesizes an impression of contemporaneity with a succession of modern media myths, drawing on the London of glib working-class parodies familiar enough to viewers of populist British television. Keith Talent and his world are gleaned more from the prism of television renditions of working-class culture such as *EastEnders*, *The Sweeney*, *Minder*, and so forth rather than any direct quotidian reality. What Amis adds is a ruthless logic of amorality, desire and a lack of ethics that transforms this into a synthesis of myth and parable. Elsewhere, Amis's concern for the contemporary British urban environment – as is the case too with McEwan – is often quite residual. Significantly, Keith Talent – a most talentless individual – appears unable to distinguish reality from the televisual world, and in a flux of always potentially reflexive and self-parodic narrative, 'Nicola Six was a performing artist, nothing more, a guest star directed by the patterning of spacetime, and there it was. It was written' (202–3). In its exaggerated apocalyptic futurity and performativity, this London does not represent the city itself, but no less than a meta-vision, a parabolic myth to which we return. Amis focuses on the degenerating pub, milieu of the populist vision of identity and familiar from 'the Jack the Ripper, the roughest and least local of my many locals' (156) from which John Self discovers he had been banned in *Money*.

In contemporary writing the *code of space*, to repeat Lefebvre's term, may itself vary with an even greater historical rapidity than in previous phases of the novel. One example of the pace of change of narrating codes – cited as a characteristic of the 'postmodern' – in terms of city experience is the emergence of a series of hedonistic, 'clubbing' and youth culture novels that were in vogue toward the end of the 1980s, only to disappear, but influence the jaunty style and self-obsession of subsequent phases of urban rites of passage such as 'chick lit' and 'boy books'. The original phase included Michael Bracewell's novella *The Crypto-Amnesia Club* (1988b) and other less polished novels such as Robert Elms's *In Search of the Crack* (1988), which mapped the city as enveloping human desire and commandeering the energies of youth, with its Thatcherite intention 'amid the myriad chatters of a dozen nations' to 'deal in delight', as one character describes his generation's expansionary hedonism (54). Elms appears to be almost as smugly satisfied as his characters themselves with the name 'Pleasure Incorporated', a fusion of 'pleasure' and 'capital' invented for Elms's vision of a new generation of supposedly reluctant businessmen exploring yet more populist avenues for commodifying capitalism (55). This reveals an underlying truth of this kind of market that appears to exonerate itself from being part of the establishment, since as Marcuse reflects in *Negations* (1968) 'Basic to the present form of social organization, the antagonisms of the capitalist production process, is the fact that the central phenomena connected with this process do not immediately appear to men as what they are "in reality," but in masked, "perverted" form' (70). As both Bracewell and Thomson seem to indicate – especially as capitalization is not entirely monolithic and given that its topographical cultural forms are capable of mutation and of being expressed through cultural commodities and fashions, one ought not to over-determine the ephemeral. Only the propensity for the ephemeral is significant, not its current mutations or 'perversions'. More traditional deceptions persist, the privileged young masking both their class and their wealth. Simon Nye reflects upon this with the denial of savings by stamp dealer, middle-class hedonist and 'man about bed-sitting land' Gary in *Men Behaving Badly* (1989).

> Gary was lying. He had a heap of liquid money and was happy watching it accumulate. If he had to be honest he was waiting for one of his rich remaining grandparents to die, leaving what one had called 'a tidy sum' and the other 'a small something for you to start with' as if a family was a dry-cleaning business. Then he would sell all his stamps, buy a house and plan a radical new future. Alternatively, he would do none of these things. (56)

The latter seems unlikely, as the text centres upon the rituals and rivalries concerning 'The problem of sex and courtship' (52) of the 'twenty-somethings' approaching thirty. The future might appear radically new for Gary in terms of his student-style lifestyle, but his trajectory is reminiscent of Barnes's *Metroland*, for as a youth 'Gary used to come down to London when he was that age, escaping from Hertfordshire' (111), and as with *Metroland* a return to middle-class conventionality becomes the subtext of the desire that is the deep ecology of this supposedly new urban lifestyle. Of course *Men Behaving Badly* spawned successive series of an immensely popular and well-known comic television programme that adopts a combination of youth cultural irony integrated into what are essentially slapstick or vaudevillian situations. A knowingness of the quip and ironic gesture are shared with the original novel, but many of the text's nuances and social implications are significantly different. Even the 'laddishness' of the series could be argued to be quite different from that of the novel.

New Generations

The generational emphasis is itself corrigible and part of the city's changing fabric. *Search In the Crack* indicates that the youth cultural emphasis of its protagonist Tony, with his synthesis of 'pleasure' and 'capital', cannot last. By the narrative's end the protagonist has to pick his way self-consciously through the next generation of hedonistic youth returning from Bournemouth and elsewhere on the coast to Waterloo. Tony faces not only the reality of one's own ageing, but stumbles upon something of the scale of the city that troubles him, reminds him of loss and mortality. He finds himself in tourist territory, looking from Waterloo Bridge, as if a stranger in his home city, 'I leaned for a little – a little self-consciously, but what's wrong with that? – over the side of the bridge. Looking west, I thought it seemed big and old, and I felt deep-down confused. One side of me felt happy, at home; the other unsure. The scale of it was difficult to accommodate' (211). Even for a characterization of a *faux-naïf* consciousness this is clumsy, and its indeterminacy does not expunge a sense of Elms's delight earlier throughout the narrative of his sub-cultural importance and pleasure. It ends with its partial continuation, with the promise of late drinking in an anonymous pub. In a society so divided as Thatcher's city, as with real urban space, the novel is a site of social contestation. Certainly it is commercial, exhibiting an exploitation re-naturalized by the Thatcher generation. In Michael Bracewell's novella *Missing Margate* (1988a) Arabella, a section editor on one of the emergent lifestyle magazines, in her search for a new journalistic angle senses the suburban and provincial identity of this 'new' generation of affluent *arriviste* consumers:

> Arabella made a mental note to write a small item for the 'In and Out' section of *Designate* about the colonisation of West One by the working population of the outer suburbs. Oxford Street was, after all, the High Street of England, indistinguishable in its cast of shops from Norwich, say, or even Croydon. This was the worn out oesophagus of London, where massive mouthfuls of money were lubricated by the saliva of retail design in order to slip effortlessly into the stomachs of business. The money was then broken down by all the little enzymes employed by business corporations to keep the process working. (16)

The metaphor is organic, but concerns a monstrous process of mass consumption that Arabella sees as the fate of the masses with their herd instinct. Arabella seems convinced her designer 'one-to-one' purchasing elevates her. The very title of the magazine indicates the secular sense of election that this generation of trendy urbanites imagine is theirs; the term 'colonisation' indicates their affinities with the imperial class, another eclectic and commercially minded generation. Its quotidian analysis makes a spectacle and subject of analysis of what is in truth an ephemeral banality, and as Guy Debord comments in *The Society of the Spectacle* (1967) 'Behind the glitter of the spectacle's distractions, modern society lies in thrall to the global domination of a *banalizing* trend that also dominates it at each point where the most advanced forms of commodity consumption have seemingly broadened the panoply of roles and objects to choose from' (38). A subsequent allusion in Bracewell's text to Shelley indicates the roots of youth's self-awareness in romanticism, and serves to emphasize the generational repetitiveness indicated in Ecclesiastes. Max de Winter, a successful architect suffering from what appears to be an enervating sense of malaise, sees a frantic spiral of prices and greed among the nation of shopkeepers, and 'Even as Max sank deeper and deeper into despair he knew that it was those sycophants to fashionable business sophistry who had ownership of tomorrow. Tomorrow most probably belonged to them by virtue of a shrewd down payment the previous fiscal' (14). Max echoing Eliot hankers for an older England and in the vocabulary of *The Waste Land* hopes he might see the acquisitive as 'well dressed corpses in rusting company Saabs' (15). As Max's colleague indicates, on the contrary the style magazine *Designate* staff are ' "Looking for stylists, figureheads of the New London. The usual lifestyle design commentary thing" ' (20).

In his disillusionment Max de Winter becomes an urban terrorist, in a spontaneous and individual manner that mirrors the protagonist of B. S. Johnson's *Christie Malry's Own Double-Entry* (1973). However, Max, unlike Christie who engages in mass murder, is guided by his underlying humanistic conscience and so avoids creating human victims – and in his campaign that is directed against himself in that he destroys the buildings that he himself has designed, Max seems to invert and yet is some ways perpetuates a negativity central to the notion of self-signification that became a cultural and literary referent of the 1980s. Max is self-obsessed, but not in a way that it would seem could be immediately capitalized, so it would appear his campaign resists commodification. His wife Rebecca is immured in this understanding of this Thatcherite social narrative. 'London never tires of success stories and why should it? Living as she had in the Green Room of Triumph, Rebecca knew by heart the discourse of Success and could follow the vapid annotations to Glamour like a script. The circuitry of Fame, the Souvenir issue – the intellectually italicised portfolio that was rushed out by the backers at the merest sniff of serious money' (46). At one level, Max's acts of destruction represent an attempt at the destruction of the self, a wish for anonymity, but ultimately this is a condition that he cannot comprehend or in any sense achieve. The campaign itself is predicated on his social success; his professional presence, and its subsequent negation possess elements of a gesture underwritten by the potlatch. There is also a self-abnegation, the fusion of satire and irony that in fact reflects the kind of social presence of knowing assuredness that Evelyn Waugh charts as the ultimate mark of social success. In a perverse way Max's campaign mimics those elevated traditionally above him and is a gesture of the Thatcherite *arriviste* against an ongoing cultural matrix they cannot fully permeate.

He considered the mess left over on history's palette by the vigorous and neurotic process of keeping the masterpiece of the urban centre alive with these inspired acts of terrorism. He walked through Lincoln's Inn Fields, smoking a cigarette and feeling his invisibility. He was fading a little more with each building destroyed, crossing out his signature on the skyline with his bare hands, the same bare hands with which he had built a glittering career and sculpted an envied marriage. Irony, the liquid engineering within the machinery that drove Max de Winter as myth, leant a pleasing symmetry to the otherwise arbitrary and chaotic bombardment of man by phenomena that was the reality of Max the Man. (41)

More broadly, Max is fighting what became the unconscious doubt of this generation, its universal inconsequentiality despite the images, the myths and the excesses of consumption. However, despite the irony of Max's gestures and his paradoxical suspicion of irony, *Designate* shows how adaptable the new globalized market can be, seeking to exploit the destruction itself, an executive enquiring ' "Given the recent and not altogether unexpected destruction of de Winter's tallest building, would it be possible for *Designate* to stage the West One Fashion Week Show on a catwalk across the rubble?" ' (55). So finally Bracewell makes it clear that irony – the great postmodern gesture – is not immune to exploitation and profitability.

In this case the cliché, in the passage quoted above from Bracewell, that expresses the quality of Arabella's thought processes indicates something of Bracewell's ironic distance from his character and this world, however, assessing the narrative and authorial position in a generation of writers that ironize, allude inter-textually and offer apparently knowing cultural analysis – given that all of these can be so formulaic as to become both unperceptive and topographic – can be complex. One specific problem in assessing contemporary fiction is that while some writers critique these hedonistic and commercial processes, others appear ultimately to revel in them and even identify with the currency of the code of the significant self. The demise of such uncritical texts as social narratives becomes more clearly evident in the fiction of the 1990s where the satiric element increases in depictions of youth and fashionability, specifically so in Will Self's *The Sweet Smell of Psychosis* (1996) and Bracewell's *The Conclave*. Bracewell began the reflective process in *The Crypto-Amnesia Club* where the manager, Merril, ruminates at the novella's opening 'These days it always feels like the beginning of the end' (13), both narratively and culturally apt, and toward its end 'There are a million stories in the strangely dressed city, and none of them makes sense. It used to be a search, if not for truth then for some acceptable substitute' (108). In fact in among this narrative searching – at author, narrator and character levels – a recognizable process began in the identifications that constituted the city narrative of the 1980s, for the diversity that has always affiliated itself with city experience was in fact being narrowed, variously channelled into a sense of belonging that could never be sustained in amid such spaces of plurality.

Self's vision of the city is curiously contained and yet panoramic, a site of contradictions of limited consciousness and psychic potential. Comparing himself in conversation with Martin Amis in *Junk Mail*, Self believes his London is more literal than Amis's (390) and finds that 'our perceptions are different – in my London there is a lot between the signs and the sky. I'm very concerned with the physical reality of the buildings, the landscape. I'm harping on this, I suppose, because of what you said about Nabokov. About geography just being a critical corrective for him, because when you look at his work it isn't really there' (391). In Self the placement of the geographic or spatial provides a psychic-phenomenological grounding and not an expression of a realist paradigm (or ambition). Certainly the idea of scope and scale cartographizes his vision; Self challenges the arguably far narrower vision of the world of Robert Elms, and reworks the fashionable city elements found in the narratives of Michael Bracewell and Rupert Thomson so as to make of them something more grotesque. There is little residual lyricism in the lives of Self's characters, nor a narrative narcissism, but there is an underlying emotional referent, often as subdued as it appears to be in British social mores. As Self says in *Junk Mail* of his own fiction when in conversation with his *éminence grise*, Ballard, 'I am a writer who is very attached to the idea of place. I am concerned with the notion of topography, of visceral shape underlying the imaginative skin of the book' (331). Marking out the mores of a post-Thatcherite 'New London' and its contradictions, Self renders masculinity at least topographically as something challenged, almost perverse and strange. This has a number of manifestations. Firstly there is the middle-class male who nevertheless exhibits a desperation, as with the actions of the sexually deprived hack journalist Richard in *The Sweet Smell of Psychosis* of whom the narrator comments 'He'd had no sex of any kind in the past year, save for two frenzied couplings with his immediate boss at the magazine, a successful anorexic in her forties who turned out to be a glove fetishist. He had balked at a third coupling, when she'd asked him to don oven gloves before scratching her pork' (13). Additionally there are the contradictions in the street-wise life of Danny in 'The Rock of Crack as Big as the Ritz' in *Tough, Tough Toys for Tough, Tough Boys* (1998) who rejects his African name, and after army service discovers a fortune in the form of an enormous rock of crack underpinning the house that he had bought from illicit earnings, perhaps somewhat improbably ripped off from Yardies. These parodic masculine identities, which nevertheless capture the shift in gender roles, at times seem tied inextricably to images and conceits of excess and incomprehension. As Self writes in 'The Burnt-Out Shells of Men' in *Junk Mail*,

> On the marginalized estates of modern Britain, devastated by unemployment and economic deprivation, the traditional gender-based social distinctions have been fractured. With young unemployed men thrown back into the physical spaces normally

occupied by women, they exorcize their impotence in the form of internecine warfare. The burnt-out cars that litter these suburban landscapes are poignant symbols of male destruction, as a function of male impotence. (151)

In some senses the whole frame of constant reference points in Self's fiction refer to a range of such transformed social realities, some to do with deprivation, others to shifting gender roles and social values, and the details of this displaced, almost grotesque reality are alluded to in rapid narrative transit, and the helter-skelter image of lives in muta-tion are part of Self's satirical ambition for social relevance and sym-bolic contemporaneity. In *The Sweet Smell of Psychosis* the reader encounters a version of The Groucho Club – one key habitat of the new cultural media figures of the Thatcherite world – which is the centre for their ephemeral professional and personal pursuits.

There was a ratio of hacks to non-hacks in the bar at this time of about one to one. And these weren't principled journalists, or hardened reporters, oh no. No one eased his leaning position at the bar in order to relieve the pressure on the shrapnel wound he'd caught covering the Balkan crisis. Nor did anyone huddle in a corner earnestly discussing *her* view of the Neo-Keynesian implications of the treasury's management of the Public Sector Borrowing Requirement. Not a bit of it.

The hacks who frequented the Sealink, yakking in the bar, gobbling in the restaurant, goggling in the television room, wobbling in the table-football room, and snorting in the toilets, occupied a quite different position in the cultural food chain. They were transmitters of trivia, broadcasters of banality, and disseminators of drek. They wrote articles about articles, made television programmes about television programmes, and com-mented on what others had said. They trafficked in the glibbest, slightest, most ephemeral cultural reflexivity, enacting a dialogue between society and its conscience that had all the resonance of a foil individual pie dish smitten with a paperclip. (10–11)

Bell, who is the centre of the clique with whom Richard mixes, becomes an almost devilish figure, each member appearing to be subsumed into his presence, Richard at the end finding the object of his love, the beautiful Ursula, transmogrified into another version of Bell. On one level this characterizes the lack of individuality in this culture of apparently rampant individualism. Self's narrative and metaphoric technique involves reference to culturally imbued con-texts, a world of glib cultural commentary set among the conflicts generated by the desire for and cultures surrounding class privilege, sex, ethnicity, drug culture and social fashions. This world becomes one of grotesque and increasing arationality. Self's characters exist among the paradoxes of new masculinity contending with more traditional roles, all of which are conveyed by comic or oblique verbal significations, each quip offering an entry into another range of social and discoursal activities. 'The Rock of Crack as Big as the Ritz' starts with the luxurious connotations of the hotel building itself encoded in a dream, touches upon the army and Desert Storm and delves into the multi-layered cultural identities suggested by migration, African ethnicity and the urban reality of Bantu's friend Stan 'who ran the Montego Bay chippie in Manor Park Road' (4). None of Self's conceits leads to resolution, leaving a chaotic and changeable environment, its strength being in the persistent grotesque survival of the characters.

The Provincial Perspective

Jonathan Coe reflects the machinations of economic and political power in which London is a site of symbolic and literal exchange, and essentially of conflict. In *What a Carve Up!* his version of the city in 1990 focuses on the researcher and writer, Michael Owen, and exhibits the quotidian side of a world of publishers and the images of the media, both print and televisual, in an age of an onslaught of images and narrative, often either banal or devious. The influences and origins of this world are the experiences and memories of the immediate postwar past as a kind of legacy, made evident by the long section preliminary to the main text entitled 'Prologue 1942–1961'. Images of the Gulf crisis intersect with the past lives of those around the increasingly powerful and yet corrupt Winshaw family, an image of Thatcherite free enterprise achievements. The literal quality of the city is made clear in the oppressive tube ride when Owen faints in the total darkness in a crammed carriage: 'I could hear someone say, Watch out, he's going! and the last thing I can remember thinking was, Poor guy, it's no wonder, with asthma like that: and then nothing, no memory at all of what happened next, just blackness and emptiness for I don't know how long' (98–9). The city, like so much else in Coe's world, is not only corrupt, but replete with such incongruities. Owen's background is on the fringes of the provincial city, 'the point where Birmingham's outermost suburbs began to shade into countryside, in a placid, respectable backwater, slightly grander and more gentrified than my father could really afford' (159), echoing Coe's own origins and a territory to be used again as the setting for *The Rotters' Club*. On his return after his father's illness to the market town hospital closest to this fringe area, Owen discovers its smallness and provinciality compared to its scale in his childhood and adolescent memories. As we will see in the chapter concerned with the modes of myth and parable, Coe explores youth, origins and the laboratory of emotions and experience found in the mass of the city, an ideological matrix, demonstrating as he does in all of his novels Lefebvre's sense that 'Space is at once result and cause, product and producer; it is also at *stake*, the locus of projects and actions deployed as part of specific strategies, and hence also the object of *wagers* on the future – wagers which are articulated, if never completely' (143). In *The Rotters' Club* Birmingham becomes a site for contestation and desire, often obliquely understood, but confirming a need for location and cultural significance.

In both texts Coe uses a quasi-mythic dimension to look at modern life and the city, indicating the symbolic order of the present in the making of new readings of mythic presences. Especially in *What A Crave Up!* and *The Rotters' Club*, Coe reworks mythical configurations including those of return and origin. In the latter Coe recovers the adolescent urban provincial perspective that is the setting that Michael Owen escapes for London. In *The Rotters' Club* he describes life in 1970s Birmingham, peopling the city of this Cold War era with both the facts and the experiences that mirror and subvert the myths of the past. Benjamin Trotter outside of his middle-class school discovers a city of multiple perspectives, Coe describing the adolescent bands, the schoolchildren, their parents involved in the trades union and man-agement conflicts of that era, the propaganda and prejudice of the National Front, and the reality for victims and survivors of the IRA bombing campaign. History is recovered in its mundanity, a corrective to the collective loss of the detail of the past, but it cannot be con-tained in the simple facts of the concrete and finite world. Toward the end of the novel the aspirant teenage writer, Benjamin Trotter, in an immensely long stream of consciousness while sitting in a pub, can reflect on the object of his desire.

> Cicely is thinking about Helen but I don't believe she is, I believe she is thinking about me, but is she imagining me or remembering me? I shall never know, but here's an idea, I could imagine her remembering me, or I could remember her imagining me, and that way it could go on forever – which of course is exactly what I want! – like a hall of mirrors or indeed a Hall of Memory, yes, I like that phrase, I could use that, I could put it in a poem or use it as a title of a chapter or a tune or something, and what makes it so perfect is that I am looking at the Hall of Memory right now, because I am sitting in The Grapevine which I have noticed, only

this morning, I never noticed before, but it is situated in a square called Paradise Place, and straight through the window I can see through to the civic square, with the Masonic Hall and Municipal Bank on one side, to the left, and Baskerville House to the right, and between them is the Hall of Memory, built of Portland stone and Cornish granite [...] even the city is transforming itself around me, I am sitting in Paradise Place and looking on the Hall of Memory and suddenly it's as if everything refers to me and Cicely, everything is a metaphor for the way we feel, somehow the entire city has become nothing less than a life-size diagram of our hearts, and I could shout with the joy of it, I want to run out into the square and shout to anyone who will listen, I LOVE THIS CITY!, I LOVE THIS CITY! but as you might have guessed I am not going to do that. (372–3)

In this epiphanic moment, Coe expresses the possibility of the city being not so much a literal place but a fusion of phases of lives, an archaeology of presences mixing together realities, desires, imagination and their constant transformations and deformations.

Emergent Identities

Another intriguing fictional rendition of a youthful vision of a city with a similar synthesis of elements is the sub-cultural, multiethnic northwest London suburb that is the backdrop to Kureishi's *The Black Album*, but as indicated in Chapter Two, it is perhaps primarily in terms of class and cultural referents of belonging that the city is explored as a rite of passage of the young Asian protagonist, Shahid. It is certainly in terms of class that he responds to his relationship with his lover and lecturer, Deedee, negating her need for a mutual analysis of their need and commitment for each other. '"Fuck off, Deedee. Who cares? I'm drained. I can't do a middle-class kind of relationship discussion tonight"' (208). In *The Black Album* the optimism and expectations of *The Buddha of Suburbia* are subsumed in a series of crises that seem more threatening. Seen in part through Shahid's eyes, the city is in conflict, with urban youth seemingly in a search for values and a sense of belonging, with a cult arising over mystic shapes perceived in an aubergine through which Kureishi indicates the potential insularity of uncritically indicating cultural boundaries and interests. The old leftists, the skinheads and the militant Muslims that are all drawn into the conflicts that permeate the texts, tempering its comedic tone, all mark a further breach of any residual consensus. The liberal freedom of the 1960s, from music like Jimi Hendrix's *Electric Ladyland* to Anthony Burgess's *A Clockwork Orange* (1962), appear in the text as if youth were seeking a new identity or commitment somewhere in a lost Golden Age, but finding instead a world of intersecting and potentially conflicting factions and interest groups based around belief systems; finally the book burning offers a catalyst for reviewing the uneasy balance of an indifferent world unable to perceive the threat in the youthful aspirations as an agent for disruptive change:

> A singed page lay in the gutter outside the college. But the buses were running, the kebab houses were open, people pushed prams and walked home from work. On the steps of the subway a priest squatted to read the Bible to a teenage beggar who sat there all day. None of these people knew a book had been burned nearby. Few of them would, perhaps, have been concerned. Nevertheless, that morning there had been another bombing in the City: many roads had check-points. He knew it would be wrong to assume that everything would remain all right. (227)

Shahid wants to retreat to his room, write in an act of self-reclamation, and finds he cannot accept this attack on free expression in which he is implicated whatever its motivations and the injustices from which it arises. He is even more shocked at a firebombing of a bookshop, indicating the threatening potential of a narrow reading of belief or ideology. His notion of class is an instinctive response shaped by the forces of his lived experience, rather than the rationalized divisions identified by Brownlow, Deedee's husband, who offers another extremist view, attempting to superimpose his notion of class, a recuperation of the radicality of his 1960s youthful protests, in his rejection of liberals supporting 'literary freedom' in an echo of the Rushdie affair. '"They're just standing by their miserable class. When have they ever given a damn about you – the Asian working class – and your struggle? Your class is fighting back. No one will colonize you, put you down or insult you in your own country. And the liberals – always the weakest and most complacent people – are shitting their pants, because you threaten their power"' (215). Kureishi's position is complex, since in Shahid's equivocation lies an uncertainty about such a categorization, and yet in Brownlow's analysis (the character named after the middle-class rescuer of Oliver Twist in Dickens) there is a residual persuasiveness. The city is a site of conflict, of forces vying for affiliation and loyalty, an amalgam. The social order and British identity is a site of flux and corrigibility; and enigmatically and offering no resolution, Deedee and Shahid run off together.

Caledonian Perspectives

As Lars Ole Sauerberg says in *Fact into Fiction: Documentary Realism in the Contemporary Novel* (1991): 'Although the traditional realistic novel has been pronounced dead on several occasions since the modernist break-through in the 1920s, it has shown a viability which must be surprising to those who have busied themselves predicting its demise' (1). For other writers virtually the opposite of imagining oneself as being elect or chosen within the city is true, and they convey a sense of rejection and marginality among alienating structures for the dispossessed individual without social signification or elevation. The typical form is a consciousness of the problematic of everyday life, a narrative based on re-patterning or revising concepts of social realism. The common feature is the mundane and the motif of failure as thematic and existential realities, a literary response shared by Coe in his descriptions of a provinciality that potentially opposes metropolitan London chic. As a contrast to the latter, which emerged from a commodified Thatcherite city, three Scottish writers typify a more mundane and sceptical approach to the urban: for James Kelman, A. L. Kennedy and Irvine Welsh urban life both synthesizes and resists an experience of the anonymity and despair. They offer a narrative of ordinariness, and of the threat to it by the pathological and the criminal, an environment of potential failure and neglect. The world so depicted is not constructed primarily through a modernist vision (although its generic perspective remains part), but is firmly a world of multiple practical problems, of violence, addiction, loneliness, unemployment, poverty, fracturing or fractured relationships, and the inconsequentiality in terms of the hegemonic or macro-culture of the lower classes. In Kennedy's *Night Geometry and the Garscadden Trains* (1990) in 'Night Geometry' a betrayed wife comments of her existence: 'We have small lives, easily lost in foreign droughts, or famines; the occasional incendiary incident, or a wall of pale faces, crushed against grillwork, one Saturday afternoon in Spring. This is not enough' (34). The narrator in 'Didacus' confirms this sense of contemporary urban living, with people's sense of existential inconsequentiality:

These are small people. On the whole, on the average, on the pavements, the people here are small.

Small in body.

And we are speaking of a time here when small things were thought unimportant and the figures who now fill our bus stops were withered by lack of belief. In the larger world they were steadily forgotten and they woke up every morning, lost in their beds. (47)

In 'The Fiction of James Kelman and Irvine Welsh: Accents, Speech and Writing' (2003) Drew Milne specifies Kelman was himself a marginal writer, first publishing with a small press in the US and his first two novels with Polygon, Edinburgh University's publishing house, when it was still student-run (158). Kelman focuses intently upon dispossession and abjection. In 'the same is here again' in *Lean Tales* the unnamed narrator complains in great detail of his physical decline as he endures homelessness. He reflects: 'Explanations sicken me. The depression is too real' (13). In Kelman's novel *The Bus Conducter Hines* (1984) the narrator, Rab, ruminates at length and obsessively over his dissatisfactions with life. The dialect of the narrator that is close to Rab's own speech emphasizes a male perspective of working-class marginality, detailing a world of drinking, boring work, marital worries and relative poverty. This is a common view of the city in this new realism, emphasizing an undeniable conjunction of dispossession and inequality. Nevertheless the influence of modernist narratives of fragmentation and chains of diverse causalities remain strong. The city is not simply successive actions, but encompasses conscious resistance of the past and present. Within its incoherence, Hines thinks of how he might educate his infant son, Paul, into his reality.

> Come with me son and I'll show you the ropes. How d'you fancy a potted history of this grey but gold city, a once mighty bastion of the Imperial Majisteh son a centre of Worldly enterprise. The auld man can tell you all about it. Into the libraries you shall go. And he'll dig out the stuff, the real mccoy but son the real mccoy, then the art galleries and museums son the palaces of the people, the subways and the graveyards and the fucking necropolises, the football parks then the barrows on Sunday you'll be digging out the old books and clothes and that and not forgetting the paddy's by christ for a slab of last year's tablet son plus the second-hand pair of false teeth right enough, aye, very useful indeed [...] you'll be able to do it son, control, take control, of the situation, standing back, clear sighted, the perspective truly precise and into the nub of things, no tangents, just straight in with an understanding already shaped that that which transpires shall do as an effect of the conditions presented. (90–1)

His very incoherence and confusion reveals the inability of the social narrative to reflect the dispossession of such lives as his own, of their resentments. Beyond the imperial pretensions, which have little relevance to such an existence, lies a new order of control and power by which access and knowledge of the urban space is defined. As Milne comments of Kelman 'His work deliberately resists the dominant terms

of the capitalist media and the culture industry, articulating a politi-
cised critique of trends within literary modernism' (159). Rab's job is
threatened by one-man buses and he faces immediate dismissal after a
series of infractions such as lateness and wearing an incorrect uniform,
and he resigns. The city is full of activity, initially seemingly indifferent
to Rab, but after leaving work it is as if he is reintegrated into another
pattern. After leaving his son at his nursery

> Instead of going home immediately he crossed the road and went
> into the nearest pub and ordering a pint he walked to a table at
> the wall and dumped the bags on the floor there. Back at the bar
> the man serving nodded to him and commented on the weather.
> Farther along a man named Michie was trying to attract his
> attention and when Hines acknowledged him with a nod he asked
> if it was his day-off. Hines smiled and said it was. He borrowed the
> *Daily Record* from the barman and took it back to the table; he
> read it until finishing his pint. A man was coming in as he was
> going out and held the door for him to pass. (229)

Suddenly the pace of the city is transformed, its spatial code revised.
Rather than his resignation providing a denouement, the daily life of
apparently little consequence continues, the novel ending as 'he wiped
the condensation from the back window and looked out' (237). In
Trainspotting (1993) Irvine Welsh writes in Scots dialect, an aggressive,
conversational style, and as Milne makes clear 'Both Kelman and
Welsh attack the class basis of written English' (160). This influences
the perspective of their descriptions of the urban, foregrounding
working-class lives that normally fall into the interstices of texts.
Unlike Kelman, Welsh's encounter with the streets is situated centrally in a world of drugs, drug paraphernalia, petty criminality and
violence. Although Welsh is populist in his appeal especially in the
sensationalist, cinematic and fast-moving aspects of his prose, and as
Milne says of these aspects, they 'have disguised the underlying
sociological enquiries in his writing. [. . .] Welsh is not uncritical of
the sensation-seeking immediacy he portrays, but much of the critique
is left implicit' (159). Welsh's Scotland is not only defined by its social
malaise, but is furthermore a site of conflict and identity crisis.

> Ah hate cunts like that. Cunts like Begbie. cunts like that are
> intae baseball-batting every fucker that's different: pakis, poofs, n
> what huv ye. Fuckin failures in a country ay failures. It's nae good
> blamin it oan the English fir colonising us. Ah don't hate the
> English. They're just wankers. We are colonised by wankers. We

can't even pick a decent, vibrant, healthy culture to be colonised by. no. We're ruled by effete arseholes. (84)

As Milne indicates Welsh retains a narrative distance, offering the possibility of an ironic separation from this view. And yet, the abjection of these lives is reflected symbolically in the fabric of the city. 'Their destination is a pub which seems to prop up a crumbling tenement set on a side-street between Easter Road and Leith Walk. The streets have missed out on the stone-cleaning process its neighbours have enjoyed and the building is the sooty-black colour of a forty-a-day man's lungs. The night is so dark that it is difficult to establish the outline of the tenement against the sky' (258).

Detecting the City

Almost diametrically opposite to such revisions of social realism, there are novels that re-work the generic, exploring the city through an elaborate intertextuality, creating a subtextual alternative. In these parodies of genre fiction, set among lives of relative affluence, the urban points of reference appear to create an opportunity for an implicitly diachronic vision of the city, one where contemporary mores are implicitly set against other codes of behaviour that one understands to be subtextual, the reader implicated in reconstructing a territory typical to the original examples of the genre, offering a culturally composite allusion. Joan Smith renders a feminist version of the mystery detective novel in a series featuring protagonist Loretta Lawson including A Masculine Ending (1987), Why Aren't They Screaming? (1988) and Don't Leave Me This Way (1990). Loretta is an academic and in the tradition of the amateur sleuth, an updated Miss Marples. Loretta's world might seem different with its mixture of Islington, Camden, Paris, Charlotte Street restaurants, feminist literary conferences, a Greenham Common style protest and academic intrigues and research. However, Smith makes Loretta a respository for a range of residual snobberies that indicates a continuity of unworldliness and awareness. In Why Aren't They Screaming? she is surprised to find a student residence in Hackney (184) and she appears unsettled in Don't Leave Me This Way to discover a policeman with a foreign name and complexion (92), but like Miss Marples she finds herself amongst worldly intrigue, retribution, passion and violence. Of course in the narratives she has various lovers and affairs, but ultimately one senses she is no more knowing than the characters upon whom she is based and compared with whose presence her contemporaneity rests. This is a recurrent feature of the re-visioning of contemporary writing. One wonders if these texts escape from their predecessors in quite as meaningful a fashion as many of the writers appear to assume. In one even more self-aware and consciously self-referential recent fiction, Toby Litt turns to genre fiction to thematize contemporary mores and allude quite specifically to the conceptualization of the 'postmodern'. In *Corpsing* (2000), because of the corrigibility of narrative and reality, the shifting ground of perception, the protagonist, Conrad Redman, is able to pass off his public brandishing of a gun as a rehearsal for a film. However, as Litt indicates something of the perceptual persists, for the textual replay of the bullets that strike Conrad and his girlfriend reminds the reader of an ultimate physical law, that of materiality, causality and death. He might not understand or be able to account for the death, but its occurrence sets a chain of events in motion. If the text is ironic, it cannot subvert this appeal to factuality, simply rework its significance. In this context, the contemporary urban experience and its narrative representation can have a double effect. In the Thatcherite and post-Thatcherite world reference to transformations are tempered by the re-emergence of cultural variations upon tradi- tional themes. Thatcherite success as Miller makes evident in *Smiles and the Millennium*, modelled itself in terms of a grandiose image based at least on the past. This apparently contradictory tension exists in much of the fiction of the period that focuses upon the city. The intellectual image of contemporary urban living is that it is knowing, referential, image conscious and postmodern. As a cultural and literary trope, its image making is supposed to be more allusive and telling than simple narrative reflection. Toby Litt's ersatz and allusive quasi- mystery novel creates from such dualities and the undermining of self- conscious reference points, a narrative based upon the destruction of the myth of both fashionability and knowledge, in a text whose own provenance is a site of contestation. In this context it is significant that in his acknowledgements the author cites as a precursor and influence J. G. Ballard's *Crash*, rather than Agatha Christie who, once decoded from critical prejudices, offers the underlying template for most of Litt's 'ironic' strategies and who arguably offers herself as an equally ironic chronicler of the self-consciously fashionable young (of course of a different era than Litt).

The revelations and structures of *Corpsing* are both offset and in some senses constituted by the knowing detail of the topography of contemporaneous London, mapping studiously the fashionable, con- sumerist lives of the young postmodern professionals, focusing on the media world of Conrad and his erstwhile actress girlfriend, Lily. Without the fulsome cartography the irony could not be sufficiently heightened to sustain the plot. The initial setting is juxtaposed by the painful physical and psychic recovery of the protagonist. The pair is gunned down in a trendily expensive restaurant, Le Corbusier in Frith Street, Soho, by a Day-Glo-clad cycling assassin. The murder is in full view, graphically described in a textual version of slow motion and repeated image, breaking the conventions of the classic murder and mystery genre it draws upon. Unlike his girlfriend Conrad recovers to investigate the murder and explore his feelings of revenge. The mystery is mixed with the social references of a world that, emerging from his coma, Conrad explores with new eyes, sensing an alienated emptiness and overwhelming sense of contingency. Despite its cultural quips, the text shares at least as much of the Victorian and melodramatic as Christie's *The Murder of Roger Ackroyd* (1926) with its peripheral hidden relationship secrets and offers no major reworking of the minutiae of technical and chronological detail upon which the plot depends for its coherence than one finds in any of the classic Poirot narratives. Litt's mostly implicit intertextuality finds him not so far from his predecessors; in fact like Litt Christie subsumes emotional referents in a kind of intellectual, ludic alienation. Rather than being postmodern, although this critical term is alluded to playfully, Litt's social critique demonstrates a kind of cultural continuity underlying the surface, an ethical engagement. This is the whole moral cartography of a detective pattern, the chaotic truth reconfigured comfortably, but only partially by the detective figure. Even cultural referents resurface. Litt's Lily as a minor theatrical has progressed from parts at Euro Disney to star in a dramatic series of breakfast cereal ads. In his contemporary city a self-defining fashionable generation seem confronted by tortuous realities mirroring the twists of the generic plotline, but this is the case too in Christie's city novels. In *Lord Edware Dies* (1933) the sketch artist 'Carlotta Adams was quite the rage in London at the moment. The year before she had given a couple of matinees which had been a wild success. This year she had had a three weeks' season of which this was the last night but one' (7). Both writers convey a sense of the superficial. The immediacy, the illusion of success and the desire to signify socially and personally, all conspire both in Christie and in Litt to create deadly consequences for these theatrical women. In Litt, Lily is the author of her own fate; in Christie, Carlotta is a victim. One might remember that, very much in contrast to Conrad, when Jane Marple is accused by her nephew, Raymond, of not understanding 'REAL LIFE' in *A Caribbean Mystery* (1964) the narrator reflects

> People like Raymond were so ignorant. In the course of her duties in a country parish, Jane Marple had acquired quite a comprehensive knowledge of the facts of rural life. She had no urge to *talk* about them, far less to *write* about them – but she knew them.

Plenty of sex, natural and unnatural. Rape, incest, perversions of
all kinds. (Some kinds, indeed, that even the clever young men
from Oxford who wrote books didn't seem to have heard about.)
(9–10)

Conrad inherits Raymond's *naivety*. Hence by reconfiguring the generic, formulaic setting Litt achieves simultaneously a revocation and a
recuperation of the narrative structures of the past and thereby reaf-
firms existential and ethical difficulty – of the kind posited by the
excesses underlying detective and mystery genres – and he indicates
that the cartography of youth and success is an ongoing illusion, with
both its Thatcherite and its post-Thatcherite versions superseded in a
millennial mood of recognizing limitations, reflected by Lily in the
posthumous tape that Conrad hears. She says ' "I want you to die. I just
hope I get to see you die. Cunt. Cunt. Cunt. that's what I think of you.
You talentless little fucking shit-shit. Oh, what's the point. Conrad,
you cunt – " ' (367). If even the knowingness of 'postmodernity' can
evoke a space for reasserting the past and thematic continuity, the
question then remains concerning quite what is it of the contemporary
urban experience that fiction of this period foregrounds.

Endnote

Any amount of postmodern knowingness cannot in truth efface a shift
in both the cultural and the real-life experience of the city in Britain,
one that Will Self touches upon in *Junk Mail*. In 'The Valley of the
Corn Dollies' he reports in almost Orwellian tones from the mid-1990s:

> The fact remains that, in the past decade and a half in England,
> the poor have got resolutely poorer while the rich have got
> resolutely richer. Statistics came out a month ago (rating minimal
> column inches in newspapers that had more important things to
> comment upon, such as new trends in advertising) that, while the
> middle classes in England have doubled their wealth in real terms,
> the least well-off have got progressively poorer. (208)

Even current fiction has not reflected such realities with any ful-
someness, rather it mirrors Self's other observation in this piece that
the superstructure of our culture is reflected upon and not its base, for
'The superstructure of English culture is still overwhelmingly white,
middle-class and metropolitan. The people we are forced to listen to on
matters cultural have by and large seldom actually immersed themselves in the culture they purport to be explaining' (217). Encoding or
recoding the space of city-life cannot efface or reduce the informing
relevance of these phenomenological factualities.

Note

1 For a discussion and exemplification of these issues concerning the city, see Chapter
   Four 'The City', pp. 133–208, in Christopher Butler (1994) *Early Modernism:
   Literature, Music and Painting in Europe, 1900–1916*, Oxford: Clarendon Press.

Further Reading

Ackroyd, Peter *London: The Biography* [see bibliography].
Ackroyd's book is an interesting historical and cultural account of London that is
recommended for students considering the capital in a literary-cultural context.

Debord, Guy *The Society of the Spectacle* [see bibliography].
This is an engaging theoretical text emerging from the radical anarchistic dissent of
France in the 1960s, which deconstructs the performative (and oppressive) nature of
capitalism and its social practices, recommending a Situationist response. The book is
recommended for all advanced students given the permeation and influence of its ideas.

Keulks, Gavin (ed.) (2006) *Martin Amis: Postmodernism and Beyond*, London: Palgrave
   Macmillan.
This surprisingly is the first full collection of academic essays on Amis, offering a comprehensive and critically informed reading by leading scholars. It is recommended as
suitable for all levels of student.

Lefebvre, Henri *The Production of Space* [see bibliography].
This is a complex and yet rewarding analysis of the ideological, social and literal production of space and social relations. It is recommended for all postgraduates and theoretically confident students since it has become such an influential and seminal text.

Lynch, Kevin *The Image of the City* [see bibliography].
This is an accessible, intriguing text for the more advanced student. This analysis of
urban space and planning can provide conceptual ideas that might be useful for those
involved in literary and cultural studies.

McMillan, Neil (2003) 'Heroes and Zeroes: Monologism and Masculinism in Scottish
   Men's Writing of the 1970s and Beyond', in Daniel Lea and Berthold Schoene (eds)
   Posting the Male: Masculinities in Post-war and Contemporary British Literature,
   Amsterdam and New York: Rodopi, 69–87.
This chapter outlines the historical and ideological contexts of largely depictions of
working-class Scottish male identity in a broadly contemporary period.

Summers-Bremner, Eluned (2004) '"Fiction with a Thread of Scottishness in its Truth":
   The Paradox of the National in A. L. Kennedy', in Emma Parker (ed.) *Contemporary
   British Women Writers*, Cambridge: D. S. Brewer for the English Association, 123–38.
This accessible essay looks at marginality, sexuality, perversity and Scottishness in
Kennedy's work.

Tew, Philip (2003) 'The Fiction of A. L. Kennedy', in Richard Lane, Rod Mengham and
   Philip Tew (eds) *Contemporary British Fiction Post-1979: A Critical Introduction*,
   Cambridge: Polity Press, 120–39.
This is an essay on marginality and muteness in selected fiction by Kennedy that is a
good introduction to certain key aspects of her oeuvre; recommended for all levels of
student.

CHAPTER FOUR

The Past and the Present

KEY THEMES
Archetypes • Biblical and Fairy Tales • Children's Mythopoeic Worlds •
Darwinism • Death and the Dead • Dreams and Fantasies • History •
Modernism • Myth and the Mythopoeic • Re-reading the Postmodern •
The Parabolic • The Symbolic

KEY TEXTS
Ackroyd, Peter *Hawksmoor*
Ballard, J. G. *Crash* / *High-Rise* / *The Unlimited Dream Company*
Barnes, Julian *A History of the World in 10½ Chapters*
Byatt, A. S. *The Biographer's Tale* / *Possession*
Crace, Jim *The Gift of Stones* / *Quarantine*
Diski, Jenny *Only Human*
Fowles, John *The French Lieutenant's Woman*

Litt, Toby *deadkidsongs*
McEwan, Ian *Atonement*
Norfolk, Lawrence *In the Shape of the Boar*
Rushdie, Salman *The Satanic Verses*
Self, Will *How the Dead Live*
Sinclair, Iain *Lights Out for the Territory* / *White Chappell, Scarlet Tracings*
Swift, Graham *Waterland*
Thorpe, Adam *Ulverton*
Winterson, Jeanette *The Passion*

History and Myth

> He appeared on the hill at first light. The scarp was dark against a
> greening sky and there was the bump of the barrow and then the
> figure, and it shocked. I thought perhaps the warrior buried there
> had stood up again to haunt us. I thought this as I blew out the
> lanterns one by one around the pen. The sheep jostled and I was
> glad of their bells. (3)

These initial images of the first section '1650' in Adam Thorpe's
Ulverton (1992) picture the return of a Civil War soldier from the
slaughter at Drogheda, suggesting an intermingling of life, landscape
and death. Even before it becomes evident that the novel is an
intermixture of various different sequences from different periods set
in the same landscape, the apparent, the natural, the mythic, the

perceptual and the ghostly have created a symbolic interpenetration. The hint of death is suggestive, especially as it is for the soldier the result of the ensuing encounter to which the novel returns in its final section set out as a contemporary 'Post-Production Script' with a character named as the author. Such patterns of interpenetration are repeated throughout the novel, with the historical past interfused both with the present, *and* with the imaginary and supernatural modes of interpreting reality. This kind of reworking of long-established modes of narration, in order to synthesize apparently irreconcilable qualities within the imaginary, marks out one major strand of contemporary novels that transform history, parable and myth into something contemporaneous. These heavily allegorical, symbolic and metaphoric structures respond to the constraints or crisis of the genre: that of the rationally based naturalist (realist) narrative structure, of modernist fragmentation of such structures, and postmodern revisions of correspondence and hierarchy by reversing at least partially the early separation of a 'coincidence' of the linguistic sign and its intuitive content so that as Cassirer indicates in *Mythical Thought* 'the word still belongs to the sphere of mere existence: what is apprehended in it is not a signification, but rather a substantial being and power of its own. It does not point to an objective content but sets itself in the place of this content [. . .] a power which intervenes in empirical events and their causal concatenation' (237).

One needs this understanding to place texts such as Lawrence Norfolk's *In the Shape of the Boar* (2000), which integrates a novelistic account of the Greek myth of the hunt for the Boar of Kalydon and a more contemporary narrative, which centres on the evils of the Second World War and its post-war effect on several lives. The incongruity of the account reflects its attempt at mythopoeic effects, setting the scene and listing the qualities of the hunters, footnoted at great length in common with much of the first section narrated expansively and evidently drawing very explicitly on classical sources. There is something preternatural and archetypal concerning the qualities and symbols. The effect is cumulative, but the traces of myth structure its consciousness.

> The country which yet divides them is a place of accidental transformations. Its hinterland has been foreshadowed, its instabilities prefigured. Here, brothers turn into uncles, women may be men and men form themselves in the harsh races of rivers, wade out and stand dripping on the banks, a minute old but full-grown. The terrain narrows with every step. Its coordinates are their untrammelled bodies and what they do. Those who die here can do so only by fluke or carelessness. (7)

And the night-hunter leaves no trace in a land where silence is mysterious, where 'The hush on the far side of that noise was now their language, proper to lost men, their memories and ghosts' (59), and the hunters merge with the very landscape after a muddied flood. 'An archipelago of hump-backed islands extended peninsulas, spits and spurs whose flexings transformed them into mud-coated bodies: chthonic beings disinterring themselves from their formative clay, bones heavy with damp, eyes crusted and hair matted' (60). The novel's other main narrative concerns the fate of Sol Memel, a Romanian Jew, who in his escape from the Nazis finds himself at the site of the classical tale. After the conflict he becomes famous for a modern epic poem, that the novel indicates is of uncertain quality. The mythic and the past collide in 1970s Paris, where Sol encounters his pre-war lover, Ruth, who is involved in a film version of his poetic efforts. Sol's poem has fused the wartime struggle between a German officer, Oberstleutnant Heinrich Eberhardt and the resistance in Greece with the classical confrontation between the boar and the night-hunter. Ruth's revelation appears to destroy the myth. ' "The truth is now, Solomon. Not then. Here is the time for the Tellable. Your Thyella never existed. Your 'boar' was an insignificant desk officer. The boar didn't die at all, Sol. The boar won" ' (301). And yet such literalness cannot subsume the symbolic order of myth, for significantly the novel concludes with Sol's aspect of the tellable, that is the tale of the destruction of the boar, the mythic despatch of the symbol of evil. Norfolk's text draws together these apparently disparate features, epitomizing the kind of generic transformation of consciousness that critics have struggled to concede, simply noting instead the integration of paradoxical formal elements.

Winterson and Rushdie

Given myth's relationship with finitude, where as Cassirer states 'death by no means signifies a sharp division, a parting, of the soul from the body. [. . .] Such a distinction, such a definite contrast of the conditions governing life and death, is contrary to the mythical mode of thought' (159–60), almost invariably death is a motif or occurrence that helps centre the disparate formal and thematic elements that also characterize what is a new phase of mythopoeism rather than a new form of historicism. This common mythological thinking or framing of events has a number of implications for reading such texts. Jeanette Winterson conjures a commingling of both the unexpectedly mundane and the fantastic with a historically familiar context of Napoleon's campaigns in *The Passion* (1987). The interplay and yet the very instability of these elements on one level allow Winterson to challenge conventional narrative assumptions concerning situating the historical. The fourth section commences with an affirmation of continuance and recurrence that appears beyond any naturalistic interpretation. 'They say the dead don't talk. Silent as the grave they say. It's not true. The dead are talking all the time. On this rock, when the wind is up, I can hear them' (133). This observation concerns neither the real nor any naturalistic sense of the imaginary, and yet it is rooted in the myth of Napoleon, a 'solidly' historical figure, and as such the text represents a reworking of inscribed elements outside of the normally established bounds of facticity. Thus its historicity becomes more than the 'magic realism' Frederick M. Holmes identifies in *The Historical Imagination: Postmodernism and the Treatment of the Past in Contemporary British Fiction* (1997), Winterson's text achieving a quasi-mythicality in its subversion of itself, both in its proffering the past in the present, and in its making of history as a kind of referential narrative something akin to Lucien Dällenbach's observation of myth in *The Mirror in the Text* (1977).

> The tale is suited to the propagation of universal truths, since it can be universally appreciated. As for myths, even if they are being brought into an allegorical context, they never quite lose all of their original character: 'symbols extended into narrative form', they 'make one think', and in moving the narrative into an unreal register, none the less produce an inexhaustible supply of meanings. (59)[1]

It is this multiple movement that characterizes and links the mythic, parabolic and allegorical strands of contemporary fiction which are various. Winterson's fictional impulse is traceable and open to comparison to the historical facts, period knowledge, textual expectations, and naturally the stuff of life. As Holmes points out this cannot achieve the certainties of 'authorized' history, but as with the diary of the initial protagonist, it appears to offer an ontological reference and validity. Holmes says 'Henri's journal is characterized not by such black-and-white certitude but by diffidence and a self-conscious questioning of the validity of his own historical record' (42), but he and Villanelle do account for things in what Holmes describes as 'a language of feeling' (42). This extends what Aleid Fokkema in *Postmodern Characters* (1991) describes as 'more seemingly referential texts' that constitute what he persists in categorizing as a postmodern continuum of experimentation (15). The strength of the mythic that underpins this literary consciousness needs careful theoretical placement, since as the work of Cassirer suggests in this narrative strategy there is an important consciousness that allows an aesthetic mediation of many of the paradoxes created in postmodern and supposedly post-enlightenment consciousness. Its understanding 'begins with the insight that it does not move in a purely invented or made-up world but has its own mode of *necessity* and therefore [...] its own mode of *reality*' (4), potentially offering 'an empirical intuition' (19), and certainly a rooted 'characteristic creative elaboration' (23). This contextualizes the kind of narrativity and symbolic consciousness Rushdie achieves repeatedly in *The Satanic Verses*, something beyond metaphor or irony. The novel begins with the concept of rebirth as over the English Channel Saladin Chamcha and Gibreel Farishta fall from the sky. Rushdie invokes the ritualistic and mythopoeic in the chanting and babble of Gibreel. This is present in mundane commencement of the flight to which the narrative returns. 'Once the flight to London had taken off, thanks to his magic trick of crossing two pairs of fingers on each hand and rotating his thumbs, the narrow fortyish fellow who sat in a non-smoking window seat watching the city of his birth fall away from him like old snakeskin allowed a relieved expression to pass briefly across his face' (33). The significance of Saladin and Gibreel is far from literal and not simply cultural. The merging of two characters is an event on which the whole consciousness of the novel is predicated, their falling from the sky unscathed from an air crash, and the transformation of their selves is characteristically mythic. Some of its interrogative tone is significant.

Is birth always a fall?

Do angels have wings? Can men fly? (8)

As Cassirer comments 'Myth lives entirely by the presence of its object – by the intensity with which it seizes and takes possession of consciousness in a specific moment. Myth lacks any means of extending the moment beyond itself, of looking ahead of it or behind it, of relating it as a particular to the elements as a whole' (35). This helps explain the incongruities (often nonsensical qualities) in Rushdie, and the intensity of this and similarly mythically centred narratives.

The Historical Novel
A mythic dimension underpins the curious impression of inertia that runs counter to the plot in McEwan's *Atonement* which is not just a matter of reflecting an English sense of pre-war nostalgia for the age of the country house surviving into the 1930s where the bulk of the novel is set. Alongside other Woolfian elements McEwan retrieves from Woolf's oeuvre a preternatural consciousness, similar to a mythic

intuitiveness, centred on the mother of the house in question, the hypochondriac Emily Tallis who possesses 'a sixth sense, a tentacular awareness that reached out from the dimness and moved through the house, unseen and unknowing' (66). And yet this is divorced from the continuity of time and ironically misread by her so that she fails to intervene when her niece, Lola, is raped. Her sense mirrors the mythic consciousness of an undifferentiated existence.

> She would soothe the household, which seemed to her, from the sickly dimness of the bedroom, like a troubled and sparsely populated continent from whose forested vastness competing elements made claims and counter-claims. She had no illusions: old plans, if one could ever remember them, the plans that time had overtaken, tended to have a febrile and over-optimistic grip on events. She could send her tendrils into every room of the house, but she could not send them into the future. (70–1)

Much like Emily herself overall the narrative seems to be ultimately powerless in its relations with the past, simply transforming it into the ever-present, a kind of reverberation back and forth.

As Franco Moretti explores in *Signs Taken for Wonders: Essays in the Sociology of Literary Forms* (1983) James Joyce, T. S. Eliot and W. B. Yeats in particular re-instituted a new literary concern for myth, approaching these perspectives in two major ways: firstly a narrative incorporating myth, and secondly a mediation of old mythic forms to produce new symbolic figurations from the contemporaneous (192–3). The perceived differences of Moretti's distinction are significant for describing contemporary approaches since 'The question of myth returns to the centre of *Ulysses*, but in a completely different way from that in which Eliot posited it: not as a meta-historic image of the fable and several typical characters, but as a relationship between subjective intellectual consciousness and intuition of objective reality; not as a metaphoric pattern for the narration, but as its technique' (194). Certainly both modes of the mythic offer specific literary models and characteristics that persist, and at times writers achieve at least partially a kind of fusion of the two. Holmes situates Fowles's *The French Lieutenant's Woman* as part of 'the nostalgia pervasive in British high brow culture for the Victorian past, with its unambiguous social hierarchy, its reassuringly solid and densely cluttered interiors, its seeming confidence, stability, and unclouded sense of purpose' (49). The ways in which this is historicized and destabilized (along with Charles's fragile social pattern of behaviour) reveal another set of layers or interpretative possibilities extending Holmes's tentative 'proto-existentialism' of the protagonists (66–7). The novel also exemplifies an early mythic hybridization of the contemporary novel form. There are meta-historic images of the fable and typical characters, but there is something strongly intuitive. The narrator informs the reader authoritatively enough (substantiated by Sarah's reading of Charles Smithson and Mrs Poulteney) that Sarah has an 'uncanny' way of assessing people almost instantaneously, applying an 'instinctual profundity of insight' (50) to others and this allows her to act outside of the conventional moral code of the Victorian middle classes. Her thinking mirrors a mythic comprehension, which Cassirer indicates differs from the scientific-rational view. 'For where we see a mere analogy, i.e. a mere relation, myth sees immediate existence and presence' (68). Moreover, this emphasis on Sarah's intuition and its effectiveness in breaching restrictive moral codes is suggestive since as Cassirer asks 'Does myth not signify a unity of intuition, an *intuitive* unity preceding and underlying all explanations contributed by *discursive* thought?' (69). Given that, in myth, reality and imaginary realms intersect, then Alison Lee's notion (in *Realism and Power* [1990]) that in Fowles 'fictional characters, then, are given the same ontological status as "real" characters' (46) can be reconfigured very differently from the implied postmodern reading consequent upon her concept of a 'historiographic metafiction' and this enables one to recontextualize Fowles's 'mixture of fiction and "reality"' (92).

One account would situate the mythopoeic as a part of a post-war nostalgia reacting to the loss of Empire. As Connor sketches in *The English Novel in History 1950–1995* such fiction confronts or explores the 'waning of confidence in the power of history', but as he notes cultural changes after the 1960s have created the conditions for 'a huge expansion of history and history-making' (135) in the novel that engages more broadly than simply working through imperial loss. Nostalgia and myth-making have synthesized with and transmuted the historical. Such narratives are differently centred than postmodern artifice, that Lee, following very much in the footsteps of Linda Hutcheon, labels 'historiographic metafictions' while noting that they 'are, particularly in their play with Realist conventions, paradoxical. While they use Realist conventions, they simultaneously seek to subvert them. Yet they do so from within precisely those conventions which they are clearly trying to undermine' (36). There are more subtle readings where the question of history is not simply set against a previously rational and/or patriarchal hegemony. Connor attempts a number of critical placements of the historical novel, at one point evoking two broad categories: firstly those writing of the past in language contemporary with authorship (140) along with others that attempt a mix of the historical and this 'authoritative impersonal

narration' (141), and secondly novels that problematize language cit-
ing as an exemplary text John Fowles's *The French Lieutenant's Woman*
(141–2). Connor says 'The second kind seem to highlight the difficulty
of translation, by displaying the lack of fit, or ironic incompatibility,
between past and present viewpoints and languages' (142). Certainly
Connor is correct in situating Fowles's novel as a seminal one. Initially
he wonders whether one can contrast any fiction of continuous history,
placing in opposition to a *historicized* type where one can 'discern a
general movement in postwar literature and culture generally, away
from the first kind of history and the confident authority it assumes
towards the more sceptical or relativised view of history exemplified in
the second' (143), but immediately expresses reservations over this
categorization and its essentially relativistic reading by Alison Lee and
Linda Hutcheon. As Connor observes in terms of Peter Ackroyd's
Hawksmoor (1985) one might read such novels as a challenge to
'Western time by attempting to escape time as such'. (145) I would
situate this as part of what Cassirer calls in *Mythical Thought* a

> mythical consciousness [which] is not, like the theoretical con-
> sciousness, concerned with gaining fundamental constants by
> which to explain variation and change. This differentiation is
> replaced by another, which is determined by the characteristic
> perspective of myth. The mythical consciousness arrives at an
> articulation of space and time not by stabilizing the fluctuation of
> sensuous phenomena but by introducing its specific opposition –
> the opposition of the sacred and the profane – into spatial and
> temporal reality. (81)

I would add that this is the quality that elevates *Hawksmoor* from the
detective genre with a parallel historical narrative. As Adriana Neagu
and Sean Matthews say in their e-critique of the novel, that it

> was inspired in part by Iain Sinclair's poem 'Lud Heat', written in
> 1975, which inferred a mystical power from the positioning of the
> six churches which the architect Nicholas Hawksmoor built in
> the East End of London during the reign of Queen Anne. The
> novel gives Hawksmoor a diabolical motive in the siting of his
> buildings, and creates a modern namesake, a policeman investi-
> gating a series of child murders, a seeming consequence of
> Hawksmoor's work. (n. pag.)

The motive is an avowal of the power and influence of death, and Dyer
says of one of his buildings,

It is a vast Mound of Death and Nastinesse, and my Church will take great Profit from it: this Mirabilis once describ'd to me, *viz* a Corn when it dies and rots in the Ground, it springs again and lives, so, *said he*, when there are many Persons dead, only being buryed and laid in the Earth, there is an Assembling of Powers. If I put my Ear to the Ground I hear them lie promiscuously one with another, and their small Voices echo in my Church: they are my Pillars and my Foundations. (23–4)

This ongoing life of the dead and quest for rebirth is a basis of the mythological existence. Ackroyd's detective is named Hawksmoor as if to identify him with the malevolent or mythic spirit of the novel's architect, Nicholas Dyer, who is based on the genuine historical figure of the detective's name. Underpinning this conflation is a sense of a Manichean struggle between good and evil, a meta-historical, elemental force, and by the novel's end the image of the dead child is conjoined with the character, Hawksmoor, speaking enigmatically and yet in unison: 'And then in my dream I looked down at myself and saw in what rags I stood; and I am a child again, begging on the threshold of eternity.' Whether illusory or mythic, this is a fusion of elements, less a decentring than a unification of the disparate and inchoate beyond the self-evident and prosaic. As Holmes says readings such as Alison Lee's over-prioritize the postmodern features negating 'transcendent identities'. He adds

Is it the novel which categorically forecloses on this interpretative option, or is it the ideology of the critic? Lee cleverly explicates the novel's self-reflexive tendency to dissolve its patterns of significance in an ambiguous, unrestricted play of textuality, but equally pervasive are contradictory references which ground the novel's reality in the corruption of the earth, in the certainty of death, and in the ubiquitous evil inherent in existence. (15)

A consequence of such readings is to diminish the historical to a textualization, and fail to observe the recent historical novel's development of a broader mythopoeism. David Leon Higdon in *Shadows of the Past in Contemporary British Fiction* (1984) observes in this recent consciousness a different historical perspective in contradistinction to that of the modernists. 'In post-war art, however, the past in its three major manifestations of memory, tradition, and history, has reasserted itself, demanding attention, allegiance, and even homage from the present' (6). However, he conflates the mythic simply with ideological misinterpreting of historical contexts, incidentally privileging implicitly apparently 'radical' readings over the traditional (13), achieving a Foucauldian 'fragmentation and dispersal of the subject of history' (10).

Coe's use of myth alluded to earlier demonstrates that the kind of texts grouped in this chapter – the mythic, parabolic and by extension the analogical – are diverse, some apparently conventionally 'realist', others characterized by elements drawn from the fantastic and the 'metafictional'. Connor notes astutely that historical texts can be read in quite a contrary manner, and are in opposition to Linda Hutcheon's reading of indeterminacy since they do take 'possession of the past' (147), a theme he sees as explicit in Byatt's *Possession* (147). Connor's notion of this text's hybridity is acute, and as he indicates the collapse of boundaries between past and present (149) might well be less to do with the text's partialities, and yet there resides an effect drawn from another key element that could be suggested by a quotation to which Connor draws attention, taken from one of Byatt's epigraphs, from Browning's 'Mr Sludge "The Medium"' ' (Connor, 149). Here history is equated with 'Life in stones,/Fire into fog, making the past your world', and one senses not simply the 'fabrication' Connor prioritizes but, however ironized, by Browning, a residue of a mythic account of the past, a state that Cassirer describes as where 'History dissolves being into the never-ending sequence of becoming' (106) with its sense of 'perpetual coexistence and interpenetration' (127). Such a sense of the past in the present can explain the integration of the deathly into the objective relic analysed by Holmes in terms of a significant set of themes and contexts in *Possession*.

> The significance of Roland and Val's dank and dreary basement flat in this connection is obvious: Roland is symbolically interred with the dead, shut out by his landlady from the garden of fulfilment outside his door. This act, the novel implies, discloses the true significance of his obsession with the material objects owned by Ash. Cropper seems to believe that Ash somehow lives on in these items, or at least that they constitute a metonymic path that will lead him to that enduring, originary pleasure. He does discover the letter buried by Ash's wife, Ellen, but the trail finally ends at Ash's lifeless corpse. Buxton is probably right to say that at bottom his interest in the dead poet is 'necrophiliac and ghoulish.' (81–2)

In part this broader fictional turn to myth and history situates the process by which Byatt can perceive what Connor calls a 'fiction [that] is justified on the grounds that it is a kind of conjuration, an authentic medium for allowing the past to speak' (149) for as Cassirer comments 'The beginnings of creative art seem to partake of a sphere in which creative activity is still embedded in magical representation and directed toward specific magical *aims*' (25). Faced by the oppositions to both modernism and a traditional mimetic, diverted by metafictional fragmentation, it appears fiction retrieves in history and in metaphor the residue of another symbolic mode, a mythic consciousness, that works toward what might be described as a fictional 'historiographic mythopoeism'.

Death and Dreams

One finds the mythopoeic that is not historically contextualized, but still integrates the two mythic traditions indicated by Moretti, in Ballard's *The Unlimited Dream Company* (1979) whose protagonist, Blake, in the novel's first chapter steals a Cessna and through his ineptitude and inexpertise crashes it into the Thames in the London suburb of Shepperton. 'The starboard wing sank between the surface. Dragged by the current, the Cessna rolled onto its side. Breaking free from my harness, I forced back the door and clambered from the flooded cabin on the port wing strut. I climbed on to the roof and stood there in my ragged flying suit as the aircraft sank below me into the water, taking my dreams and hopes into its deeps' (19). Throughout the text one suspects Blake of multiple pathologies, a madness that persists on the fringe of the contemporary myth as a resistance to notions of normality. Either rescued or reborn, Blake's world is transformed, and Shepperton literalizes its part of the production of the modern myth in the film industry. Blake's exploration of a symbolic and mythic dream-world is actualized, intruding into and reshaping the world of the suburbanites that he encounters. The narrative becomes the site of an alternate reality, a zone apparently on the fringes of life and death, where the unconscious and a new sense of reality merge. This is more than a fracture of reality, for as Cassirer comments in *An Essay on Man: An Introduction to a Philosophy of Human Culture* (1944):

> We are in the habit of dividing our life into two spheres of practical and theoretical activity. In this division we are prone to forget that there is a lower stratum beneath them both. Primitive man is not liable to such forgetfulness. All his thoughts and his feelings are still embedded in this lower original stratum. His view of nature is neither merely theoretical nor merely practical; it is sympathetic. If we miss this point we cannot find the approach to the mythical world. (82)

Ballard's nether and yet proximate zone is encountered in several of his novels including *Crash* and *High-Rise*, the former defined by a pathological desire and the latter by the collapse of the matrix of social interaction with a bloody conflict emerging in the high-rise development of the title. London provides the setting, but so defamilarized that it is offset from the reader's shared reality. Will Self incorporates a similar strategy in *How the Dead Live*. Such fiction's dimensions are different from the metafictional, seeking to redeem and deepen the strengths of traditional narrative forms without destroying narrative coherence. Thorpe's *Ulverton* defamiliarizes and reconfigures the historical; he particularizes fragments of history so that the single location is variously a sign, a symbol and a palimpsest. *Ulverton* becomes more than a historical or experimental landscape, and the strength of the symbolic landscape and the recurrent character types and situations are both linked to a metaphysical dimension, with desire and death linking the historical vignettes. The tracing of historical moments makes the text almost a fusion of the mundane and the incantatory. For Ballard death, dreams and pathological desire suggest both an adjacency to and a difference from reality; for other authors these elements together with history and established myths provide the grounds to what Dominic Head describes in terms of Thorpe's technique in *Ulverton* as a means of ensuring 'that the personal is integrated within a broader historical drama. [...] part of a larger fabric that builds into a poetic social history of place' (200). In this novel the historical is fragmented and in the manner that it is particularized, as Head indicates, it supersedes the social and fuses with the symbolic and mythic possibilities of the landscape. The first section commences in 1650 with the return of one of Cromwell's soldiers, Gabby, from the New Model Army's campaign of slaughter in Ireland, only to be murdered by his wife, Anne, and her new husband, Thomas Walters. Gabby claims to have shaken Cromwell's hand, his tale transforming experience of history into a symbolic gesture. The soldier is compelled to narrate in guilt his experiences, evoking forgotten stories, inconsequential to his listener, a friend and neighbour. The act of Gabby's murder goes unpunished, for his skeleton to be discovered hundreds of years later by builders toward the narrative's end, thus becoming a sign of the very mystery and elusiveness of the past. For Gabby's friend after his supposed disappearance, his stories recur, irrepressibly and irrationally.

> I thought of how he had shook hands with General Cromwell in all the smoke and all the women and children of Drogheda spilled like empty sacks that Gabby had helped empty. And I saw Ruth among them, I don't know why. She had her legs open like the times we made a babby or like a ewe ready for a ram. And there was General Cromwell shaking hands with Gabby and both

smiling while Thomas Walters clacked his teeth together next to them and turned round and saw me looking on my damp log and shot me.

   These were dreams but I was awake. I shook my head free of them and took to making dolls out of straw but always they had their legs wide open and they smiled like General Cromwell or Thomas Walters. And sometimes as I was lifting out a lamb I thought of Anne with my hand inside her which was really Ruth and the ewe kicking out its legs as the lamb came out in a slither, all new. (16–17)

The symbolic order is more vivid and appears to convey more immediacy than the literal. The text's integration of historical and aesthetic testament counters the traditional concept of history, restoring a naive and yet pervasive presence and consciousness. As Cassirer comments, there is a recovery of past perception that may underwrite the blurring of boundaries and rational forms in this symbolic manner.

The primitive mind [...] its view of life is a synthetic, not an analytical one. Life is not divided into classes and subclasses. It is felt as an unbroken continuous whole which does not admit of any clean-cut and trenchant distinctions. The limits between the different spheres are not unsurmountable barriers; they are fluent and fluctuating. There is no specific difference between the various realms of life. Nothing has a definite, invariable, static shape. By a sudden metamorphosis everything may be turned into everything. (81)

This metamorphosis of meaning and understanding is at the heart of the contemporary adoption of myth, parable and analogy. In *Ulverton* the recovery of the past recurs and is suggestive of an order of communication that is both phenomenological and of hidden potential.

He handed them to me one by one: the bronze dagger, and the iron hair-pin; a polished greenstone wrist-guard (or so we guessed) with nine holes at each end capped with sheet-gold, and broken – probably as part of a ritual; and a bone pendant, stained by the corroding dagger, found beside the ribs, carved into the form of a leaping animal (a hare?) and painfully crude. Hardly a treasure. But each, as it lay in my hand, had an extra weight; of silence perhaps, 'deep as Eternity', and the value of silence, that had lain unstirred under tussocks and cloud for four thousand years, until the Squire smote through the turf with his blade. (256)

Moreover, the revival of the 'Curse of Five Elms Farm' does not simply evoke the unknown, but as Head details a nostalgic urge. One can go beyond this observation, since there is more than this; this very nostalgia is affiliated to a range of atavistic emotional motivations, most particularly greed. This recurrence and repetitious motif is significant as Cassirer says in *The Metaphysics of Symbolic Forms* 'the means for understanding living forms is analogy. Analogy unveils history's language of forms. It shows that the number of forms that appears in world history is strictly limited, that ages, epochs, locations, and persons recur according to types. [. . .] Knowledge by analogy also presupposes insight into specific, objective facts, and without them it would have no footing and no definiteness' (109). As Head notes, Thorpe's tales, although they involve 'Misunderstandings and misrepresentations [that] abound as the sedimented layers of history obscure the past' (200), are more primarily concerned with a sense of pattern and indelibility, and as Head indicates the appearance of Thorpe as a character is quite separate from the metafictional use of this device and more akin to Ballard's self-reference in *Crash* which is concerned with being part of and within the moral and ethical dimensions of the depicted world. If the contemporary scene verges on the pathological, this explains more fully Head's observation that the novel 'reproduces the extreme it seeks to anatomise' (234).

Myth and the Child

One lively exposition of such extremity, with a strong sense of the mythopoeic as susceptible to the pathological, is the incongruous narrative of childlike perspectives by Toby Litt in *deadkidsongs* (2001), an intersecting series of documents of an apparent 'Gang' of boys whose obsessions with soldiers, war and discipline, and the traditions of a Churchillian military spirit, seem to synthesize with a generic cultural sense of the mood of post-war children's narratives and a narrowly historicized Britishness. The text commences with – or is prefaced by – a map of Amplewick in Midfordshire, evoking a nostalgic mood and the co-ordinates of the childhood of the four boys Andrew, Matthew, Paul and Peter, who share appropriately Ayrean looks and a circumscribed world-view. The apparent cartographic precision and solidity of this fictional middle-English village are in stark contrast to the text that seems to be a playful reinterpretation of the rural quotidian in terms of a combination of wartime and Cold War conflict. Together as a curious collective of naïfs, the boys imagine Russian invasion, Soviet T-64 tanks and paranoia. They are subsumed into a historicized fantasy, played out with toys, models and the paraphernalia of incipient adolescence.

> The Battle of Britain was taking place about six feet above our heads. The Allied Air Force, represented by two Spitfires, and two Hurricanes, was surrounded by a swarm of twelve or thirteen Messerschmidt 110s and 109bs. [. . .] Above each plane, a transparent fishing-line or two stretched up towards the ceiling. Brass-topped drawing-pins held in place the most important air-battle in History. (37)

The innocence of the boys and their surroundings is deceptive. They become brutal and uncaring within the community itself, quite unlike William Golding's *Lord of the Flies* (1954) which has the moral absence of adulthood at its centre in terms of initiating a more atavistic violence, something that Litt's text questions. In *deadkidsongs* it is more directly from the adult world, epitomized by the complicity and inadequacy of Andrew's bullying and misogynist father, wife-beater and child-beater, that these boys draw consciously their sense of purpose and justification for their communal and destructive narrative of theirs and most particularly others' lives. Andrew's father encourages them, quite specifically militarizes them, but the knowing narrative voice in the section concerning Andrew's role admits 'His father's denial of love, of the bland statement of love, out of a greater love, was the greatest force in our lives. Only later did we fully realize this. (Those of us that were still around to have realizations.) At the time, we merely felt awe, awe far greater than had been inspired in us by Hell or PC241 or the Headmistress, or Russia, even' (52). However, it is a mythic view of the world, a desire for archetypes and concrete simplicities that is an even stronger motivating force. They are inspired to kill a dog, and plan the death of Matthew's grandparent guardians, the pensioners they label 'the Dinosaurs', pledging they must die before Christmas in Operation Extinction (206). Their actions and world spirals apparently out of control, and yet the novel conjures quite explicitly a nostalgic, almost elegiac knowingness concerning the loss of innocence and the past.

> The delights of the earth's various smells: acrid, cow-patty, decay-sweet, decay-sour, alcoholic, honeyed, old-flower-vase-water-like, powdery, sulphurous, dank, petalled. And above all, the heavenly odour of grass new-cut. A Purcell smell, so delicate it is, so laced, so graced with the immanence of nostalgia. Every child should be told to breathe deep of the effluvium of grass and hay, and all cut-stalks. This, they will remember always. And by preparing for their decrepit futures, by deliberate memory-making, they will know they did justice to their childhood, whilst living and loving it. (14)

When this feeling is intertwined with other accounts, such as their celebration of conflict and simplistic accounts of struggle, a sense of masculine realities and the power of imagination merge dangerously. The boys are essentially a *tabula rasa* upon which a strong immoral impulse has been inscribed or cultivated by Andrew's father, ironically called by them 'the Best Father', with platitudes such as 'Life is War. Life is conflict' (85). His own failures, which allow him to reject any broader perspective and accept a universalizing or common humanity, are at the heart of the reconstructed moral, adult sense of the events that Litt implicitly invites his reader to undertake. It is for Peter after Matthew's death as if he is possessed by his spirit, 'the spirit of Gang' (384). By the end of the novel, in the second version of the thirteenth chapter, the wartime aspects of the imaginary, mythic past subsume the co-ordinates of the map, when confronted with the adult world Peter reflects 'I sat with my arms folded, gazing at the wall above their heads as if there were something incredibly interesting upon it: a rare butterfly. Actually, I was staring through it at an imaginary version of events taking place elsewhere – a version, it has to be said, that in all but the smallest details was uncannily accurate' (393). Although Peter claims he is looking through things, in fact it is a return to the ghost of the concrete world which reasserts a limit to his perception, which just like those of myth, according to Cassirer's account in *Mythical Thought*,

> are fixed on man's self-limitation in his immediate relation to reality, as a willing and acting subject – on the fact that in confronting this reality he sets up specific barriers to which his feeling and his will attach themselves. The primary spatial difference lies [. . .] between two *provinces* of being: a common, generally accessible province and another, sacred, precinct which seems to be raised out of its surroundings, hedged around and guarded against them. (85)

This has been the mythopoeic reality the boys inhabit without understanding its need to be universal, since they depend on its textualization, very specifically so in Peter's 'The Archives'. Their world destroys itself. Peter may appear to succeed in narrative terms in negating any moral and material centre to his understanding, but finally he cannot sustain his visionary, archaic view of England.

In his drawing upon mythopoeic elements and setting them in contradistinction to the failings of populist historical mythic narratives, thereby interrogating cultural and narrative traditionalism, Litt suggests different ways to reconsider culture beyond the postmodern historiographic – which Linda Hutcheon in *The Politics of Postmodernism* (1989) claims renders the public world as discourse and is entirely synonymous with the real (36) – with its potential for a relativistic absence of values. This typifies a contemporary emphasis or literary inclination.

Reconsidering the Metafictional

Other novels that engage their readers very explicitly in a historiographic consciousness, most often in fact supplement the metafiction's discomposition of rational and universalizing grand narratives and centre the texts away from such metafictional structural concerns. As even Fokkema concedes, 'When readers construct the sign of character, they do not draw on literary conventions alone. [. . .] Some of the codes that constitute character are not so much literary conventions as conventions drawn from knowledge of the real world' (47). Perhaps this in part explains why there even appears, as Gąsiorek indicates, a recurrent underlying strand of quasi-mimetic realism in much post-war writing, but even more significantly for the trajectory of the British novel subsequently is increasingly the mythopoeic element. In analysing this trend it is insufficient to gesture toward the mythic, without offering some critical framework beyond evoking some vague connection to magic realism. In fact such fictions are characterized by quite a different interplay of elements than either the metafictional or the magic realist, one characterized by what Cassirer describes in terms of the mythic, similarly capable of perceiving and expressing experience through

> heterogeneous mythical explanations, [which] chaotic and lawless as they may seem in their mere content, reveal one and the same *approach* to the world. Whereas the scientific causal judgement dissects an event into constant elements and seeks to understand it through the complex mingling, interpenetration, and constant conjunction of these elements, mythical thinking clings to the total representation as such and contents itself with picturing the simple course of what happens. (47)

In literary texts this supplementary mode allows a transformation and transcendence radically different from postmodern negations of rational, enlightened thinking, although certainly some of these metafictional elements remain part of an ongoing generic hybridity. This very hybridity helps to initiate an appropriate form for myth since as Cassirer maintains 'Mythical thinking, even where it raises the question of origins as such, has a free selection of causes at its disposal. Anything can *come from* anything, because anything can stand in temporal or spatial contact with anything' (46).

Writers have adopted enthusiastically such mythic perspectives, but generally not followed a single model in what has become a complex and adaptive strategy, a kind of fictional extemporization. This mode is identified with a certain caution since arguably there remain residual mythic and parabolic patterns underlying most forms of literary discourse. Literature seems apart from the life-world and yet retains a comparative, suggestive and hence overall an analogical set of relations to reality; this analogical reference is reflected in the oppositional structures that determine myth, summarized by Shlomith Rimmon-Kenan in *Narrative Fiction: Contemporary Poetics* (1983), and its characteristic doubling of narrative reference and transformations between deep and surface meanings (23–7). In contemporary fiction foregrounding such analogical patterns is not essentially a structural or postmodern characteristic, for as Bataille says in *the unfinished system of nonknowledge* 'The myth, the symbol of the eternal return, cannot be considered in isolation. It is related to the conditions in which life attains the impossible. I've already said it twice: the impossible is only reached through the possible; without the possible, there would be no impossible' (24). Drawing upon the past and the present, the imaginary and the real, the concrete and the symbolic, this is the impetus of the new phase of mythic prose; it emphasizes traditional mythic structures, the meta-symbolic quality of symbols, institutions and naming, and in their synthesis creates a meta-imaginary where the real appears to be secondary to these determining archetypes. These elements contribute to a displacement where understandings or resolutions are implicit, intuitive, counter rather than irrational, and the quotidian acquires an often surreal or highly suggestive edge. The blending of the anecdotal, the sacramental, the extreme and the familiar is one mode of its development. Often seen as a quintessential writer of contemporary mythic forms, in *Lights Out for the Territory* (1997) Iain Sinclair reconfigures both aspects in his narrative engagement with London (where Sinclair's form invites the question of whether it is history, narrative, documentary, personal account, a series of cultural symbols or so on), which in this mythic bifurcation is neither realist nor simply imaginary; he assembles cumulative references to, descriptions of and evidence from the city as evidence of a mythic realm where one encounters 'A delirium of coded information, hot text, cancer-grey lampposts frantic to declare their allegiances. Scribbles stacked like battle honours. Scudding clouds, an avenue of disappointed nautical ambition' (49), an extemporary world of 'the transcendent oddity of airport perimeter roads, Ikea warehouses, neutral buffer zones between town and country. Landscapes of the id, such as riverside Shepperton, that have developed – from long exposure to the presence and the fiction of JG Ballard – their own peculiar microclimates' (306). Sinclair refers to a climate of belief, of perceptual understanding; he speaks in fact of challenging the confusion of the mundane with the rational, the naturalistic. The symbolic order shares with the metaphoric the transformative possibility that once resided in myth, which is why its recurrence in the current literary field is so significant. Earl R. Mac Cormac in A Cognitive Theory of Metaphor (1985) sees

> Metaphorical truth [...] in this evolutionary process in which the stability of the ordinary, banal perceptions and expressions of the world in literal language provides an objective base for metaphor. Metaphorical truth and literal truth exist on a con-tinuum; one does not necessarily need to reduce metaphors to literal language in order to assess their truth value. Truth value arises from the new possibilities and new insights that metaphors provide, and metaphoric suggestions presume an integral semantic and cognitive connection with the ordinary world, hence the assertion of a continuum. (224–5)

Significantly Sinclair makes two direct references to the comtem-porary mythopoeic when he dedicates his book to the late Angela Carter and Michael Moorcock, two writers who both draw upon the metaphysical potential of the city, while incorporating the fantasy and otherworldly mundanity of Mervyn Peake's Gormenghast trilogy, a critically understated, but major contemporary influence. In White Chappell, Scarlet Tracings (1987) Sinclair combines archetypal landscapes and interiors with the cumulative listing of objects, such as the items in a car ferrying bookdealers around 'The mid-England dark, torpid and thick, a kind of sluggish ignorance' (12). Items and names attain a symbolic quality; Jamie is known by the auction ring in cul-turally suggestive terms, 'The Old Pretender'. Book dealer Mossy Noonmann seeks almost explicitly to attain archetypal presence. 'He affected the trappings of the trade as they might have been described in a 1930s detective novel' (16). Sinclair emphasizes this potential when he comments 'He looked like an ill-shaved bison but had a will that could only be measured in geological time. His stock might need carbon dating, but he wouldn't crack' (19). The text includes a letter to Sinclair referring to his imaginative/poetic vision as a creator of 'phantasm' and thereby 'visionary' and the 'coincidence of contraries' (161). Sinclair uses a significant vocabulary, referring spe-cifically to dream, vision, illusion, invisibility, performativity, synthesis, instinct, 'Rituals of obscure transformation' (208), and 'A heightened perception of the trivial' (209). Sinclair confirms the otherworldliness inherent in our existence, the fusion of the imaginary and the past with the familiar concretion of the present. Zygmunt Bauman in *Modernity and Ambivalence* (1991) proposes 'under-determination/ambivalence/ contingency as a *lasting human condition*' (16). Daniel R. Schwarz in *Reconfiguring Modernism: Explorations in the Relationship between Modern Art and Modern Literature* (1997) defines the progression from the realistic to expressionist initiated by Thomas Hardy in *Jude the Obscure* (1895) and climaxing with *To the Lighthouse* in terms of a literary culture and certain modes of fiction that for all the apparently expressed plurality that apparently resists a notion of the real world creates a new dichotomy of artistic rendition. This sees artists and critics as being divided between those with an outmoded sense of the real set against others conceding its very impossibility:

> Influenced by English romanticism, developments in modern art, and a changing intellectual milieu that questioned the possibilities of universal values or objective truth, these novelists erased the boundaries between art and life. They no longer believed that they could or should re-create the real world in their art, and they questioned the assumption that verisimilitude was the most important aesthetic value. They realized each person perceives a different reality [...] (24–5)

In similar vein, more recent fiction continues to draw upon a range of narrative traditions that defer or reconfigure the real. In some senses the dynamics that create metaphor are foregrounded in the structures of these kinds of texts, a drawing upon the prosaic to suggest a transformational awareness, a determination of meta-contexts.

Tracing Darwin

The contemporaneous mythic and parabolic allow an engagement both with these possibilities and with the dynamics of the real (habitually concrete social forms). In her epigraph to *The Biographer's Tale* Byatt cites Goethe and his reference to the playful potential in analogy. She describes the rejection by research student Phineas G. Nanson of contemporary and postmodern theory. Of his tuition he comments in his growing dissatisfaction

> All seminars, in fact, had a fatal family likeness. They were repetitive in the extreme. We found the same clefts and crevices, transgressions and disintegrations, lures and deceptions beneath, no matter what surface we were scrying. I thought next we will go on to the phantasmagoria of Bosch, and, in his incantatory way, Butcher obliged. I went on looking at the filthy window above his head, and I thought, I must have *things*. I know a dirty window is

an ancient, well-worn trope for intellectual dissatisfaction and scholarly blindness. The thing is, that the thing was also there. A real, very dirty window, shutting out the sun. A *thing*. (1–2)

Certain reference points are established early, one a factuality, another a sense of repetition within the ontological. However complex time or history, Phineas senses intuitively by the end of his quest that these elements can neither be dissolved nor rationalized. One is reminded of Bergson's caution in *An Introduction to Metaphysics* that 'The unrolling of our duration resembles in some of its aspects the unity of an advancing movement and in others the multiplicity of expanding states; and, clearly, no metaphor can express one of these two aspects without sacrificing the other' (12–13).

Throughout Byatt sets the text in opposition to the theoretical proponents of critical theory, exploring the proto-mythic – historiography, biography and the recuperative possibilities of its research – where despite its elusive qualities language becomes ontological, appearing patterned and recurrent. The text is haunted by the ambitions and achievements of the researchers and biographers of the past, a tradition that appears enshrined only to be debunked and demystified. Even Phineas's urge must be defined in terms of *things*. 'I was pleased with the safe, solid Anglo-Saxon word. I had avoided the trap of talking about 'reality' and 'unreality' for I knew very well that postmodernist literary theory could be described as a reality. People lived in it. I did however, fatally, add the Latin-derived word, less exact, redundant even, to my precise one. "I need a life full of *things*," I said. "Full of facts"' (4). The narrative is a quest for the elusive fact and an encounter with a range of things that become part of Phineas's exploration of Destry-Scholes's biography of Sir Elmer Bole. His decision to write a biography of a biographer becomes not so much reflexive as symbolically and factually elusive. Bole's romance writing, his disguises travelling in the Ottoman Empire, and the motif of the lost Turkish manuscript that Bole may have written recur in Phineas's discovery of Destry-Scholes's life. The search brings sex and romance into Phineas's previously contracted existence and, influenced by a new Swedish love, Fulla Biefeld, takes him off to Turkey to study bee pollination. He concludes 'The too-much-loved earth will always exceed our power to describe, or imagine, or understand it. It is all we have' (259). And yet the urge of the mythic is to approach those qualities that exceed human powers of perspective. The figure of Darwin and his theories are woven into the narrative, not as a reductive discourse, but to draw from a quotation from a letter of Francis Galton that forms part of Destry-Scholes's archive that becomes part of Byatt's text. It suggests one might 'know how conscientious Mr Darwin is in all he writes, how difficult it is to put thoughts into accurate speech, and how again, how words have conveyed false impressions on the simplest matters, from the earliest times' (160–1). Earlier Fulla attempts to explain her notion of the reciprocity and interdependence in the natural world, and rejects the inaccuracies she sees in Linnaeus. ' "Linnaeus," she told me, "knew nothing about insect pollination. He invented anthropomorphic fairytales and thought the bees were blundering about damaging the marriage-chambers, accidentally deflowering the virgins, and robbing the seed-stores. He didn't see – he didn't need to see – the interdependence of things" ' (121). In the narrative this very dichotomy and yet adjacent relevance of a mythic propensity and the things of a larger order or pattern of the world lead Destry-Scholes, and ultimately Phineas, away from biography and its elusive factuality, to a recognition of invention. However, this is not a postmodern critique of the world, but one suggestive of a symbolic and metaphysical order or system that is concerned with a lack of knowledge, and yet concerned with the excess of understanding, for as Cassirer comments in *The Philosophy of Symbolic Forms, Volume 1: Language* (1955a) 'Beside the world of linguistic and conceptual signs stands the world of myth and art, incommensurate with it and yet related in spiritual origin. For deeply rooted as it is in sensibility, mythical fantasy also goes far beyond the mere passivity of sensation' (88). Phineas reflects upon Destry-Scholes's untruthfulness and perceives something else of the fictive, narrative urge despite the mundanity he claims for his existence:

> I had a sudden moment of appalling vision. I knew that whatever had driven Destry-Scholes to write the three fictive (lying, untruthful) biographical fragments, was whatever was (is) now driving me to form this mass of material into my own story [...]. I saw also that all Destry-Scholes's fiction had concerned ghosts and spirits, doubles and hauntings, metamorphoses, dismemberment, death. There are very few human truths and infinite variations on them. I was about to write that there are very few truths about the world, but the truth about *that* is that we don't know what we are not biologically fitted to know, chemistries, physics we have no access to and never can have. (237)

None of the subjects of Destry-Scholes's putative biographical fragments are sufficient: taxonomy, statistics and drama, but each is revealing of some aspects of engagement. As Phineas reflects it is not the eugenicist Galton who has most antipathy toward the lower classes, but Ibsen. Byatt's tale is full of paradox and incompletion, but it sustains a notion of a truthfulness that coheres in the nature of things. This is a mythic structure and mediation. Phineas comes to see a link between the scholarly and imaginative, and ironically comes to the same conclusion about the narrativity of biography as another history. And yet Phineas's tale of his rejection of modern theory, his leaving behind of the study of literature is a kind of partial engagement with another sense rather than a postmodern concept of ending grand narratives and meaning. Phineas successively acknowledges the experiential, the romantic, the mysterious, the unknowable and finally sees a new form of mythic suggestion, a structure of unknowingness, an aporia in the narrative effort of factuality that can only be approached by more narrative of the otherness unworldliness of objective aspects of being.

In one sense Byatt's reference to Darwin reflects a contemporary literary obsession as well as a culturally historic one. Currently, Darwinism is much debated in terms of new readings of new and old science. The populist postmodern suggestion that science is simply another narrative is much contested. Its integration into narrative seems almost irresistible. Darwinistic motifs and themes are recurrent in contemporary fiction, particularly as a point of reference where rationality displaces a world of belief, and as a mythic point of reference in the construction of new science and knowledge. Jenny Diski charts in *Monkey's Uncle* (1994) the genetic or narrative relationship of Charlotte Fitzroy, distant descendant of Robert FitzRoy, captain of Darwin's ship, the *Beagle*. Charlotte is perhaps appropriately a genetic researcher and activist and the novel opens with her visit to London Zoo during her bereavement for her daughter who had been killed in the car Charlotte was driving. Suicide is a pattern in her lineage and it lurks as a possibility in 1990 after her 'descent into madness, at the age of forty-nine' (1). At the Zoo Charlotte loses grip on reality and like Carroll's Alice – whose language she mimics – Charlotte descends into a hole of some sort to meet her ancestor and share his terror. In these apparently delusional phases, Diski combines the historical, the imaginary and the intertextual contexts of Carroll's work to create a realm of cultural archetypes and symbols, offering the unconscious mythic resolutions. This world is both absurd and familiar. Charlotte is served tea with milk and no sugar by a pedantic and bossy orang-utan in a floral frock, which berates Charlotte for her ignorance. This place of imaginings is suffused with qualities of the sixth sense, a higher order of intuition, to which the monkey refers, although Charlotte and the orang-utan encounter a picnic party of Freud, Darwin and Marx. Intermittently, Charlotte is drawn back into this world of archetypes and fantasy. At the time of her daughter's funeral, reading her ancestor's biography draws her into his world and its encounters with Darwin. In explaining his previous crisis it is FitzRoy who warns that a pragmatic engagement with a task may be insufficient. '"What I understood was that there is no absolute certainty. And such a degradation of confidence in what one knows in one area, means one can never be entirely confident about anything. Not about *anything*"' (77). Charlotte's own existential crisis from the age of sixteen splits her consciousness between innate knowing and scientific rationality, and finally confronts the irregularity or 'Humpty Dumpty Effect' that had so troubled her ancestor in his costal mapmaking explained to her by Mandelbrot. Facing the sea in such a troubled and yet reflective state may represent an oblique intertextual reference to Arnold's 'Dover Beach'. This contemporary combination of the imaginary and the mythic leads her to review history, experience and the objective presence of the world.

> A great dichotomy of all things striving to become one thing, and all things infinitely separate, filled her with the most extraordinary surge of hope, which had no name or purpose, but which spread through her, being itself, and needing, therefore, to be nothing else. It was now perfectly clear to her how everything fitted together and never would, and how movement and stillness, light and dark, truth and deception, feeling and numbness were created out of that single contradiction which kept winds blowing and hearts beating and minds racing to and from conclusions which never could, would or should be conclusive. (251)

Mimi in Diski's *The Dream Mistress* (1996), like Charlotte, is confronted in both the memory of things and its perceptual uncertainty by a world of unreliability and yet curious power. Mimi might see a 'spurious power' in 'The images and feelings [that] attempted to suck her in, trying to convince her that her present existence was nothing more than the sum of her past. This was nonsense, of course, because memories were unverifiable, absent shadows' (35) and yet the picture that they constitute remains persuasive. The homeless derelict, Bella, who appears to be her mother, has reached a state where dates and order no longer have any relevance, a more patterned and yet chaotic order of things, following a routine that exists but that she cannot fathom, a world of non-recognition and anonymity, where the past is irrelevant, a wordless existence (150–2). Bella is trapped, existing ritually as if expressing the mythic element of her own conditions, and perhaps in a negative sense representing the failure to 'master' the past which is a function according to Mircea Eliade in *Myth and Reality* (1963) of the return to origin within its meticulous and exhaustive recollection of personal and historical events. To be sure, in these cases too the final goal is to 'burn up' these memories, to abolish them as it were by reliving them and freeing oneself from them [...]. The important thing is to recollect even the most insignificant details of one's life (present or past), for it is only by virtue of this recollection that one can 'burn up' one's past, master it [...]. One frees oneself from the work of Time by recollection, by *anamnesis*. (89)

This recollection of the minutiae of the past and of mythic reference itself becomes a compulsive element in the kinds of narratives considered in this chapter.

Biblical and Fairy Tales

For Julian Barnes in *A History of the World in 10½ Chapters* (1989) the past and the present becomes a series of vignettes or episodes, the first imagining a woodworm's perspective of Noah's ark (and, perhaps only Barnes could make a Biblical woodworm articulate its opinions through a knowing middle-class voice). The chapters refer to the sinking of the *Titanic*, a Victorian woman's pilgrimage to Mount Ararat, and the sinking of the *Medusa* and Géricault's painting doomed to pigmental and chemical instability. Once more the places, themes and even expositions recur. The past becomes something of the present, although the imaginary and unconscious persist. In the last chapter it appears that the narrative is of heaven, where wishes are fulfilled, and the exaggerated and unlikely victories of Leicester City and its players are sandwiched by the same beginning and end that makes of the narrator's consciousness something surreal or improbable. 'I dreamt that I woke up. It's the oldest dream of all, and I've just had it. I dreamt I woke up' (283; 309). The notion of heaven and the ark attract the contemporary mythmaking consciousness.

If myth contains elements of transcendence, a continuity of human aspirations, and a tentative symbolism of the unknown, it may also recuperate a sense of the miraculous. In *Quarantine* (1997) explored below, Crace humanizes Biblical narratives, as does Diski in *Only Human: A Divine Comedy* (2000). Diski opts for the Old Testament story of Abraham and his barren wife, Sarah, at one level foregrounding the comedic. In the interstices of Diski's ur-Biblical text is God's own narrative, alternately bemused and irritated at humanity, but in some senses feeling paradoxically increasingly marginal. This is unlike Crace who dismisses the undecidable issues of God and belief. Diski's confirmation of this presence is not so much an act of faith as it allows two perspectives from which Diski reconfigures Biblical narratives and perspectives. God ruminates: 'Death, of course. I knew nothing of death as they invented it. How could I? I created life. I had to ask the boy, the farmer, where the shepherd was, just like I had to ask the first pair where they were in the garden that I had made for them. Hiding, always hiding. From the boy, a shrug. "Am I my brother's keeper?"' (41). Sarah offers Diski a gendered vision of this parabolic and mythical world of the Bible. In a world of scepticism and fragmentation, such new formulations of myth allow writers to return to ideas of origin, of death and afterlife, of historical and pre-historical identity, and the counter-rational that sustains a notion of truth, relevance and existential definitiveness.

In terms of subject matter and themes, Byatt and Diski both combine scientific reference consciously with a new surge of interest in the relationship of narrative and history, but rather than being concerned with the end or deconstructive displacement of history, this perspective is determined by its intersection with factuality and myth. Perhaps the other classic text of this kind of this period – responding subversively to the persistence of authorial control and certain postmodern ludic qualities in Fowles's *The French Lieutenant's Woman* – is Graham Swift's *Waterland* (1983). For Swift history consists of cartographizing the past, where the very landscape and the weight of time diminishes and swamps the individualistic urge that Fowles maintains, creating an exploration of the cultural images that make up the co-ordinates of both the present and the past. Various time sequences intersect in a narrative of family guilt, desire and secrets; its structure and motifs have classical and Biblical resonance from the incestuous (a re-gendered Oedipal) to sibling rivalry and dynastic ambition. As Wendy Wheeler argues in *A New Modernity? Change in Science, Literature and Politics* (1999) one can identify 'Graham Swift's exemplary treatment of an intensified nostalgic melancholia as a representative mode of affect in Western societies (but perhaps particularly Anglo-American ones)' (71). In fact there is a further dimension, as Swift's echoing recovery of the past in *Waterland* can be read variously as a sedimented family history, official and unofficial classroom narratives, a series of wartime experiences and memories, a confessional and rites of passage, and an expression of the current exigencies of Thatcherism. All stress the relevance of Moretti's observation that 'myth ensures that culture is no longer a mere superstructure in relation to the symbolic "neutrality" – and therefore potential disorder – of historical existence: rather it presents itself as that value-system which pervades and ascribes "significance", and hence humanizes all manifestations of that existence' (220). Crick is involved in a species of myth making; his narrative threatened by the inchoate intervenes into historical existence and mythologizes it all, resolving certain elements of his crisis. His yearning is atavistic in terms of history, a longing for a mythic time, for the archetypal.

> And where history does not undermine and set traps for itself in such an openly perverse way, it creates this insidious longing to go backwards. It begets this bastard but pampered child, Nostalgia. How we yearn – how you may one day, if that day comes, yearn – to return to that time before history claimed us, before things went wrong. How we yearn even for the gold of a July evening on which, though things had already gone wrong, things had not gone wrong as they were going to. How we pine for Paradise. For Mother's milk. To draw back the curtain of events that has fallen between us and the Golden Age. (118)

Reaching for a sense of the fall of man in its symbolism, nevertheless this is not simply a prelapsarian desire. Hence the promise of childhood, that is disappointed. It also helps orient our reading of quite how and why Swift's narrative mythologizes the immediacy of history as a localized and contained event, not immune from and yet diminishing the grand narratives. Swift emphasizes this quality of the area when the narrator reflects 'And it is strange – or perhaps not strange, not strange at all, only logical – how the bare and empty Fens yield so readily to the imaginary – and the supernatural' (15). It is 'A fairy-tale land' into which the Cricks weave external history 'as if such things were not the stuff of fact but the fabric of a wondrous tale' (16). The threat of nuclear war that obsesses Crick's pupil is a return to primeval structures of understanding, for 'Once upon a time people believed in the end of the world' (291). Crick's past and present intertwine, the symbols and motifs intermingling. Swift's narrative circles the return to archetypal form and meaning, resonates of the ancient. Although as Wheeler indicates the Fens are a product of industriousness and modernity (79), a reclamation, and as she indicates 'Love, for Swift, and along with art as the telling of stories, is what humans do to ward off the fearful sublimity of natural existence' (82). And of course, like the Fenland water, Swift's narrative runs away from simple specificity and meaning. Its contexts are brief and elusive, the chapters merging not in narrative continuity, but in the recovery of an interconnectedness that is unspecified and not articulated. Why does Crick engage in this intervention and incompletion? As Moretti comments 'If, turned toward the past, myth disarranges the course of history to the point of making it unrecognizable, when turned toward the future, it is the ideal instrument for preselecting historical events, and therefore ridding them of all unpredictability' (223). Unsettled by the past, Crick recovers it mythically and the avoidance of any such future 'unpredictability' is Crick's failed and perhaps always unconscious ambition; which makes his championship of history and change an ambivalent position for him to adopt, since in its apparent certainty he finds a protean reality. And yet patterns surface, inconsequential and minor. Chased by history, Crick is called up for the army as his father had been thirty years previously. By the time of the breakdown of his wife, Crick's existence and grip on reality appear ambivalent and fragmentary; only in the mythological, the 'magic' and 'visionary', (297) can he frame his existence, prefacing his lessons with the incantatory phrase that initiates all fairy tales and their analogical irreal realms of the imaginary: 'Once upon a time –' (297).

Secular Parables: Jim Crace

A novelist significantly developing possibilities interfusing myth and parable is Jim Crace, recently of great critical interest in America.[2] Each of his fictions creates a world that although recognizable is explicitly alternate, full of archetypes and conceits. *Continent* (1986) describes lives in an imaginary continent; *The Gift of Stones* (1988) explores a stone-age community under the technological threat of the bronze age; and *Quarantine* imagines a secular version of Christ. Crace's symbolic structures combine a signification of objectification, death and the miraculous. These are not the conditions of modernity or post- modernity. None of Crace's fictions is topographically about the contemporary British scene. As Milton Scarborough says of a rejection of or scepticism toward myth offering a meta-consciousness in *Myth and Modernity: Postcritical Reflections* (1994): 'If myths are about nature, then they must be about a nature comprised of secondary qualities. Such a nature, however, exists only in the human mind as a figment of the imagination; it is unreal' (12). Although Crace fore-grounds aspects of the 'unreal', yet he accords his world the direct determinacy of familiar ways of dealing with people and situations. The imaginary and the narrative urge are central to the acts of storytelling that permeate Crace's novels, and his fiction exists on the very margins of worlds in transition. Crace's characters share common behavioural parameters and familiar motivations. Crace's re-centring is more a displacement and mythological edging rather than fantasy or a full-scale imaginary. The tales are conceptually and geographically taut, the scope of consciousness localized and implicitly framed by a familiarity of perceptual range. The verbal repetition patterns the narrative in the manner of Biblical and evangelical accounts, as if they might offer transcendence or poeticism, and yet they persist mostly in the utterly mundane.

In *The Gift of Stones*, questioned by the Stoneys about his story of the woman Doe who returns with him from the margins to the village (later to subsist through prostitution), the storyteller declares:

> 'This is a story made by life,' he said. 'It's true in every way.' That caused some cautious laughter and some shouts. 'You know that when I want to make your eyes stretch wide, I stretch my stories wide to match. You know that when I want some fun, I let my stories tickle truth. You all know that. You are not fools. Well, now, here is a tale that's meant to make you weep. There is no need for camouflage. The world out there is sad enough. So this is not a dream. This, to a hair, is fact.' He'd never heard an audience so quiet. (105)

'Tickling' a truth is to undermine its commonly considered, but spurious solidity. As J. Hillis Miller states in *Tropes, Parables, Performatives: Essays on Twentieth-Century Literature* (1990): 'The paradox of parable is that it is a likeness that rests on a manifest unlikeness between what is given and what cannot by any means be given directly. A parabolic "likeness" is so "unlike" that without interpretation or commentary the meaning may slip by the reader or listener altogether' (136). The storyteller's status on the edge of his community's activities and Doe's home on the margins of the community are both revealing. In Crace marginal people, fields of vision, expressiveness, *mythos* and places intersect. As Miller concludes this is appropriate to parable since: 'parable is a mode of figurative language which is the indirect indication at a distance, of something that cannot be described directly' (136).

In *Quarantine* significantly the trader Musa's near escape from death and Jesus' demise activate the urge to account for the visionary and spiritualized rendition of the unknown. Musa retrieves Christ as the subject matter or possession of his own story from the 'Gally's' state of death, inspired by profit and need. Such is the manner and placement of Jesus' resurrection. In this transition and appropriation we can discover perhaps elements of Walter Benjamin's exposition in *Illuminations* (1955) of finitude and narrative: 'Death is the sanction of everything that the storyteller can tell. He has borrowed his authority from death. In other words, it is natural history to which his stories refer back' (93–4). For Musa, joining a train of travellers after his travails and Jesus' death, this movement or progression authorizes him and provides him with a new voice beyond the mere stories woven around and deriving from his goods and the act of their exchange that he had used previously. Transformed he can lay claim or discover a voice speaking of disconnected and more expansive tales that strengthen his haggling and enhance his prices in quite a different manner. He can sell the storytelling possibilities of a belief system beyond the self and the material. In *Quarantine* a story becomes the object of Musa's trade and thereby offers a thing or quality beyond things themselves:

> They were amazed at all the stories he could tell. He'd come from forty days of quarantine up in the wilderness. He hadn't drunk or eaten anything. He'd gone up thin and come back fat, thanks to god's good offices. He'd shared his cave with angels and messiahs; he'd met a healer and a man who could make bread from stones. His staff had come to him one night, a dangerous snake which wrapped itself around his arm and turned to wood. They could hold it, for a coin. One touch of his staff would protect them against all snakes. (240–1)

Clearly it is significant that Musa's new trade is in belief and image beyond simply the objective form, as if enhancing the object within the moment of exchange. There are traces of the miraculous, since his demand for belief elevates the act of exchange by a manipulation of the benefit (the *goods*) anticipated. The deceit that underpins the trade of muddy water and caves that Musa does not own, and further of the selling of unstable wool dyed with urine that deceives initially even the trader with its alchemical stench possesses a movement that is parallel to that which he perceives in Jesus' death. In his ascetic descent Jesus is separated from form and presence; he is made into something beyond. Musa redeems these events as a form of exchange. He both reinforces and yet defies the parabolic. He turns their significance into a materiality, that of the word which nevertheless requires a kind of transcendent referentiality. He trades the equivocal nature of the miraculous and its effect upon those who believe in his tale. As Miller explains parable is itself implicated in contradictions and paradox. Particularly instructive is his: 'Fourth paradox: the economy of equivalence, of giving and receiving, of equable translation and measure, of the circulation of signs governed by the Logos as source of proportion and guarantee of substitution or analogy, is upset by the parables' (141). Jesus' appearance as a character evokes the parables and their ministry, the given word and culturally the miraculous. Musa's appropriation and vision of the dead man exhibit features of Bataille's critique of death and the miraculous found in *The Accursed Share* (1991). We perceive in Christ's fate and its place within Musa's intended (parodic) ministry something that was inherent in the latter's cajoling and cheating, which transforms the nature of relations and the world. His trade shares an absence and negative power with the description of Christ's death:

This *negative miraculous*, manifested in death, corresponds quite clearly to the principle [...] according to which the miraculous moment is the moment when *anticipation dissolves into* NOTH-ING. It is the moment when we are relieved of anticipation, man's customary misery, of the anticipation that enslaves, that subordinates the present moment to some anticipated result. Precisely in the miracle, we are thrust from our anticipation of the future into the presence of the moment, of the moment illumi-nated by a miraculous light. (207)

Musa offers belief that is located in the moment of immediacy and being. His vision is toward something present and universal where in Musa's own account: '"I am the living proof." [...] "He came into my tent," he'd say. "He touched me here, and here. "Be well," he told me. And I am well. And I have never been so well. Step forward. Touch me. Feel how well I am' (242–3). Crace positions the miraculous appropriately as both elusive and mundane. Sighting what appears to be the resurrected figure Musa opts for practicality and the vision or occurrence's exploitative potential: 'He would not wait, he persuaded himself, because it was not sensible to wait. There were practicalities to bear in mind [...]. The Galilean might be a healer and the lord of miracles, but he was not a cart' (242).

The decline of Christ that precipitates or allows this transition for the merchant is charted by Crace as a peculiarly immanent union with the forces of nature within the world.

Quarantine had been the perfect preparation for his death. His body was quiescent and reduced; dry, sapless, transparent almost, ready to detach itself from life without complaint. A wind this strong could pluck him like a leaf [...]

It seemed to Jesus, when he woke and put his hands out to the wind, that he was already dead and living it. [...] There was no future there for him. No fleshy future anyway. He had surren-dered food for dreams. [...] (191)

Crace's Jesus prepares himself for an immediacy that expresses a condition where momentarily: 'The "miracle" of death is under-standable in terms of this sovereign exigency, which calls for the *impossible coming true*, in the *reign of the moment*' (Bataille, 211). However, as the narrative of *Quarantine* clarifies, such transition engages and redeems only itself:

There was a light, deep in the middle of the night. He tried to swim to it. He tried to fly. He held his hands up to the light. His hands were bluey-white like glass. The light passed through. The mountain shivered from afar. He felt the cold of nothing there. He heard the cold of no one here. No god, no gardens, just the wind. (193)

Narrative and storytelling are performative, and it is this capacity Miller finds in parable; a performativity that exploits an evocation of a heavenly parallel that exists in the interstices of its words:

> A true performative brings something, a 'meaning,' that has no basis except in words or something about which it is impossible to describe whether or not there is an extralinguistic basis. [...] Secular parable is language thrown out that creates a meaning hovering there in thin air, a meaning based on the language itself and our confidence in it. The categories of truth and falsehood, knowledge and ignorance, do not properly apply to it. (139)

It is this secular aspect of parable that contemporary writers extend to the neo-mythopoeic view, fusing performatively parable and myth. Hence Biblical and religious reference remains newly suggestive. The narrative engagement with apparent facts, events, characters and objects is in essence informed by the dynamics of the mythopoeic-symbolic realm. The often profuse systems of both familiar and obtuse reference in such texts is indicative of Bataille's tentative formula expressed in *the unfinished system of nonknowledge* that 'Sense + Nonsense = Profound meaning' (248). Crace's refiguring of the sacred as profane exemplifies these contradictions that cannot yet escape the metaphysical, preternatural urges, instincts and intuitive consciousness that underpin this adaptive mode of narrative of 'historiographic mythopoeism' where even the recent past becomes the site of the mythological.

Endnote

All of the methods of the mythopoeic outlined above are responses to the kinds of impasse that for a time postmodernism seemed to indicate, which led as Nancy J. Peterson notes in *Against Amnesia: Contemporary Women Writers and the Crises of Historical Memory* (2001) 'to skepticism concerning access to the past but also instigated a debate about whether historical narratives can be regarded as objective narratives or are (merely) subjective constructions' (8), but as she specifies such a position would make ascertaining anything almost impossible, and make a more comprehensive access to the public domain almost impossible for previously marginal communities. It is in this sphere that British fiction has blossomed in this period, accessing its own 'counterhistories' to use Peterson's terminology in terms of the contemporaneous as well as that which concerns the past but is of relevance to what Walter Benjamin describes in *Illuminations* as 'a presentation of the circumstances, in which they themselves have learned what is to follow' (91), but like the symbol of the potter's clay vessel with his hand imprint to which Benjamin alludes in defining storytelling, this remains in emphasis intersubjective and expressive of the eventful. In the next chapter certain themes recur in examining texts framed by a cultural decentring of literariness and Britishness that has allowed a new sense of not only cultural hybridity and adaptation, but the serious narrative reflection of previously marginal identities marked by either effacement or stereotypical representation, those best understood in terms of class, sexual orientation, gender, ethnicity and regionalism. These are the sites of these 'counter-histories' and the cultural (not necessarily formal) hybridity of fictional consciousness. Continuing the impetus of the issues under consideration in the present chapter, the first texts considered will be of a historical mythic nature, exploring literary and cultural myths, including Pat Barker's *Regeneration* Trilogy.

Notes

1 In this Dällenbach reflects M. Rifaterre as he makes evident in his citation.
2 On the television chat show that accompanied the broadcast of a Booker Prize award ceremony, Crace's importance was certified publicly with A. S. Byatt's description of Crace as the most significant writer in English fiction of the last ten years. Although the academic world has been slow in exploring her endorsement, in 2000 the US National Book Critics Circle awarded its 26th annual book prize for fiction for *Being Dead* (1999).

Further Reading

Bataille, Georges *the unfinished system of nonknowledge* [see bibliography] [see Further Reading in the Introduction].

Carroll, Joseph (2004) *Literary Darwinism: Evolution, Human Nature and Literature*, New York and London: Routledge.
This is a complex and persuasive study of the place of literature and literary study within evolutionary theory and structures that attacks poststructuralist dogmas; suitable for advanced students only.

Cassirer, Ernst *Mythical Thought* [see bibliography] [see Further Reading in the Introduction].

Crossan, John Dominic (1976) *Raid on the Articulate: Comic Eschatology in Jesus and Borges*, New York, Hagerstown, San Francisco, London: Harper & Row.
This offers a detailed analysis of the structure and signification of parable as a form, drawing upon Biblical and other examples. Although not concerned solely with literature it is a good starting point for further reading on this topic.

Hidalgo, Pilar (2005) 'Memory and Storytelling in Ian McEwan's *Atonement*', *Critique: Studies in Contemporary Fiction*, 46 (2), 82–91.
This journal article looks at history and storytelling in McEwan's novel, establishing their wider literary context and assessing reviews of the text. Its complex, detailed close reading makes it an excellent critical reading for students studying this work.

Makinen, Merja (2005) *The Novels of Jeanette Winterson*, Basingstoke and New York: Palgrave Macmillan.
This is an accessible introductory overview of Winterson's early and middle work that is recommended to all students.

Meletinsky, Eleazar M. (2000) *The Poetics of Myth*, New York and London: Routledge.
Complex study and overview of myth and the mythopoeic, which although theoretically informed is a good starting point for all of those seriously interested in engaging with these aspects of the literary-cultural field.

Mengham, Rod (2006) 'Fiction's History: Adam Thorpe', in Philip Tew and Rod Mengham (eds) *British Fiction Today: Critical Essays*, London: Continuum, 177–85.
This essay considers *Pieces of Light* and *Ulverton*, offering an intriguing reading suitable for all levels of students.

Tew, Philip (2006) *Jim Crace* Manchester: Manchester University Press.
An introductory criticism that is suitable for all levels of student that covers all of Crace's major works, and contextualizes his emergence as a writer.

Tiffin, Jessica (2006) 'Ice, Glass, Snow: Fairy Tale as Art and Metafiction in the Writing of A. S. Byatt', *Marvels & Tales*, 20 (1), 47–66, 136.
A close reading of Byatt's text, including *Possession*, that serves as a useful introduction.

Zipes, Jack (1979; rev. 2002) *Breaking the magic spell: radical theories of folk and fairy tales*, Lexington, KY: University Press of Kentucky.
This is a detailed analysis of fairy tales and fantasy as a genre suitable for most levels of student; it remains a seminal and influential text, particularly informed about revolutionizing or radical elements.

CHAPTER FIVE

Multiplicities and Hybridity

KEY THEMES
British Hybridities • Contemporary Identities • Class • Ethnicity • Historicity and Multiplicity • Hybrid Identities • Liminality • Migrancy • Multiculturalism • Regionality and Regional Identity • The Postcolonial

KEY TEXTS

Amis, Martin *The Information*

Barker, Pat *The Eye in the Door* / *The Ghost Road* / *Regeneration*

Harris, Wilson *Jonestown*

Phillips, Caryl *Cambridge* / *A State of Independence*

Rushdie, Salman *Imaginary Homelands* / *The Satanic Verses*

Smith, Zadie *White Teeth*

Welsh, Irvine *Trainspotting*

Winterson, Jeanette *Gut Symmetries* / *Oranges Are Not the Only Fruit* / *The Passion* / *Sexing the Cherry* / *Written on the Body*

Hybridity and the Contemporary

In Zadie Smith an ambivalent symbiosis is the basis of the relationship between two wartime comrades, Archie Jones and Samal Iqbal, joined in an experience that Archie finds anachronistic and embarrassing to subsequent generations as cultural markers shift, and the world changes. 'An unlikely compadre possibly, but still the oldest friend he had – a Bengali Muslim he had fought alongside back when the fighting had to be done, who reminded him of that war; that war reminded some people of fatty bacon and painted-on-stockings but recalled in Archie gunshots and card games and the taste of a sharp, foreign alcohol' (12). Smith's world is a suburban multicultural secularized London defined by oddities, incongruities and humour as her narrative follows the fate of the men's two interlinked families. This symbolizes the hybridity which as a legacy of colonial migrations influences both the migrants and the former imperial cultures, especially in the lives of oppressed and ordinary people, the truly marginal. As Richard Lane and I say in our introduction to *Contemporary British Fiction* (2003b), 'The theme of cultural hybridity features strongly in

contemporary British fiction, not just as subject matter but as part of
the creative act of writing itself [. . .]. Hybridity is not simply an issue
of migration but of plural cultural identities' (143). Attributing any
unique and separable categorization for postcolonial 'subalterns' is to
be seduced by a subliminal and unconscious imperial (and racist)
structure, a legacy inherited by white liberal intellectuals who see
themselves positively in terms of an unpalatable mixture of radicality,
virtuous interventionism, and perhaps a secularized form of Christian
Salvationism. Robert J. C. Young argues in *Colonial Desire: Hybridity in
Theory, Culture and Race* (1995) that to believe intellectuals of previous generations held a view of a 'fixed centre' distorts the past.

> Even what is often considered a founding text of English culture,
> Matthew Arnold's *Culture and Anarchy* (1869), is predicated on
> the fact that English culture is lacking, lacks something, and acts
> out an inner dissonance that constitutes its secret, riven self. For
> the past few centuries Englishness has often been constructed as a
> heterogeneous, conflictual composite of contrary elements, an
> identity which is not identical with itself. The whole problem –
> but has it been a problem? – for Englishness is that it has never
> been successfully characterized by an essential, core identity from
> which it has been excluded. (3)

Recent negations of any 'core identity' perversely encourage both a
sense of dislocation and loss, *and* a nostalgia for the illusory lost centre
evoked. Fiction mirrors the living process in that both are a making
anew of things, which is in part what Salman Rushdie indicates in his
much-quoted comment in *Imaginary Homelands* (1991): 'The past is a
country from which we have all emigrated, its loss is part of our
common humanity' (12). John Erickson in *Islam and Postcolonial
Narrative* (1998) talks of the borrowing and two-way interpenetration
of Anglo-Indian culture (134–5), but adds that 'The Indian in Rushdie's narrative, even at home, assumes thus the figure of the migrant
undergoing constant mutation' (135).

Rushdie makes clear the constant mutation is wider. In *The Satanic
Verses*, the transformation of Chamcha is grotesque – or simply
metafictional according to some accounts – and his shifting self symbolizes a hybridization of identity. The borrowing and interchange is
evident, even in the residue of the colonial that is symbolized textually
with his father's unread evidence of colonial exoticism and appropriation, 'a ten-volume set of the Richard Burton translation of *The
Arabian Nights*, which was being slowly devoured by mildew and
bookworm' (36), a magic lamp that is unused. Significantly Chamcha
supports the English cricket team and is offered an English education

despite his mother's fears of the uncivilized habits of the English. ' "It is inconceivable, Ammi, what you say. England is a great civilization, what are you talking, bunk" ' (39). Despite his aspiration to be English, he becomes a 'fauntleroy' on his return home and much later is beaten unconscious by the thuggish police and immigration officers, indistinguishable from football hooligans in attitude and interests, as he becomes goat-like in his physical metamorphosis. ' "Who're you trying to kid?" inquired one of the Liverpool fans, but he, too, sounded uncertain. "Look at yourself. You're a fucking Packy billy. Sally-who? – What kind of name is that for an Englishman?" ' (163). The details are myriad of these multiplicities of viewpoint and its implications for the division of the self. It remains the case that as Stephen Baker says in 'Salman Rushdie: History, Self and the Fiction of Truth', 'Salman Rushdie's writing is based on endless conflict and revision, particularly in its engagement with cultural, literary and socio-political history. There is little or nothing in this world that is fixed, settled or secure' (146). This is Rushdie's paradigm for a cultural hybridity, and as Baker describes it the writing of 'nation' through what he calls later a 'playful contemporary eclecticism' (154). This is what led to the so-called 'Rushdie Affair' of the Iranian *fatwa*, understood by Robert Fraser in *Lifting the Sentence: A Poetics of Postcolonial Fiction* (2000) to represent a conflict of cultural affiliations, with Rushdie the product of Rugby school and King's College, Cambridge (48). He concludes: 'The problem lay essentially in the clash between a deconstructive tendency almost endemic to literature of what we have termed the "transcultural" phase and a deep-seated attitude in the Islamic world regarding the sacred texts of the Qur'ān as of absolute and infallible worth' (209). Very characteristically Rushdie's class origins are elided in Ashcroft, Griffiths and Tiffin with their exaggerated appeal to a colonial and subsequent postcolonial experience as separable, isolatable and discrete which position raises all sorts of problems, especially curious given their defence of hybridity and cultural, aesthetic forms. Clearly aesthetic hybridization is localized and countercultural, and may appear even within Western cultures, in the interstices of classes and regions. This is a fact Ashcroft, Griffiths and Tiffin seem to concede, at least regarding the textual, in a revised edition that adds 'The concept of literary studies in general will be revitalized by the perception that all texts are traversed by the kinds of complexities which the study of post-colonial literatures reveal' (222).

If Jaina C. Sanga is correct in asserting in *Salman Rushdie's Postcolonial Metaphors: Migration, Translation, Hybridity, Blasphemy, and Globalization* (2001) that 'By addressing the experiences of migration and displacement, and the imaginations they engender, Rushdie postulates the condition of migrancy as transcending the nationalist myth' (19), this will have broader implications if the wider socio-cultural process and its aesthetic reflections gain critical impact. The 'nationalist myth' was never uniform even in the 'Mother Country' as some termed it in part ironically, and nor were postcolonial states immune from its impact, and the historical changes of which migration was part suggest a general re-evaluation of cultural co-ordinates. Moreover, in terms of an earlier migrancy and its effects, as Edward Brathwaite perceived in the early 1970s in looking at the incomplete 'creolization' in *The Development of Creole Society in Jamaica 1770–1820* (1971) 'it was a two-way process, and it worked both ways' (300). Interestingly in *Contradictory Omens: Cultural Diversity in the Caribbean* (1974) he describes art and its visibility as being part of the process of intermixture (54–5) which has tensions within it, as Brathwaite indicates, 'The term creolization, then, is a specialized version of the two widely accepted terms acculturation and interculturation: the former referring [...] to the process of absorption of one culture by another; the latter to a more reciprocal activity, a process of intermixture and enrichment each to each' (11). It is the dynamics of this process that I wish to trace in narrative responses to the contradictory conditions that have been referred to as alienation, but affected as I hope to demonstrate by this broader examination of the conditions of the self and the community.

This features in recent fiction quite explicitly. According to Brad Buchanan's analysis in 'Caryl Phillips: Colonialism, Cultural Hybridity and Racial Difference' (2003) the historical emergence of 'creolization' is the subject of Caryl Phillips's novel *Cambridge* (1991) (183–7). In a literary context, Head is correct to caution that it is 'misleading to cultivate a facile celebration of a post-nationalist experimentalism. There may well be some affinity between postcolonialism and the self-conscious forms of the post-war era; but the implication that needs to be resisted is that a contemporary form of narrative is more "truthful" than earlier forms it comments upon or extends' (155). I would add additionally one must recognize (as I indicated earlier) that 'post-coloniality' may be a misleading term for the general reader since imperial forms persist differently centred. As Aijaz Ahmad says in *In Theory: Classes, Nations, Literatures* (1992)

> Not only did the United States emerge as the hegemonic capi-talist power, but by the end of World War II its levels of accu-mulation were already far greater than Britain or France had ever enjoyed even at the height of the colonial period; in 1945, it alone accounted for roughly half the world's output. One of the many

contradictory consequences of decolonisation within a largely capitalist framework was that it brought all zones of capital into a single, integrated market, entirely dominated by this supreme imperialist power. (21)

It may be that most usefully the term postcoloniality indicates what remains at many levels essentially an aesthetic and cultural concept, since the recent global triumph of imperialism that Ahmad perceives would indicate that the supposed geo-political consciousness that some assume is inherent in postcoloniality is of limited relevance (21). As E. San Juan Jr observes in *Beyond Postcolonial Theory* (1998): 'Post-colonial theory [...] occludes its own historical determinacy by deploying psychoanalytical and linguistic conceptual frameworks that take market/exchange relations for granted. It takes as given the ideological assumptions of utilitarian individualism as normative and natural' (9–10). Holmes indicates astutely that many critical attacks upon hegemonic discourses have often simply purveyed or at least tacitly assumed a notion of the 'straw man' of Western male violence and oppression, of which qualities or characteristics he correctly observes such figures have no historical monopoly (59). Perhaps one should concede in contrast a more complex sense of history leading to a broader aesthetic and cultural focus potentially offering a responsive set of cri-tical and creative positions, from where one can articulate the conditions for understanding a broader, less bipolar contemporary cultural con-sciousness, within which literature is embedded. One can perceive culture and criticism existing among a set of relations that are shifting and evolving at both a local and an intersubjective level. Or perhaps simply it might aid the raising of consciousness to apply a more dated and universalizing terminology. This is another matter of ongoing critical dispute. For instance, in *Beyond Postcolonial Theory* San Juan Jr might well object since he argues that 'Cultural pluralism via what I call the "multicultural Imaginary" [...] may be regarded as the principal ideo-logical strategy of the ruling bourgeoisie in the post-Cold War era' (12).

Countercultural currents recur in contemporary aesthetic responses to culture, and perhaps recently, at the level of a general cultural influence the postcolonial decentring of the subject, which alongside the apparently deconstructive effects of postmodernism, has accelerated in part a more general critical and aesthetic sense of how Britishness itself, as a communal or intersubjective series of identities, is both historically inscribed and is historically being reformulated as a ground for a reflection of a more general cultural multiplicity. Ahmad reflects an apparent 'explosion of theory' and claims to new forms of knowledge, but sees in both a lack of political force and engagement, where such theory is 'mobilized to domesticate, in institutional ways, the very forms of political dissent [...] to displace an activist culture with a textual one' (1). As San Juan Jr says there are other dangers in this area of postmodern theory. 'Hybridity, heterogeneous and discrepant lifestyles, local knowledges, cyborgs, borderland scripts – such slogans tend to obfuscate the power of the transnational ideology and practice of consumerism and its dehumanising effects. Postcolonial discourse generated in "First World" academies turns out to be one more product of flexible, post-Fordist capitalism, not its antithesis' (7–8).

Localities and Boundaries

As a process any diversification of reflection, perhaps a more accurate term for what Head in *The Cambridge Introduction to Modern British Fiction, 1950–2000* labels 'Post-Nationalism' (182), has its limits. Certain of Will Self comments in 'The Valley of the Corn Dollies' alluded to in Chapter Three emphasize what is by and large both a middle-class and an urban intellectual bias to be found in cultural and critical commentaries, and very prone to such a bias in its undercurrents and subtexts is the majority of literary-critical responses, often in the subtlest of ways despite an often implicit claim for transparency (217). Although it may be as Parrinder claims in *Authors and Authority: English and American Criticism 1750–1990* that 'Literature in English today reflects the growing diversity and rich cultural vigour of the English-speaking world. Global in its extent, it also seems faced and perhaps threatened by cultural decentrement and dispersal. The growth of cultural studies reflects this dispersal. There is, however, a kind of narcissism inherent in a study which nourishes local and sectional identity' (348), yet locality and its spatialization are an essential element of any changing culture. All cultures are diverse – for Francisco Bone, the protagonist of Wilson Harris's *Jonestown* (1996), this is exemplified in part in the mythic and in part the ethno-geographical aspects of history – and it is simply the accounts of them that in certain periods appeal to an ideological centring. As Harris indicates in various novels even imperial narratives were always illusory and self-deluding. John Thieme comments 'Harris's whole oeuvre has been dedicated to the promotion of communal, cultural and psychic heterogeneity' (31). It is my sense that many contemporary authors may be at least attempting in their fiction to be more proactive than the kinds of 'other commentators' to whom Self refers, and this chapter suggests many such novelists, following in the tradition established by writers such as Harris, are capable of reflecting upon and engaging in a form of critique upon these processes in many different ways, and additionally that the cultural adaptability and variability that fiction may reflect are becoming increasingly characteristic. Harris himself is not simply noting hybrid identity, for as Stuart Murray comments in 'Post-coloniality/Modernity: Wilson Harris and Postcolonial Theory' (1997) one must 'stress the ways in which his work intersects and challenges the dominant dynamics of contemporary postcolonial theory' (54). The endless disappearance of the author in a premodern manner that Murray identifies has resonances of a residual mythic view of the world, and express 'his desire to retain the resonances of both colonizer and colonized within the imaginative fabric of his fiction' (56). As Mary Lou Emery says in ' "Space Sounds" in Wilson Harris's Recent Fiction' (1997) 'Harris's writing does not homogenize the imperial European eye but finds within its failures and in its encounters with African and Amerindian worldviews the potential for renewed vision expressed in the ongoing epiphanies of his prose' (99). Two comments from San Juan Jr seem particularly salient at this point: firstly, 'Power is always situational, not dispersed in abstract space. [...] In short, crisis is where we work, suffer, meditate, rejoice and fashion our destinies. This provides access not only to dangers and solipsistic dead ends but also to opportunities for rupture and liberation' (8); and secondly, 'There are still "internal colonies" within the advanced industrial societies [...] the "inner cities" inhabited by what has been called "the truly dis-advantaged," the now proverbial lumpen "underclass"' (14).

In Harris's *Jonestown*, where Bone, whose supposed letter to W.H. inscribed on a 'Dateless Day' (3) commences the text in the manner of Hawthorne, he describes explicitly a process of writing overlaid in part upon actual events. 'In my archetypal fiction I call Jim Jones Jonah Jones. All of the characters appearing in the book are fictional and archetypal. In this way I have sought to explore overlapping layers and environments and theatres of legends and history that one may associate with Jonestown' (3). This of course relates to the kinds of intuitiveness discussed in the previous chapter. And yet through the fusion of traditions and cultures, myths and even the 'unpredictable keys to tradition within the terrifying legacies of the past' (6) Bone indicates a commonality of resistance to colonialism and materialism (that is of the oppressive forces that he names specifically). He insists on perceiving the form of his dream-book both materially and meta-physically, but not generically. 'Composite epic is rooted in the lucidity that fractions or fictional numbers, fictional multitudes, bring. The walls of ruined schools and houses and temples and hospitals and theatres are full with presences and voices though apparently void and empty. Such is the mystery of chaos. The weight of Chaos is sometimes apparitional, sometimes concrete' (6). 'Robbed' of his heritage and roots in a mythic, dream-world Bone accesses the identities of the past, one being an ancestor who has been a slave and another on becoming one again with his 9-year-old self in 1939 with his mother of whom he has a premonition (an apparently proleptic knowledge at that point of return) that she is on that very day about to die. His teacher, Mr Mageye, is significantly taking a class in history on his late arrival for the class and as part of a curiously intellectual discussion between them explains the child's association with the past, ' "The spontaneous linkage that you make between the organs of the past and the present (your long-dead great-great-grandmother and your poor mother today) is a kind of synaesthesia or simulation of different moral ages and visions" ' (34). Bone's experience, and the cultural reference points of the narrative more generally, articulate a cultural hybridity in historical consciousness that is centred upon the diffuse and hybrid nature of origins and of motivations.[1] The text extends itself into both the pathological (the massacre) and the ghostly and ineffable (as with the tradition of the day of the dead).

As indicated earlier, the kind of cultural centring and continuity alluded to in 'The Fall and Rise of the Middle Classes' is being challenged, by new fictions which explore the very hybrid identities that have existed within concepts of a supposed traditional British identity, now suppressed and marginalized. Such extensions are important in recognizing an overall shift in cultural perceptions. Hence I would argue one must extend Head's sense that migrant communities define their relationship to a broader identity in essence historically, when he says:

> Much migrant writing in Britain, chary of identifying with unaccommodating England, seeks, ostensibly, to enlarge perceptions of 'Britishness' in pursuit of propitious hybrids [...]. It is often the case, however, that it is 'Englishness' that is really at issue in the new reformulations, for it is England, the original colonial mother country – found wanting in its historical obligations – that must be seen as the focus of critical migrant revisionism. (182)

Critics are often subject to an almost opposite process, appearing to respond to flux and its declared radicality, whilst in almost contradictory fashion avowing simultaneously a cultural uncertainty that concedes a sense of an implicit conservatism since an established literary-critical culture precedes (and often subtends) their scepticism. Head is right to alert the reader of fiction to Homi K. Bhabha distinguishing between an 'authoritative national identity' and a 'living principle', but the same objection could be applied to any terminological ascription (whether it is either pedagogic or practical). Many critics in the field of postcolonialism object to Bhabha's underlying assumptions. San Juan Jr believes that he defers to a textualizing discourse. 'With structuralism and dialectics refused, Bhabha elevates the "language" metaphor to transcendental aphoristic status' (26). Interestingly, in addition he attacks Bhabha for his distortions of Fanon (27–9). Certainly, the oblique insinuation of minority challenges to a dominant discourse is not a matter of simply defining cultural difference, but one element in the hybridity of the dialectical interplay between on the one hand intersubjectivity and enculturation of all kinds (including subaltern and counter-cultural forces) and on the other the capriciousness of social interaction. In *Absolutely Postcolonial: Writing Between the Singular and the Specific* (2001) Peter Hallward comments on Leela Gandhi's position in *Postcolonial Theory* (1998) that 'Surely we don't need a *post*colonial theorist to tell us that colonialism installed an "ambivalent and symbiotic relationship between coloniser and colonised", if we recognise from the beginning that *all* human relations are to some degree ambivalent and symbiotic, that every subject is constitutively related to its others' (xiv).

White Teeth and Multiculturalism

Such an understanding of ambivalence helps situate more broadly the multiculturalism that Head sees as the focus of Zadie Smith's *White Teeth* which is not idealist, but a comic deflation of the overburdening elements of the quotidian, where all of the events are revealing in terms of identity and the notion of culture. Importantly, the narrative is inextricably interwoven with the realities of everyday London life. Certainly in conjuring an almost Dickensian concept of the grotesque and coincidental, Smith interweaves an ongoing subtextual and stylistic gesture to this cultural underpinning, however partial and ironic its inclusion and depiction. Head says in *The Cambridge Introduction to Modern British Fiction, 1950–2000* of the central characters and their cultural identifications:

> The novel questions the extent to which the attitudes of Samad and Archie amount to a reliable understanding of first-generation immigration and its reception. Smith is also careful to embed the representativeness of her characters more deeply, both historically and culturally. Samad's identity is fashioned from his pride in his great-grandfather Mangal Pande whose actions are said to have triggered the Indian Mutiny of 1857. Archie's sense of self, on the other hand, is rooted in the transformative experience of being saved from suicide (by a halal butcher): a personal revelation results, and within hours, in a new state of euphoria, he meets his future wife Clara whose Jamaican mother was sired by a colonial Englishman. (184)

He adds in a later essay, 'Zadie Smith's *White Teeth*: Multiculturalism for the Millennium', that 'Given Smith's understanding of cultural misrecognition it is remarkable that this does not generate a stark and unproductive opposition. The focus, instead, is the sense of cultural confusion. It is this aspect, which lends the book a serio-comic tone [...]' (113). That fate and the effect of personal experience that is consequent on such chance effects which are always active elements of cultural referents is emphasized by the separation of Samad's twin sons, Magid and Millat. As Head indicates Magid on his return has become Anglo-Indian and therefore innately and conservatively 'English' in much of his outlook. Millat is more influenced, in a very similar fashion to Kureishi's adolescent males, by popular culture that leads him to an affiliation with a militant Islamic group. Rather than develop a hybrid identity, in fact, Millat regresses as fundamentally as much an imperial-style nationalist might, wanting to identify types where he might project himself. Significantly Smith details a revealing episode about the nuances of cultural references when the family suffer the effects of the 1987 hurricane attempting to escape from their home following the advice of Archie despite the insistence of Archie's wife, Alsana, con-cerning the infamous reassurance from the BBC weatherman:

> Even when the lights went out and the wind was beating the shit out of the double glazing, Alsana, a great believer in the oracle that is the BBC, sat in a nightie on the sofa refusing to budge.
>
> 'If that Mr Fish says it's OK, it's damn well OK. He's BBC, for God's sake!'
>
> Samad gave up (it was almost impossible to change Alsana's mind about the inherent reliability of her favoured English institutions, amongst them: Princess Anne, Blu-Tack, Children's Royal Variety Performance, Eric Morecambe, *Woman's Hour*). (220–1)

Smith suggests culture is difficult to locate, but a feeling for its pres-ence persists within the cultural objects of our lives. As in darkness they are forced to move, Samad insists the family only 'grab the essentials, *the life or death* things' (221), and feels both amusement and depression over Millat's '*Born to Run* (album) Springsteen', 'Shrink-to-fit Levis 501 (red tab)', and Alsana's '*Linda Goodman's Starsigns* (book)', and 'Huge box of beedi cigarettes', part of the list that the text presents in parallel columns. Smith plays with this urban myth of the incongruous items people grab in a crisis to emphasize the impracti-cality and commercialized nature of people's lives in the contemporary city, and the generational element (Samad like Archie being much older than his wife) which adds another element to this cultural snapshot. Life is not simply ideological, and that ideoplogy is played out in terms of dispositions. Samad notes the failings of their choices: ' "No pen knife, no edibles, no light sources. Bloody great. No prizes for guessing which one of the Iqbals is the war veteran. Nobody even thinks to pick up the Qur'ān. Key item in emergency situation: spiritual support" ' (222). These items are literal and symbolic, representing cultural as well as personal selections, a theme that recurs in the novel. This might be regarded as constituting a characterization critics like Aleid Fokkema describe as offering typically

> The postmodern 'borderline' character which is both signified according to some established literary conventions and, tied up in intertextual references, linguistic structures, and discourses, is representational in that it represents a concept about the world of human culture. Such postmodern characters are not mimetic because they represent universal human beings, but because an understanding is offered of contemporary Western culture (even when the fiction is set in the past or in the East), of which discourses, other fictions, earlier conventions, and certain hierarchical power relations are part. (189–90)

These are the elements that hybridity explores dialectically as both a mimetic particularity and a broader category of being. Smith defers judgement at times, but much like Kureishi, a notion of consensus, change and adaptation still appeals to a certain liberal notion of humanity. A subsequent crisis reveals the differing responses of the Iqbal family to Rushdie's *Satanic Verses* (a text implied rather than named). Millat sees his own marginalization and identifies with the *fatwa*. 'Millat recognized the anger, thought it recognized him, and grabbed it with both hands' (234). Alsana mocks Samad for responding without having read the book (much like Millat), at which Samad dismisses ' "Rationality! Most overrated Western virtue!" ' Alsana responds by identifying a context for choice, compromise and restraint, confronting Samad's avoidance of defining the meaning of being a Bengali by consulting the 'number three of their 24-volume set *Reader's Digest Encyclopedia*' (236) concluding from its reference:

> 'Oi, mister! Indo-*Ayrans* ... it looks like I am Western after all! Maybe I should listen to Tina Turner, wear the itsy-bitsy leather skirts. Pah. It just goes to show,' said Alsana, revealing her English tongue, 'you go back and back and back and it's still easier to find the correct Hoover bag than to find one pure person, one pure faith, on the globe. Do you think anybody is English? Really English? It's a fairy-tale!' (236)

There is an irony in her appeal to and use of the terminology that characterized the Nazi regime against which Samad fought over forty years previously as a very young man, around Millat's age, who appears engaged in a very different kind of ideological battle. Nevertheless, Alsana seems to offer an almost oracular, quotidian truth that is unpalatable for Samad, to which he refuses to respond and it is only when she catches sight of Millat on television at the book-burning of Rushdie's novel that his discomfort ends. Outraged, she makes a funeral pyre of 'his secular stuff.' ' "Everyone has to be taught a lesson," Alsana had said, lighting the match with heavy heart some hours earlier. "Either everything is sacred or nothing is. And if he starts burning other people's things, then he loses something sacred also. Everyone gets what's coming, sooner or later" ' (237).

Hybridity underlies the literal scientific and symbolic meaning of the 'FutureMouse©' project with which the novel ends and which as Head notes in 'Zadie Smith's *White Teeth*: Multiculturalism for the Millennium',

> is the work of Marcus Chalfen, and it is the Chalfens that bear the main brunt of Smith's social satire. This family of seemingly well-adjusted middle-class rationalists appears to embody a normative model of genetic health and stability; but the family is also a model of asocial exclusiveness: the Chalfens, having no friends, interact only with their extended family, 'the *good genes*'. The boredom that results from this enclosed perfection, with the family members seeming 'like clones of each other' leads the Chalfens to reach out, and to interfere in the lives of Magid and Millat, and in that of Irie, daughter of Archie and Clara. Thus a mild but debilitating form of eugenics is halted by its interaction with divers migrant bodies, though this necessary 'grafting on' is misperceived by the Chalfens as a channel for their own condescending patronage. Smith explodes the stereotypical middle-class Englishness of the Chalfens and demonstrates that the notion of biological 'purity' is destructive, not just as a biological falsehood, but also as a historical falsehood: the Chalfens are 'immigrants too (third generation, by way of Germany and Poland)'. (113–14)

The past recurs variously. Toward the end of the novel Abdul-Colin (with his hybridized name) reflects on the statues in central London and the English love of the icons of the past, on how they lack faith; ironically Millat seeks a particular bench where his father had years before just after his arrival in Britain carved his name. Millat remembered his father's words.

'A great shame washed over me the moment I had finished. [...]
It meant *I wanted to write my name on the world*. It meant *I
presumed*. Like the Englishmen who named streets in Kerala after
their wives, like the Americans who shoved their flag in the
moon. It was a warning from Allah. He was saying: Iqbal, you are
becoming like them. That's what it meant.'

No, thought Millat, the first time he heard this, no, that's not
what it meant. It just meant *you're nothing*. (505–6)

However, both in his disappointment at his father and in his attempt
to revenge himself, Millat more than anything else acts out his lifelong
Pacino fantasies. The strands of the novel are far too diverse to
summarize (a significant formal point in itself), but the tying together
of such strands toward the end – those of the effects of the war when
Samad and Archie meet, the episode that leads to the escape from the
two by a German scientist, who coincidentally re-emerges as a bio-
geneticist, and the very thematic neatness of the origins of the Chal-
fens – and the apparently ironic inclusion of '*endgames*' (540), is despite
the various postmodern ironies of a generically English kind in the
aesthetic sense. It seems as if Smith reminds her reader that at some
level a cultural teleology of historical effects of all kinds mirrors the
kind of complexity of life itself and this remains inescapable.

Rushdie's Hybridity

Of another text dealing explicitly with hybridity, Rushdie's *The Satanic
Verses*, Fokkema argues that

The real, historical worlds of religious strife in India or of
Thatcherite Britain figure in the dialogues between the characters,
but are mixed with the world of fantasy: London suffers an
apocalyptically tropical summer ending in hellish fire, the police
are involved in black magic, Thatcher becomes 'Mrs Torture,' the
Imam takes on huge proportions and literally flies off to an imaginary country in order to drive away the Empress Ayesha, and in
India a girl (also called Ayesha) works miracles. [...] This mixture
of fantasy and the real finally destabilizes the real and points to
other possible 'worlds' (or ontologies as McHale would say). (154)

One might equally argue that it destabilizes the imaginary, distancing it
from referentiality and sociological immediacy, if it were not for the
elements of life-world that repeatedly sustain the novel's critique of
cultural forms, suggesting even the imaginary and bizarre may well help
one challenge the epistemic provisionality that makes up a large part of
cultural formations and actions. Moreover, the apocalyptic summer

and cases of people flying that Fokkema invokes might be offered as intertextual allusions to the fantastical and often grotesque world of Ballard, where the imaginary and the real play out archetypal obsessions. I disagree fundamentally with the final emphasis of Fokkema's critical account of Rushdie's novel, that 'The narrative action is not guided by epistemological questions, but by the middle ground between knowing and its opposite, ignorance. Between knowing and ignorance are believing and doubt. Salman, Mohammed's scribe, whose name links him to the real author of *The Satanic Verses*, actively questions the truth about Mahound's revelations. Doubting that Gibreel truly speaks Allah's words to Mahound, he starts to corrupt his text, testing Mahound's reliability' (156). This is more than balanced by the world of contemporary events, which when overlaid with the struggle between good and evil, that Fokkema identifies as a central characteristic of the text, situate these abstract concepts, for without this backdrop they would be devoid of human meaning. As Andrew Gibson says in *Postmodernity, Ethics and the Novel: From Leavis to Levinas* (1999), 'Rushdie is concerned with the moment when the "real thing" is challenged by its "diabolic opposite", the godly by the satanic verses, homogeneity by radical alterity; with *tentō* – and reception – recast, perhaps, as the ethical moment itself' (209). However, as he indicates not only do Rushdie's concerns include a concept of reality, but its 'middle ground' expresses intuitive, radical knowledge and understanding, seeing in the complexity of experience and lives surreal, symbolic oppositions to dogmatic versions of humanity, which is why Fokkema finds 'a curious optimism that is rarely found in the postmodern text, and makes its characters more representational' (158).

British Cultural Hybridities
Cultural hybridity is not confined to writing from formerly or new 'migrant' communities. Writers such as Martin Amis, Michael Bracewell, James Kelman, A. L. Kennedy, Hanif Kureishi, Martin Millar, Will Self, Irvine Welsh and many others have captured the nuances of a range of urban voices demanding attention, and these fictions have highlighted the victims of late capitalism in the urban despoliation within the previously colonial centres of Bristol, Glasgow, Edinburgh and London in robust vernacular styles of language. This is despite some of these writers emerging from close to whatever passes for a cultural centre (Amis and Self for instance). Amis in *The Information* reflects on 13, a young black male involved in crime as a 'gofer' street criminal, 'The black kid cannot just be a black kid anymore. Nobody can just be somebody any more. Pity about that' (34). These represent

challenges to the past, and to conformity variously conceived and influenced. They edge British narrative away from the centre of traditional literary concerns and create a centrifugal space reaching outward both in geographic and in class terms. Such texts confront the epiphanic notions of transcendence and wish fulfilment conventionally associated with the literary, drawing in underclass, ethnic, radically gendered, socially subversive and working-class subjects who articulate profoundly non-conventional senses of community and self via dialect, humour and profanity. *The Information* might appear self-conscious and postmodern, but through his protagonist, failing writer Richard Tull, Amis disavows its presumptions. The narrative spirals among street life, criminality and the intrigues of upper-middle-class writers, but the process of fiction suggests parallels in the processes of urban life, observation, wit and adaptation. Richard reflects on a young prostitute drug-user and he feels a separation from things and events:

> Maybe they all had what Richard didn't have.
> 13 had it. Walk down any street with him and you wouldn't be seeing any of the things he saw. He saw earners and turners and leavers and levers, he saw locks and catches, what was unguarded and what protruded, what was detachable, what was transferable. In any shop his eyes glittered with compound calculation.
> Scozzy had it, though he had it the wrong way round. Animal thermovision, in the city; the night-sight of the wild boy.
> Belladonna had it. In the business of reinvention, the first act is that of renaming. The novelist does this all the time, on the page. On the street, the only thing you can rename is yourself, and everyone else you know, if you like, so that everyone had two names, just as everyone on television has two names. (255)

The narrative consciousness quite explicitly adds that despite 'representational difficulties' 'If writers drain life out of those around them, if writers are vampires, are night-mares [...] To be clear: I don't come at these people. They come at me. They come at me like information formed in the night. I don't make them. They're already there' (260). In fact Richard's son comes to him later with the demand that he be called 'Nothing' as if he recognizes the forces that can efface the individual (403–4). Richard's novel in progress that is his focus for the first part of Amis's novel is published finally by an obscure publishing company, ironically called Bold Agenda, attempting to balance the ethnic and social mix of its list, to maintain its funding. After a disastrous tour, after various professional readers have been hospitalized during the process of reading the book, he cannot find anyone who has completed a reading of the manuscript or established some criteria for its appearance. The title remains *Untitled*, the reflexive joke being finally on Richard himself since his ethnic middle-class English identity is the only reason he finds himself in print after successive rejections, and it seems to suggest that his class has lost itself in language games and a fear of identifying the self-evident or real.

> 'Basically,' said Leslie Evry, 'basically to balance the list. We felt the mix was wrong and may look badly. We felt it might imperil our funding.'
>
> 'Because,' said Richard, 'everyone else was called Doo Wah Diddy Diddy or Two Dogs Fucking. And you needed ...' On the wall, he noticed, was a framed poster of the Bold Agenda flyleaf or bookmark. With recognition, with love, Richard saw that one of his fellow authors was called Unsöld – Unsöld Inkuluk. 'Christ,' he said. 'A token honkie – not even *Gwyn* bothered with that. Why me? Why not someone from Boston?
>
> 'It's our policy to represent the most authentic possible –' (387)

This is an ironic inversion of tokenism. Moreover, one of the points of the humour (beyond being an amusing reflection of the dynamics of small presses) is that this intellectualizing of hybridity is sterile; it stands in stark contrast to the intermixture that is the world of street life, with an implicit manner of authenticity where as James Diedrick says in 'The Fiction of Martin Amis: Patriarchy and its Discontents' (2003) 'The inanimate world itself comes vividly to life in Amis's reifying prose' (244). Here as part of the 'patriarchal anxiety' Diedrick identifies in this novel (249), such people's lives appear chaotic and troubling only to Richard and his class, possessing a consciousness if not a logic of its own that is multicultural and variously diverse. In the trading of information that the novel's title refers to, there exists other effects, a conjoining of the lives depicted although to Richard it appears as if his supposed universal values are threatened, as does his rival, the more successful novelist and friend, Gwyn Barry, an *arriviste* in Richard's terms. Richard meets a young thug, Steve Cousins, who admires his writing and detests Gwyn's anodyne prose. 'Richard was undergoing a series of realizations. Which was just as well. He realized that the young man was not a type. Not an original, maybe; but not a type' (154). The information, a kind of view of things, also transforms Richard with its version of a hybrid consciousness. 'When Richard walked the streets with all his fingertips on his forehead he was saying to himself, am I one? am I two? am I worse? am I better? At night, as he prepared to enter the forests of sleep and temptation, things looked like two things: the ironing board was a deckchair and the mirror was a standing pool. He was being *informed* – the information came at night, to inhume him.' (150). After his return from America, over lunch Richard takes the name of his rival and in a curious process of transposition arrives at the notion of Great Britain, as if it might be some aspect of Britishness that has failed him. 'Gwyn advanced to the central window and looked down at the street and its ballroom of cherry blossom – the dance partners all the way to the bottom of the hill. How could the street not like him? The universe, the world, the hemisphere liked him [. . .]. Now the city behaved as if he wanted to break his face. The city wanted to break his face' (401).

Barker and McEwan: Historicized Multiplicities

Nostalgia for an imperial or pre-war Britain often serves to sustain the very concept of such a centre, but its central historical tenets have been radicalized in fictional re-visioning of the past. Pat Barker's *Regeneration* trilogy is intriguing in this respect since its premise is Siegfried Sassoon's resistance of the structure of power with the text of his 'wilful defiance of military authority', which it quotes in full (5). In what appears to be a naturalistic mode, Barker reconstructs the poet's stay at a hospital at Craiglockhart in 1917 where his doctor is W. H. R. Rivers, also a cultural anthropologist. Balancing this seemingly authorizing narrative of culturally centred and significant figures is the resistance in lifestyle terms of Billy Prior, a working-class officer who haunts the fringes of the first novel and emerges increasingly toward the centre of *The Eye in the Door* (1993) and *The Ghost Road* (1995). The notion of a threatened culture of nostalgia and lost innocence is clear from Rivers's reflections on the possessions that typify the young officers.

> The bookcase was already full of other books: boys' annuals, the adventure stories of Henty, *Scouting for Boys*. Games too: Ludo and Snakes and Ladders, a bat for beach cricket, collections of pebbles and shells, a strip of bladderwrack. All these things must have been brought here, or collected here, summer by summer, and then outgrown, but never thrown away, so that the room had become a sort of palimpsest of the young life it contained. He looked at Burns's sleeping face, and then tiptoed downstairs. (161)

There is something tangibly Woolfian in Barker's focus, the male world of the Ramsays and Jacob Flanders, whose ironically chosen surname evokes the conflict and slaughter at the heart of Barker's narrative, to which Prior returns and sees the ruin of the world of authority that he despises. 'An overhanging branch of laburnum flung a scattering of cold raindrops in his eyes and he was startled by the intensity of his joy. A joy perhaps not unconnected with the ruinous appearance of these houses. Solid bourgeois houses they must have been in peacetime, the homes of men making their way in the world, men who'd been sure that certain things would never change, and where were they now? Every house in the road was damaged, some ruined. The ruins stood out starkly, black jagged edges in the white gulf of moonlight' (511). As Wells says, 'The historical subject matter is infused with a conspicuous class-consciousness, covering a range of characters from the *literati* to poor women working in munitions factories' (165). And as Nick Crossley says in *Intersubjectivity: The Fabric of Social Becoming* (1996) 'Representations do not stand outside of the social, as a picture of it. They are within the social. They are one of a number of active, practical forces which combine in the constitution of the social. Moreover, subjects do not only "represent" the social to themselves. They act in it and participate in it' (75). Billy Prior's social interactions exemplify this aspect, extending the Freudianism (psychotherapy) and aestheticism (poetic expression) which are finally expressions of the self, and in some senses demonstrating something they seem unable to convey about power, what Crossley describes as negating a 'perfect mutual recognition' and distorting intersubjectivity, subordinating otherness where 'Power is a distortion of the communicative, mutually recognizing relation' (147).

In Barker's 'Author's Note', at the conclusion of the novel *Regeneration* (1991), she reflects 'Fact and fiction are so interwoven in this book that it may not help the reader to know what is historical and what is not' (220). In one sense this is disingenuous, particularly with its status as an apparently 'factually' or textually derived coda to what has appeared to be a fully fictionalized narrative with reconstructive ambitions. Moreover, despite the supposed incapacity to distinguish on the reader's part, Barker proceeds herself to outline the sources and events from which she drew certain key historical co-ordinates of the narrative set in the First World War, and yet Barker's cautionary comment is in many respects salient and correct in certain implicit assumptions. Barker adds such a note to each of the novels in her trilogy and these additions or supplements are suggestive in a number of ways in terms of part of what might be regarded as a paradoxical element in the narrative. The naturalistic elements of narrative indicate the text's apparent aspiration toward verisimilitude, and yet the blending of themes such as uncertain sexuality and class awareness far more contemporaneous to the author's world suggest a trans-historical perspective, and other modes of more internalized modernist awareness seem to mirror something of the emergent aesthetic consciousness of the period of its setting. This combinatory mixing of incompatible elements is neither as paradoxical as it might at first appear, nor even so unusual as a fictional stratagem and was discussed at length in the previous chapter. Many contemporary novelists position their fictional events curiously between the present and the past, exploring the irreal and the imaginary as they impact upon the concrete and the specifically signified.

Notably, instead of focusing upon a fictionalization of the historically recognizable and aesthetically inclined figures of Siegfried Sassoon and Wilfred Owen, both patients in the hospital where shell-shocked soldiers are sent, Barker chooses to explore what appears initially the far more prosaic relationship, that of Prior, and his psychiatric doctor, Rivers. Prior's sexual abuse as a child, his eliciting of similar memories from Rivers, Prior's homosexual adventures, and his contempt for authority are telling. The relationship is clearly a fictional construct, and yet such themes and interactions are more indicative of a contemporaneous narrative design than the past and exemplify characteristics of such fiction in its hybridization of elements. This re-invokes the past to reinforce its sense of crisis and instability for these historical subjects, thus redefining the imperial illusion of social cohesion. Barker undermines the class assumptions of such narratives. She explores Prior's seduction by a more upper-middle-class (or in populist terms much 'posher') officer, Manning, and signifies the underlying tensions. 'He'd transformed himself into the sort of working-class boy Manning would think it was all right to fuck' (235). He later appeals on behalf of Beattie Roper who has been imprisoned for supposedly being part of a pacifist conspiracy to poison Lloyd George, but recovers from the encounter a broader social awareness that is reinforced for the reader by its historical resonances. Prior realizes that Manning thinks that he is abusing their relationship, and his perception on the historical evidence of hindsight becomes authorized in the exchange of periodizations implicit in the act of reading.

> Prior had a sudden chilling perception that Manning was right. 'Rubbish. Because Roper's a working-class woman from the back streets of Salford. You don't give a fuck about her. I don't mean you personally – *though that's true too* – I mean your class.
> Manning was looking interested now rather than angry. 'You really do think class determines everything, don't you?'
> 'Whether people are taken seriously or not? Yes.' (368)

Barker reinforces our sense of this exchange by adding details of the plot in 1917 on which it is based and adds in the 'Author's Note' to *The Eye in the Door* apparent 'facts' that confirm not only this moral sense, but a curious half-confirmation (given it is drawn from the historically parallel, real case) of Prior's concern that Beattie will not last until the end of the war as Manning suggests she ought before release. 'Beattie Roper's Story is loosely based on the "poison plot" of 1917. Alice Wheedon, a second-hand clothes dealer living in the back streets of Derby, was accused and convicted of having conspired to murder Lloyd George, Arthur Henderson and other persons by poisoning. [...] After the war she was released, but, weakened by prison diet, hard labour and repeated hunger strikes, died in 1919' (422).

A similar effect underpins Ian McEwan's poignant use of historical detail in *Atonement*, where in the late 1930s Emily Tallis comes across her absent husband's work undertaken at the Ministry, negating ironically the subtextual hints that she suspects his obsessive hours serve as a cover for an affair. The reality is abrupt for the contemporary reader, but of little consequence for the wife even on the eve of war.

> It was only the mildest wifely curiosity that prompted her to peep, for she had little interest in civic administration. On one page she saw a list of headings: exchange controls, rationing, the mass evacuation of large towns, the conscription of labour. The facing page was handwritten. A series of arithmetical calculations was interspersed by blocks of texts. Jack's straight-backed, brown-ink copperplate told her to assume a multiplier of fifty. For every one ton of explosives dropped, assume fifty casualties. Assume 100,000 tons of bombs dropped in two weeks. Result, five million casualties. She had not yet woken him and his soft, whistling exhalations blended with winter birdsong that came from somewhere beyond the lawn. (149)

Emily dismisses this, reflecting that 'these extravagant numbers were surely a form of self-aggrandisement, and reckless to the point of irresponsibility' (150). Her reaction contrasts the later retreat of the British Expeditionary Force to Dunkirk that is central for the experience of the next generation, those at the centre of the incident at the heart of the book, and is detailed at length. The historical reference cumulatively indicates two kinds of Britain, one before the cataclysms, personal and public, one afterward. Thus McEwan conveys something of the almost anachronistic quality and emotional ill-preparedness of this upper middle class in an imperial period that it felt might well be an ongoing heyday. The reader conjoins with the very specific textual indications others that lie nevertheless in the implied interstices of the text, beyond the self-evident surface. In similar fashion Barker's supplementary narratives that come after each part of her trilogy extend the texts and therefore blur their boundaries.

Through such historical and other formally hybrid acts of mapping of selves, and by cartographizing the landscape and co-ordinating concepts of desire and conflict, a pattern emerges of a series of mutating narratives that help the reader understand or at least absorb the framework of what is a non-rationalist (in its simplistic sense), although far from truly postmodern, intersection of these modes of understanding. There lies in this aesthetic response a generic, formal and thematic hybridity, and certainly this is a key term in understanding the cultural and aesthetic implications of narrative and culture more generally. As Ngūgi Wa Thiong'o recognizes in *Decolonizing the Mind: The Politics of Language in African Literature* (1986) a cultural *hybridity* is an important concept both in cultural formulation and any resistance to a more hegemonic or embedded culture. He describes how a restrictive culture affects our language and thus 'our capacity to confront the world creatively [which] is dependent on how those images correspond or not to that reality, how they distort or clarify the reality of our struggles' (15). In hybridity what Thiong'o sees as a response in colonial conditions is appropriate to other hybridities of identity that have characterized contemporary Britain, often in recognizing new and old diversities. As Fanon says in *The Wretched of the Earth* considering the resistance to national cultures by postcolonial subjects, 'Each generation must, out of relative obscurity, discover its mission, fulfil it, or betray it. [. . .] We must rid ourselves of the habit [. . .] of minimizing the action of our fathers or of feigning incomprehension when considering their silence and passivity' (166). In at least a literary context, what was once perceived as the basis of chiefly a postcolonial consciousness has become a more general one both in ethnic and in other 'communities' or modes of identification of the self, as a global phenomenon, not just a British one. Dipesh Hakraharty notes Fanon's attempt to hold on to aspects of the Enlightenment idea of the human (5), and adds importantly in *Provincializing Europe: Postcolonial Thought and Historical Difference* (2000):

> The European colonizer of the nineteenth century both preached this Enlightenment humanism at the colonized and at the same time denied it in practice. But the vision has been powerful in its effects. It has historically provided a strong foundation on which to erect – both in Europe and outside – critiques of socially unjust practices. Marxist and liberal thought are legatees of this intellectual heritage. The heritage is now global. (4)

The colonial effect re-centred itself both symbolically and literally, both as a broad sociological fact and as an aesthetic effect, enabling a more general reconsideration of identities.

Hybridized Indigeneities and the Politics of Class

Significantly, from the mid-1970s many black British subjects were indigenous either in birth (within postcolonial communities that had resettled) or marginal in some sense (local working-class, Irish, Scots and Welsh), and split in consciousness, resulting in literary responses with very different concerns from the recurrent themes found traditionally in postcolonial migrant fiction, although some of these do persist.[2] Hence, given that cultural hybridity has become more widespread, far more diffuse and complex, unsurprisingly there are of course a number of different kinds of hybridity than the historiographic mythopoeism found in contemporary fiction; a range of other fictional voices that reconfigure the contemporary in other ways by decentring the cultural determinants of a range of identities. In *Trainspotting* Welsh, through Renton's reflections while visiting London, mocks a nationalistic sense of any kind, old or new.

> The pub sign is a new one, but its message is old. The Britannia. Rule Britannia. Ah've never felt British, because ah'm not. It's ugly and artificial. Ah've never really felt Scottish either, though. Scotland the brave, ma arse; Scotland the shitein cunt. We'd throttle the life oot ay each other fir the privilege ay rimmin some English aristocrat's piles. Ah've never felt a fuckin thing aboot countries, other than total disgust. They should abolish the fuckin lot ay them. Kill every fuckin parasite politician that ever stood up and mouthed lies and fascist platitudes in a suit and a smarmy smile. (234)

The dialect form of Welsh's writing, much like Kelman's at least superficially, indicates a local and specific consciousness of some sort, indicating a linguistic belonging. In refuting Bhabha, Rosemary Marangoly George echoes Welsh's character in a more critical vocabulary, declaring in *The Politics of Home: Postcolonial Relocations and Twentieth-Century Fiction* (1996) that:

> One could argue that 'the nation' is precisely that which is not inscribed by writing that is produced at the margins. Perhaps the location sought in these instances ought not to be read in terms of national subjectivity and/or national space. Immigration, one could argue, *unwrites* nation and national projects because it flagrantly displays a rejection of one national space for another more desirable location, albeit with some luggage carried over. (186)

The notions outlined above are crucial to reading contemporary fiction since clearly, many more previously marginal identities – regional,

class, gender or ethnic variations – have responded to the way in which
mainstream culture (just like 'colonial alienation') engaged in 'an
active (or passive) distancing of oneself from the reality around; and an
active (or passive) identification with that which is most external to
one's environment' (28). Certain subjects (fictional, authorial or both)
may incorporate a range of such identifications or markers of the
elements of a hybrid culture. Interestingly many writers are infused by
an awareness of class as a way of challenging and hybridizing the
hegemonic culture. Some critics resist this response, and as Terry
Eagleton notes in 'Postcolonialism and "Postcolonialism,"' 'Class
struggle is now embarrassingly *passé*, whereas the affirmation of cultural
identity is not. One of the less creditable reasons for the emergence of
postcolonial discourse, as indeed of feminism, is that certain other
forms of political conflict in the societies which breed these languages,
are currently proving too hard to crack, and a certain displacement
effect has accordingly set in' (26). On a localized level, a range of
contemporaneous, often subversive hybrid voices and even a new
sensibility have emerged in prose writing all of which reflects the
Zeitgeist of a different and emergent kind of Britain. This combines
original perspectives and experiences, synthesizing the marginal and
postcolonial, and admits quite explicitly the complexly gendered. One
has to recognize perhaps that in fiction and even in critical responses,
as Graham Huggan indicates in *The Postcolonial Exotic: Marketing the
Margins* (2001), that there may be examples of 'instances of the *postcolonial* exotic, of the global commodification of cultural differences'
(vii) in such fictional efforts. Writers like Kureishi and Zadie Smith
adapt these circumstances to an underlying tone of ironic humour.
Certainly this is what is indicated in Gandhi's description of Kureishi's
Buddha in *Postcolonial Theory: A Critical Introduction*:

> Khureishi's [sic] Anglo-Indian hero Karim, in pursuit of thespian
> aspirations, agrees to participate in an audition organised by the
> seedy and decidedly B-grade theatre director Shadwell. As it
> happens, Karim's unregenerate South London accent seriously
> belies Shadwell's expectations of exoticism. Karim, he finds, is a
> culturally impoverished and disappointingly British lad who has
> absolutely no stories to tell about eccentric aunties and Oriental
> wildlife. But Karim does land the part – as Mowgli, the native
> protagonist of Kipling's imperialist classic. Not content to let his
> new actor explore the subtle nuances of his assigned role, Shad-
> well instructs Karim to work harder on his Indian accent, and also
> to smear himself with brown polish before he appears on stage.
> (127)

The postcolonial colonial shadow is very persistent, and yet, such hybridity is a sign of an edginess and self-awareness that has marked strands of literary creativity in a manner that is distinguishably not simply postmodern, reflexive or self-aware, nor is it simply constituted by a postcolonial identity. Moore-Gilbert comments in terms of this novel that its intertextuality is complex. 'While certainly "reiterative" [...] The *Buddha*'s quotation of Kipling attests rather to a desire to 'hybridise' colonial discourse by adapting it "catachrestically" to address new cultural problematics. It could be argued that, like Rushdie, Kureishi seeks to recuperate and develop Kipling's interest in cross-cultural transactions, seeing in this aspect of his work a precedent for explorations of the contemporary predicament of cultural "in-betweenness"' (127). This is relevant more broadly as a wider series of transformations with their innate contradictory elements at any one point as Kureishi reflects comically concerning London in *Gabriel's Gift*: 'The city was no longer home to immigrants only from the former colonies, plus a few others; every race was present, living side by side without, most of the time, killing one another. It held together, this new international city called London – just about – without being unnecessarily anarchic or corrupt. There was, however, little chance of being understood in any shop' (8).

Winterson and 'Migrancy'

Hybridity is not simply an aesthetic device, but responds to a changing culture, recognizing complexities, a social priority rather than simply that of the individualistic. The literal results of 'migrancy' create responses even in the most apparently unpropitious circles. At the end of *Oranges Are Not the Only Fruit* (1985), returning home to the narrow religiosity of the northern evangelism from which she had escaped, the protagonist of Jeanette Winterson's novel finds various transformations. Head notes in the *Cambridge History of Modern British Fiction, 1950–2000*

> In the manner of Angela Carter, the realist code that governs Jeanette's narrative (the story of growing up in an enclosed community), is combined with narrative strands drawn from or inspired by fable, myth, and folklore. The combination of these disparate approaches to story is characteristic of Winterson's technique in which the reader's hold on normative reality is shaken up by an appeal to a higher kind of psychological truth. Consequently a readjustment of how that social reality is perceived is demanded. (100)

Head also outlines the reflections at the beginning of the section 'Deuteronomy: The Last Book of the Law' on history and her use of the cat's cradle metaphor where in Winterson's narrative 'History should be a hammock for swinging and a game for playing, the way that cat's play. Claw it, chew it, rearrange it and at bedtime it's still a ball of string full of knots' (91), and 'Very often history is a means of denying the past. Denying the past is to refuse to recognize its integrity. To fit it, force it, function it, to suck out the spirit until it looks the way you think it should. We are all historians in our small way' (92). And the expectation implicit in those who shape things confronts Jeanette in the present, for on her return she finds what she clearly anticipated is transformed into conditions that she could not have imagined, exemplified in the turn of events when her mother having taken up contacting other evangelists with her 'build-it-yourself CB radio' (167), literally adapts at least in some ways her localized identity and culture. Nevertheless, when with Jeanette's ex-lover, Melanie, she works 'together on the town's first mission for coloured people. [. . .] When the first coloured pastor came to her house, she [Jeanette's mother] had tried to explain to him the significance of parsley sauce. Later she had found he had lived most of his life in Hull' (166–7). Jeanette might have reflected ironically earlier in the text,

> So the past, because it is past, is only malleable where once it was flexible. Once it could change its mind, now it can only undergo change. The lens can be tinted, tilted, smashed. What matters is that order is seen to prevail . . . and if we are eighteenth-century gentlemen, drawing down the blinds as our coach jumbles over the Alps, we have to know what we are doing, pretending an order that doesn't exist, to make a security that cannot exist. (93)

Yet, despite this undercutting of enlightenment patriarchy, it is that very flexibility of the ongoing present as the site of adaptation, of the 'oozing world' (93), which surprises the reflective Jeanette of the text. She reads of one set of changes in her adoptive mother's letter concerning Mrs Butler, a stalwart of the Society for the Lost with which they were both involved, and owner of a Morecambe guest house, by implication a stereotypical figure of northern phlegm and solidity. It is not simply in sexual awareness that a hybridity of consciousness enters the text. This is literal. As Winterson says in an introduction added to the paperback edition of the text in 1991,

> *Oranges* is a comforting novel. Its heroine is someone on the outside of life. She's poor, she's working-class but she has to deal with the big questions that cut across class, culture and colour.

Everyone, at some time in their life, must choose whether to stay with a ready-made world that may be safe but which is also limiting, or to push forward, often past the frontiers of commonsense, into a personal place, unknown and untried. In *Oranges* this quest is one of sexuality as well as individuality. (xiv)

Of course in part this hybridity is expressed through her emergent sexual nature, and her affair divides her from the community, but it also expresses symbolically a moving away from the unity of soul which has been the implicit aspiration of her mother's upbringing, where the body is defilement. Jeanette's return to her mother's is a journey back from a kind of exile. As Head notes perceptively, both in the context of a home life from which she emerges and in the fantasy story of Winnet banished by a sorcerer, this explains why the author concludes with

the surprising return of Jeanette to her foster-mother [...]. In the final pages, Winnet's narrative is incorporated into Jeanette's as she ponders on her life away from home, in a metaphorical city 'full of towers'. [...] In this autobiographical work, the quest of Jeanette is linked to Winterson's search for her identity as a writer, so that when Jeanette claims that she is a 'prophet' this is also a definition of Winterson's desired role as the producer of a new feminist mythology. (100–1)

From the 'descent' or fall from grace that she undergoes Jeanette acquires an acuity absent in her mother, whose religiosity seems finally somewhere between a neurosis and the 'hobby' her daughter identifies. To return at Christmas with its implicit ceremonial and ritualistic elements, however residual in this local culture, may be significant, for as Paul Ricoeur comments in *The Symbolism of Evil* (1967) in terms of the Judaic traditions, 'There are not two worlds: a world of ceremony and a world of contrition; the latter is represented in the former as in a gestural enigma' (98). The reconciliation underlying the return is similarly enigmatic. And her mother's ire becomes first ritualized in preaching to 'other distressed parents with demon-possessed children' (169), and finally displaced when Jeanette's fate is echoed in the descent of another figure in her mother's circle.

It seemed that Mrs Butler, depressed by falling numbers at the guest house, and frustrated by the constant nagging of the health authority, had taken to drink. More importantly, she had got herself a job as matron of a local old folk's home. While there she had taken up with a strange charismatic man who had once been the official exorcist to the Bishop of Bermuda. He had been dismissed under mysterious circumstances for some kind of unmentionable offence with the curate's wife. Back in England and safe within the besotted arms of Mrs Butler, he had persuaded her to let him practise voodoo on some of the more senile patients. They had been caught by the night nurse. (170–1)

It seems significant in terms of the themes Winterson outlines in her introduction, cited above, that what might have been expected to represent an exotic alterity of a colonial and hybrid tradition has insinuated itself even in what has been described in the preceding narrative of Jeanette's upbringing as a closed and seemingly impermeable community. And the emphasis on the demonic and possession indicates the underlying multiple nature of the self even in this wider family of the saved, something her mother's dysfunctional personality mirrors.

Kim Middleton Myer argues in 'Jeanette Winterson's Evolving Subject: "Difficulty into Dream"' (2003) that 'A unitary approach, that explains away contestatory positions vis-à-vis Winterson's work, forecloses on the multiplicity that she herself seeks to engender. Thus we must allow the novels to display the author's developing theory of contradiction in identity' (210). I agree with Middleton Myer that this is not simply a concern for what she describes as 'contradiction within a singular body' (210), but is a matter of subjectivities that Middleton Myer describes as 'nomadic', a process of hybridity. Winterson's characters are in states of transition and escape, as is evident emotionally in *Written on the Body* (1992) and both emotionally and literally in *Gut Symmetries* (1997), where all of the major characters are in first-generation exile in America, Alice having an affair with Jove and later his wife Stella. Both protagonists are linked by a strong element of scientific understanding that fails to address the emotional and any ontological sense fully. Such knowledge fails to address the character's longings, as with Louise's illness in *Written on the Body*. 'In the secret places of her thymus gland Louise is making too much of herself. Her faithful biology depends on regulation but the white T-cells have turned bandit. They don't obey the rules' (115). The conflicts central to *Gut Symmetries* are in some senses less private, although it is there that their origins lie. Subtextual to the discourse on metaphysics and science that runs through the text is the location of the character's identities in the families and cultures of their youth, lost not only in time, but left in other places. Stella reflects 'I've lived my life like a serial killer; finish with one part, strangle it and move on to the next. Life in neat boxes is life in neat little coffins, the dead bodies of the past laid out side by side. I am discovering, now in the late afternoon of the day, that the dead still speak' (49). The text interlaces personal details with the shifting identities of the self and the culture around those selves, exploring more than just heterogeneity, but finally the metaphysical aesthetic aspiration with which the novel ends. 'They were letting off fireworks down at the waterfront, the sky exploding in grenades of colour. Whatever it is that pulls the pin, that hurls you past the boundaries of your own life into a brief and total beauty, even for a moment, it is enough' (219).

In *The Passion* Henri, a cook from peasant stock in France is co-opted to the Napoleonic campaign kitchen; as in Winterson's *Gut Symmetries*, points of origin and a separation from those dynamics are worthy of inclusion. If one reconstructs the detail, then a kind of complex hybridity beneath the tale of Napoleon and his imperial progress becomes evident: Bonaparte's own origins in Corsica (12); the giantess madam who originates from Sweden and Joséphine herself from Martinique, symbolized as exotic since she is associated with the whore's idol, for 'Around her [the whore's] neck on a leather thong she kept a flat-faced wooden doll. She saw me staring at it and drawing my head close forced me to sniff it. It smelled of musk and strange flowers' (13); all the talk of Egyptian failures (17); the presence of eagle-eyed Patrick, a defrocked Irish priest (21); Domino from eastern Europe, 'the colour of old olives', whose loyalties to Bonaparte are mixed (29); and, later Villanelle with her French name, from the city at the heart of the subjugated and faded trading empire of Venice, a place of exile, of disguise and uncertain identities. In his madness and passion, hearing voices and seeing the dead, Henri loses his mind in the asylum of San Servelo, and his existence seems to echo that of Napoleon in exile. In the hybridity of form, an intermixture of the real and fantastic where the retrieval of Villanelle's heart constitutes part of the grotesque form that Middleton Myer analyses (213–14), there underlies a curious division of culture and consciousness, of place and understanding which Venice epitomizes. Henri loses himself for five days, embarrassed to speak French, and appears to find Villanelle as if by chance:

> 'I need a map.'
> 'It won't help. This is a living city. Things change.'
> 'Villanelle, cities don't.'
> 'Henri, they do.' (113)

The route they take along the canal mystifies him and, as Henri later perceives in his incarceration, it is Villanelle that has taught him to see the double nature of things, and he understands that staying in exile has been by choice. Yet this is not really any reconciliation with the conditions of life, where in exile the world has become fantastic and irrational, and from that experience of the delusional and obsessive that merges with his madness, he concludes 'The cities of the interior are vast and do not lie on any map' (152). Rather than embrace the hybridity of this world, a world of encounters, desires and secret mutations, Henri withdraws, and in this there is a sense of loss and disengagement. What from? In part from the historical confusions of culture and identity, from the grotesque realities of a disorganizing life, for as Gayatri Chakravorty Spivak says in A *Critique of Postconial Reason: Toward a Vanishing History of the Present* (1999) in insisting that postcolonial sensibilities are part of a more broadly based cultural sense, 'Simply put, culture alive is always on the run, always changeful' (355). Henri retreats to the lost world of the dead and of memory, although Winterson in her authorial role has undertaken what Rod Mengham describes in 'General Introduction: Contemporary British Fiction' (2003) 'as an attempt to generate a culturally hybridized identity' (5). *Sexing the Cherry* is replete with fantastical symbols and motifs of sexual and cultural transition and hybrity, with its Woolfian androgyny of the wish 'to be free of the burdens of their gender' (31), and a historicized fantastical perspective, where 'The earth is round and flat at the same time' (81). The transition into modernity and the proto-colonial expansion of British trade and adventurism are inscribed in Jordan's travels, as Middleton Myer indicates the real blurring with the imaginary indistinguishably, and tellingly Jordan reflects what is the effect upon himself 'I discovered that my own life was written invisibly, was squashed between the facts' (10). Jordan's explanation of the grafting to the grotesque Dog Woman, his adoptive mother, is an allegory for the cultural hybridization. 'Grafting is the means whereby a plant, perhaps tender or uncertain, is fused into a hardier member of its strain, and so the two take advantage of each other and produce a third kind, without seed or parent. In this way fruits have been made resistant to disease and certain plants have learned to grow where previously they could not' (78).

Lost Origins: Caryl Phillips

A retrieval of the lost ghosts of memory, and a return from a different kind of exile to confront the mental cartography of a culture constitute the central concerns of Caryl Phillips's A *State of Independence* (1986) where Bertram Francis flies home from twenty years in London to St Kitts. Something of the land of his exile and of contemporary Britain clings to Bertram, although the Englishness of his speech is more marked at the beginning of the novel, changing subtly to a more local usage toward the end. The occasion of the visit is the island's impending independence when in fact a sense of transformation unsettles Bertram who despises the Americanization celebrated by an old rival and school friend who is a minister of state, Clayton Jackson. Bertram abandoned the scholarship that sent him to London (placing him firmly as an early migrant), and not only does he have to face the hostility of those he once knew including his own mother, but his own sense of failure combined with a growing recognition that he is between cultures. As he lands, at the beginning of the novel, he is both relieved not to have sat next to a traveller with more up-to-date local knowledge than himself, to be followed through customs by an old woman he identifies as 'a true national who had probably been to England only to see grandchildren' (13). He is subsequently upbraided by a taxi driver for rushing him. ' "I'm often picking up fellars who been living in England and America and all them places, and they coming back here like we must adjust to their pace rather than it's they who must remember just who it is they dealing with once they reach back" ' (17). Later the receptionist to Clayton's government building imagines he is an outsider saying that, ' "You're not from here and your people probably have a different way of doing things" ' (106). This comment is part of a series of telling encounters. Bertram has to confront the change in what was once his culture, alongside guilt at the abandonment of those he loved, and moreover the loss of his youth. He explains to Patsy, the girl he betrayed, and he later finds may have borne a child by him: ' "I had to go, I captured the scholarship." He paused. "After two years they tell me I must leave the college so I take a job. Then I take a next one and so on, until my time just slide away from me. I know it don't sound too impressive, but there's plenty more just like me still in England. People who went there for five years, then one morning they wake up with grey hair and wonder what happened. Well, what happened is called a life, and it just passes away from you unless you do something about it and discipline yourself" ' (151), only to confess he has nothing for him in England, unable to say whether he feels at home there or even now in St Kitts. This is exacerbated earlier after Clayton's underlying opinion of him emerges when Bertram attempts to insist that Clayton advise him on business opportunities for investment, and the latter responds not in a manner that is palatable, but rather declares certain ambivalent truths. Firstly he reflects Bertram had not ever properly left and yet adds:

'You English West Indians should just come back here to retire and sit in the sun. Don't waste your time trying to get into the fabric of the society for you're made of the wrong material for the modern Caribbean. You all do think too fast and too crazy, like we should welcome you back as lost brothers. Well, you may be brothers alright, but you lost for true for you let the Englishman fuck up your heads.' (136)

As Brad Buchanan reflects in 'Caryl Phillips: Colonialism, Cultural Hybridity and Racial Difference', 'Clayton's insulting advice is the more galling because of his own status as a kind of cultural hybrid, albeit of a more successful kind. Inspired by American activists rather than British educators (like Bertram), a much younger Clayton had gone through a brief period of militancy during which he called himself "Jackson X" as if in tribute to the famously uncompromising black leader Malcolm X' (180). Clayton's attack appears to be a pivotal moment, but it simply confirms Bertram's sense of cultural and personal malaise. He confesses to Patsy a failing relationship in England, a need for clarification in his personal life but 'his thoughts became too complex and he withdrew' (150). There is no resolution for Bertram, perhaps only the notion of change, one he fears, with the arrival of another cultural influence with American cable television, Jackson's world and source of inspiration.

Notes

1 This a term used in postcolonial studies, but draws on previous, often racist, discourses. A good outline of the origins and certain historical significances of the meaning of 'hybrid' can be found in: Brad Buchanan (2003) 'Caryl Phillips: Colonialism, Cultural Hybridity and Racial Difference', 174–90; and, Robert J. C. Young (1995) *Colonial Desire: Hybridity in Theory, Culture and Race*, London and New York: Routledge; and Avtar Brah and Annie E. Coombes (eds) (2000) *Hybridity and its Discontents: Politics, Science, Culture*, London and New York: Routledge. The reading in my present chapter explores new cultural contexts for its application in more contemporary understandings of the word.
2 These would be those outlined by Hedwig Bock and Albert Wertheim in the introduction to their edited collection *Essays on Contemporary Post-Colonial Fiction* (1986a), which includes: 'Returning from studies or exile abroad [. . .] reaction of characters from colonial and post-colonial areas to life outside their country. Similarly, much post-colonial fiction also considers the transformations of characters from the outside world who enter an alien colonial or post-colonial society' (5).

Further Reading

Easthope, Antony (1999) *Englishness and National Culture*, London and New York: Routledge.
This is a sociological and cultural critique of the nature of Englishness, its culture, traditions and historical notion of itself. It offers itself as a sound background for literary scholars unaware of other traditions of critical intervention. The literary contexts featured are somewhat trite and self-evident.

Hallward, Peter (2001) *Absolutely Postcolonial: Writing Between the Singular and the Specific*, [see bibliography].
This intriguing and original consideration of postcolonial theory and literature breaks new ground, considering both the contradictions inherent in the essentialist position of many critics and the four key prose writers. Because of the complex nature of its

argument that the postcolonial be understood as an ultimately *singular* category, it may be most suitable for postgraduate students.

Lowe, Jan (2001) 'No more lonely Londoners', *Small Axe*, 5 (1) March, 166–81.
This is am excellent close reading of Zadie Smith's *White Teeth*, looking at class, migrancy, London and a range of themes, and is recommended for anyone studying the novel.

Mączyńska, Magdalena (2003) 'Apocalytic London in the Fiction of Martin Amis', in Will Wright and Steve Kaplan (eds) *The Image of the City in Literature, Media and Society*, Pueblo, CO: The Society for the Interdisciplinary Study of Social Imagery, Colorado State University-Pueblo, 189–93.
Good essay on reading Amis's urban apocalyptic vision which situates his writing within a broad literary tradition; recommended, but published in an obscure publication of conference proceedings.

Morace, Robert A. (2001) *Irvine Welsh's* Trainspotting: *A Reader's Guide*, London and New York: Continuum.
A short, well-informed introductory guide that is suitable for all levels of student.

Mukherjee, Ankhi (2001) 'Stammering to Story: Neurosis and Narration in Pat Barker's *Regeneration*', *Critique: Studies in Contemporary Fiction*, 43 (1), 49–62.
Closely argued journal article looking at Barker's account in *Regeneration* of Craiglockhart, considering trauma, shell-shock and both the historical and the fictional interpretation of Rivers's interventions; thoughtful and to be recommended.

(1997) *Review of Contemporary Fiction*, 17 (2).
A special edition devoted to Wilson Harris covering a range of topics, and the essays are mostly short and accessible for all levels of student.

Shiffer, Celia (2004) ' "You see, I am no stranger to love": Jeanette Winterson and the Extasy of the Word', *Critique: Studies in Contemporary Fiction*, 46 (1), 31–52.
This is an excellent journal article that is theoretically informed, and uses an analytical close reading of most of Winterson's major texts. It considers the themes of loss, her use of language and *écriture féminine*; recommended for all students.

CHAPTER SIX

The Post-millennial, 9/11 and the Traumatological

KEY THEMES
9/11 or September 11 • British Dystopias • Domestic Conflicts • Chaos •
Collective Consciousness • Cultural *Zeitgeist* • Fear and Violence •
Millennial Fiction • Solipsistic Identities • Terrorism • Trauma Theory •
The Traumatological

KEY TEXTS

Ali, Monica *Brick Lane*

Amis, Martin *Yellow Dog*

Aslam, Nadeem *Maps for Lost Lovers*

Ballard, J. G. *Kingdom Come*

Barker, Pat *Double Vision*

Garland, Alex *The Coma*

Levy, Andrea *Small Island*

Litt, Toby *Ghost Story*

McEwan, Ian *Saturday*

Peace, David *GB84*

Self, Will *The Book of Dave: A Revelation of the Recent Past and the Distant Future*

Smith, Ali *The Accidental*

Thomson, Rupert *Divided Kingdom*

Thorne, Matt *Cherry: A Novel*

Winterson, Jeanette *Art and Lies*

Cultural Conflict: David Peace *GB84* (2004)

This chapter considers the aesthetic mood of post-millennial fiction, most particularly novels published after 9/11. Although characterized by uncertainty, I suggest that much recent fiction is of a traumatological rather than postmodern bent, abjuring both the latter's abandonment of certainty and meaning, and its deconstructive dissolution of identities. As discussed in the preface, the traumatological both emphasizes and responds to concrete historical conditions *and* expresses either overtly or covertly an awareness of radical simultaneous challenges to *both* personal identity and the social order. Such fictions may look back to other recent periods indelibly linked with violent fault-lines, such as with David Peace's didactically inclined novel, *GB84* (2004), which considers the ugly and conflictual dynamics of the 1984 miners' strike. Peace describes how Margaret Thatcher transformed Britain into a state resembling a civil war, ending with an almost incantatory voice that appropriates the political sloganeering of the period. 'In place of strife. In place of fear – Here where she stands at the gates of her tribe and waits – Triumphant on the mountains of our skulls. Up to her hems in the rivers of blood – A wreath in one hand. The other between her legs –' (462). As Randall Stevenson says in 'Big Sister':

> Following the strike's events week by week, GB84 juxtaposes multiple narratives [...]. Each [...] is more or less continuous, but fragmented in its presentation by repeated interruptions from the others. One set of narratives is characterized by the dialectal, first-person voices of miners daily involved in violent struggles with the police on the Yorkshire coalfields, and bitterly aware of their terrible human costs. Other sections, largely in the third person, record increasingly desperate manoeuvrings by a senior official in the National Union of Miners, intertwined and counterpointed with accounts of Machiavellian machinations conducted by the Government and its intelligence agents. (21)

By detailing the historical machinations and confrontations involved in the government's secretive rebuttal of Arthur Scargill's National Union of Mineworkers strike alongside both what Stevenson calls the 'grim idiom of crime writing' (21) and the tortured consciousness of a key character, an NUM official, Chief Executive Terry Winters, Peace thereby creates a highly original synthesis. The novel is an emphatic vision of the turbulent birth of contemporary Britain, with a rhetorical emphasis rarely articulated so directly in fiction. As Stevenson notes, Peace's 'disconnective language' reflects the novel's fragmentariness, 'heightening its stark montage of a society rapidly falling apart' (21). Individuals are sucked into the literal process of history, a concatenation of overlapping narratives, all intense and personal, each inflected by a fervour and intensity. Events become a testimony to painful change and transformation. 'For the Prime Minister is winning her war; her many, many wars – The IRA. British Leyland. GCHQ. Cammel Laird. CND. The Belgrano. The GLC' (336). Seen through the accounts of others, Peace's Thatcher ignores what Halliday calls 'the central claim of the state to authority, its ability to protect its citizens' (42), turning upon them as do those acting of her behalf. Throughout, by re-inscribing history Peace infuses the personal with the political, creates an ideological vista darkened by its sub-plot of dirty tricks, of confrontation and of murder. Stevenson concludes that 'as well as looking back, GB84 looks bleakly ahead [...] Peace's novel helps to account for the bitterer, more divisive Britain left by the Thatcher years' (21).

By foregrounding the turbulent historical uncertainties of the present, Peace's novel typifies the traumatological, in that it engages an
underlying aesthetic with a fundamentally different emphasis or
orientation to the previous literary culture stretching from the late
1980s, which was influenced by a notion of 'trauma' conceived almost
solely in terms of individual, almost solipsistic identities. Roger Luckhurst outlines its parameters in 'Traumaculture', as 'a new kind of
articulation of subjectivity [which] emerged in the 1990s organized
around the concept of trauma. This subject was brought into being in
the advanced capitalist economies of the West through discursive
statements not in themselves necessarily new [...]. It was more the
conjuncture of discourses across a variety of professional, political and
cultural sources that locked a powerful account of selfhood into place
in this decade' (28). Such 'trauma-culture' fiction explores obsessively
individual identity and a sense of one's fractious personal history, often
retrieving lost memories or addressing feelings of intense alienation
that result from being oppressed by stereotypes and conventional social
expectations. Conversely, the traumatological responds to concrete
and collective fears, exploring a notion of their radical threat to both
the individual and one's sense of collectivity.

The Traumatized Subject: Alex Garland *The Coma* (2004)

Alex Garland parodies the expectations of traumaculture in the
pointedly unpaginated (and therefore difficult to chart) illustrated
novel, *The Coma* (2004). Garland's woodcut style images vie with the
words of his episodic short chapters for prominence and dominant
meaning. Toward the end of the text strings of words vie with the
images of the scenes Carl creates (Section 3, Chapter 10, n. pag.).
When trying to protect a woman passenger, Carl is beaten and kicked
unconscious (a literal series of direct physical traumas) on the tube on
his way home from work. He is hospitalized, later apparently awakening, but subsequently his world seems devoid of tangible, locatable
meaning. Initially he sees only a series of images, then more developed,
but fragmented episodes which become both dream-like and nightmarish, as if parodying both the postmodern condition and society's
rendition of the individual through the narrative's evocation of a
traumatized consciousness revisiting a concrete traumatic experience.
'I was not suffering from psychological trauma, as I had at first suspected. Instead, as Mary pointed out, it was more likely that I had
some sort of brain damage. Which, to look on the bright side, might be
reversible. Even, in some ways, easier to address than psychological
trauma – or at least more straightforward' (Section 1, Chapter 10,
n. pag.). The illogic of the events and continued flashes of a hospital

together persuade Carl he must be in a coma, especially given the oddity of his friends and family, who seem even to Carl on close inspection to be generic individuals rather than specific ones. Garland parodies the contemporary cultural obsession with the inner self, exploring a coma where 'My one remaining protection against the uncertainties of waking life was itself an uncertainty: I had amnesia. All my movements through memories and locations still hadn't told me who I was' (Section 3, Chapter 16, n. pag.). Carl faces the ultimate lack of points of reference, after his literal trauma renders him without tangible selfhood, that is without true consciousness. His lover, Catherine, appears, as food does, within the negative logic of the dream and its own meaninglessness, chaotically rather than randomly.

> But I didn't care.
> Because why would I? Strip down my waking life, and I'm a consciousness in a void. Strip down my dream life, and I'm a consciousness in a void.
>
> (Section 3, Chapter 7, n. pag.)

For Carl, without the realm of the real, traumatic experience expands to become the truly traumatological, a lacunary fissure widening to an ontological void. He continues in his attempt to combine apparently meaningless words, to 'Crash these things together, make them exist to the exclusion of everything else, and that's it' (Section 3, Chapter 5, n. pag.). In this he continues to fail. He lacks co-ordinates and fixity.

In complex ways, Garland reflects aesthetically the end of the period of self-obsession, subtly incorporating a post-9/11 shift toward a wider ideological awareness, responding to the very sociopolitical uncertainties which appear to both permeate and transform the public as well as the aesthetic consciousness. Of course some will insist that fiction does not reflect the cultural or historical. Despite such objections to a concept of narrative *mirroring*, certainly the literary aesthetic, perhaps as a collective unconscious, represents inflections of the wider *Zeitgeist*; both are affected profoundly by historical shifts, by changes in cultural experience, and by eventfulness. John Macleod admits in 'Revisiting Postcolonial London', 'Millennial optimism has not lasted' (39). He concedes that there has been 'a shift which has been chillingly brought home in more ways than one by recent events. On a grey London Thursday morning in July 2005, 52 people were killed in a series of coordinated bomb attacks on London's transport system' (40), marking such events as profound aesthetical and critical landmarks.

Revisiting Millennial Fiction: Reconsidering *White Teeth*

In 2000 American economic and political influences appeared culturally and ideologically impermeable, as if representing an unchal-
lengeable hegemony. America's cultural permeations were noted by a
range of novelists, including both Phillips in *A State of Independence* as
discussed at the end of the previous chapter, and Zadie Smith in her
delineation of a commodified, seductive youth culture that influences
Millat in *White Teeth*, and apparently vying with the fundamentalism
that he avows under the influence of KEVIN or the *Keepers of the
Eternal and Victorious Islamic Nation*, an Islamic group agitating against
such Western influences. Nevertheless, as Macleod comments such a
contingent affiliation 'segues seamlessly into precisely the kind of
fundamentalist ardour which cosmopolitan and multicultural energies
are meant, in theory at least, to act as a kind of cultural inoculation'
(42). Smith's source may well have been hostage Brian Keenan's young
Hizbollah kidnappers who are described in *An Evil Cradling* (1992) as
paying homage to the selfsame Western icon as Millat. 'Emulating
Rambo they would conquer the world and simultaneously rid themselves of that inadequacy which they could never admit.' (133).

It is tempting to regard millennial fiction as more naive in many
respects than it was judged to be prior to 9/11, as exemplified in certain
aspects of Smith's *White Teeth*. Published in 2000, the novel looks
backwards in a celebratory style that would become subsequently more
difficult, creating a pastiche of the cultural moods and moments from
the mid-1970s that had contributed to the new multicultural Britain.
Smith ponders in her inimitable comedic, satirical fashion on divisions
within the self and the body politic, particularly those of Muslims,
which are prominent in the narrative. Macleod wonders about the
effects of 9/11 and the July 2005 London bombings, saying 'It appears
that the conflict between national and translocal discourses of
belonging may no longer be the most significant or urgent' (40). And
despite Macleod's attempts to reposition Smith's novel, its focus
remains largely familial and domestic. Nevertheless, and perhaps
presciently, the Iqbals are absent from the mock edenic return to the
Caribbean at the narrative's end. Offstage, one infers, continues the
conflictual, unresolved dialectic of the partly radicalized Millat, the
nostalgic and fissured religiosity of Samad with his rhetorical resistance
to the West and to assimilation, Alsana's pragmatic conciliations, and
the Anglo-Indian tradition upon which Magid draws despite his
father's disgust to create an anglicized Bangladeshi culture. In the final
whimsical image of a paradise regained Smith situates Irie, Joshua,
Hortense, and 'Irie's [unnamed] fatherless little girl [who] writes
affectionate postcards to *Bad Uncle Millat* and *Good Uncle Magid* and

feels free as Pinocchio, a puppet clipped of paternal wings' (541). Perhaps one is implicitly invited to set this against the despair of Samad at the Western assimilation of his family, particularly that exhibited toward Alsana's nephews and nieces whose behaviour induces him to abduct his own son and return him to the homeland and what he imagines is a true religiosity.

> 'They won't go to mosque, they don't pray, they speak strangely, they dress strangely, they eat all kinds of rubbish, they have intercourse with God knows who. No respect for tradition. People call it assimilation when it is nothing but corruption. Corruption!'
>
> Archie tried to look shocked and then tried disgusted, not knowing what to say. He liked people to get on with things, Archie. He kind of felt people should just live together, you know, in peace or harmony or something. (190)

There is much positivity in Archie's vague idealism, and it stands as much in opposition to the middle class's use of their own value system in intervening in and shaping the collective culture, as it is confused by Samad's paradoxical and self-defeating ersatz traditionalism. Smith's novel in balancing these contending forces optimistically now positions her text very much as a pre-9/11 narrative, whimsical about fundamentalism, creating a comic motif of Samad's obsession of surviving the last days, and gently satirizing Millat's opposition to his brother, the two contending like children, miming their discontents, their rivalries and their past, confronting the crisis and trauma of their separation.

> Millat uses the filing cabinet as a substitute for another one he despised, fills it with imaginary letters between a scientist Jew and an unbelieving Muslim; Magid puts three chairs together and shines two anglepoise lamps and now there are two brothers in a car, shivering and huddled together until a few minutes later they are separated for ever and a paper plane takes off.
>
> It goes on and on and on.
>
> And it goes to prove what has been said of immigrants many times before now; they are *resourceful*; they make do. They use what they can when they can. (464–5)

Smith is explicit that Magid and Millat risk a dead end in such ongoing confrontation, but adamant that they cannot manage to weave 'their way through Happy Multicultural Land. [...] They left that neutral room as they had entered it: weighed down, burdened, unable to waver from their course or in any way change their separate, dangerous trajectories' (465). Macleod comments astutely that 'Smith's attention to the less soluble problems of postcolonial London [have] been overlooked – problems of identity crises and divided consciousness have *not* disappeared in the cheerful polyphony of the city. At the heart of Smith's novel we find a deeply perplexing, disorientating dynamic which is offered as the quintessence of contemporary London life' (40). However attuned to these dynamics Smith proves, she certainly could not be expected to predict real events, although it seems clear that the novel's ending emphasizes certain historical (ideological) impasse that Irie's child unknowingly parodies. Curiously, it seems subsequently that the reading of the aesthetic emphases of the text may have been transformed by subsequent events, so that Smith's homilies above seem partially undermined by the very tension that she charts; ones which will rupture into a world-changing conflict of views, a larger polarization of ideologies and energies.

As Kevin Lynch says in *What Time Is This Place?* (1972), 'Space and time modify each other: the idea of space is built up by a temporal sequence of scenes; time is enriched by cramming it with spatial experience' (167). I maintain that this can be applied to the meaning of literary spaces, for it is as if the location and dynamic space of Smith's fictionality, the meaning of the lives of the characters and the text's significance for British culture, have been transformed and differently oriented by subsequent events. Current readings are becoming dislocated from earlier times when critics assumed that a liberal consensus seemingly underpinned and guaranteed the subject's life, although Smith does undermine such assumptions subtly. In *White Teeth*, Magid and Irie adopt a silent protest against Samad's objections to celebrating Harvest Festival, and at this time Magid adopts the name Mark Smith as part of what Smith specifies as a larger and 'a far deeper malaise' (151). Magid doesn't just want to be English, simply to assimilate and become part of a broad culture, but aspires to a very specifically middle-class intellectual existence, with cats, maternal cello music, pianos, shiny wood floors, biking holidays in France and a doctor as a father. As Smith informs the reader as a symbol of these aspirations (and one supposes to oppose his father), Magid focuses all his attention on participation in the Harvest Festival, ironically enough to be confronted by the toothless Mr J. P. Hamilton, 'an elderly English bird in Wonderland' (168), whose rhetoric embraces the past of the 'niggers' (171) he has killed in wartime Congo, of 'wogs' (172) when refuting the possibility of a Pakistani in the English army in the Second World War, and ultimately he is both half-mad and obsessed with the fact of losing one's teeth. Curiously it is obsessive brushing of teeth as advised by J. P. Hamilton that epitomizes the Magid who later returns from Bangladesh, after being abducted by his father with

Archie's compliance. The children flee this racist dinosaur, 'tripping over themselves, running to get to a green space, to get to one of the lungs of the city, some place where free breathing was possible' (174). Significantly, the literal space of the city offers nurture, redeems their presence, despite its lesser madnesses. 'These people *announced* their madness – they were better, less scary than Mr J. P. Hamilton – they flaunted their insanity, they weren't half mad and half not, curled around a door frame. They were properly mad in the Shakespearean sense, talking sense when you least expected it' (174). As Smith indicates here lies some of the wisdom of the city, its wisdom not rational. As Arthur G. Neal makes evident in *National Trauma and Collective Memory: Extraordinary Events in the American Experience* (2005), 'One of the major assumptions shattered by September 11 was that the end of the Cold War had provided [...] an increased degree of safety and security' (180), and that this traumatic event also challenges the trust that supposedly safeguarded people through certain norms found in contemporary urban culture (181), a sharing of values that in *White Teeth* convey a residual sense of familiarity and safety, however illusory, for even the mad in Willesden Green appear relatively beneficent.

Public Presences: Traumatological Crises

If 9/11 changed the collective consciousness, its kind of subsequent trauma is unlike that described by Luckhurst in 'Traumaculture'. 'The idea of a "traumatic subject" is peculiarly paradoxical: trauma is, after all held to disaggregate or shatter subjectivity ... To organise an identity around trauma, then, is to premise it on exactly that which *escapes* the subject' (28). Rather, 9/11 evokes the pathological public sense of the traumatic that exposes the victim as spectacle (3–4), which Mark Seltzer describes in 'Wound Culture: Trauma in the Pathological Public Sphere', and engages one in

the large question of the meaning of the trauma or wound in the direction of this coalescence or collapse, of private and public registers: the convergence that makes possible the emergence of something like a pathological public sphere [...] everywhere crossed by the vague and shifting lines between the singularity or privacy of the subject, on the one side, and collective forms of representation, exhibition, and witnessing, on the other. (4)

In this context one can understand the implications of the professions of the two main characters in Pat Barker's *Double Vision* (2003), a sculptor and war correspondent, which roles do not just allow them but impel them to play out their inner fears and concerns as part of their public identities, a context where both the privacy and the stability of the self are subject to extreme external forces. The image of a violated girl in Bosnia haunts the male protagonist, Stephen, partly because of its brutality, but also due to its very public dishonouring of the private, the personal, and that which should be tender and meaningful. In a curious inverse doubling on the day of 9/11 Stephen is further trau-matized by discovering over the phone that his wife is having an affair, an incident discussed below. This represents another conflation of the public and private, a collapse of boundaries. Moreover, in the post-modern, apparently hyper-real world of Martin Amis's somewhat aes-thetically unconvincing *Yellow Dog* (2003), there are dirty bombs with radioactive waste (160), extending the inherent illogical performativity of events reminding one of 9/11, events that engage in the almost total collapse of the public and private, threatening everyone with an underlying logic of the traumatological event. This is almost fathomless for Amis's Western subjects. 'Almost floundering, Brendan said, "The bomber [...] To the bomber, death is not death. And life is not life, either, but illusion"' (151).

In *Al Qaeda and What it Means to be Modern* (2003), John Gray details how 9/11 exposed what he calls 'the fragility of liberal societies' (15), and Halliday identifies therein what he calls 'an *internationalist* approach' (27), a profound 'global crisis that will, if we are lucky, take a hundred years to resolve' (24). In contrast to such readings and the 'real' world quality of 9/11 which is both paradoxically concise and complex, Jill Bennett and Rosanne Kennedy's collection, *World Memory: Personal Trajectories in Global Time* (2003) emphasizes the relativistic, allowing Jill Bennett in '*Tenebrae* after September 11, Art, Empathy, and the Global Politics of Belonging', rather curiously to propose effectively that refugees and asylum seekers should be regar-ded as much as victims as the World Trade Center victims (179), as if this were relevant to (and implicitly thereby situated as a cause of) terrorist violence. Such opposition becomes dialectically meaningful, for indeed Bennett and Kennedy's objections to the relevance of 9/11 can be read as a resistance to the meta-reality of major global events that have the power to displace and dislodge the previously prevalent notions of narcissistic victim-hood. The pair purvey the academic equivalent of a kind of Chalfenism, to adopt Smith's evocation of liberal interventionism, and might well be accused of the worst of kind of Western (late) colonialism, trading upon (and in a sense negation of) the suffering of others. However, in her own contribution at least Kennedy admits that, 'It seemed to me that in some quarters, at least, the impact was felt as profoundly in London as in parts of the US. If this was, indeed, a global tragedy and an attack on trade, the devastating impact in the financial heart of London – where many had lost friends and colleagues – brought this home' (177). Increasingly in fiction such obsessive private concerns are certainly seen to be either superseded or shaped by public ones.

Contextualizing Ian McEwan's *Saturday* (2005)

Aesthetically Luckhurst's pre-millennial individual 'traumaculture' is superseded by a broader post-9/11 traumatological culture, by a sociologically significant disposition that permeates both selfhood and artistic renditions of this perspective, a gradual process of transformation. Fictionally the transformative effects of this global trauma on the British novel can perhaps be best exemplified by the following reading of two specific texts that demonstrate the dynamics of this change in aesthetic and historical mood. First, in a London Square in Jeanette Winterson's *Art and Lies* (1994) one of the author's recognizably archetypal trans-historical female narrators, the poet Sappho, identifies an excess in nature itself, a breaching of the average, which is to be found in a cornucopia of fruitfulness, the materialization of an almost violent beauty (88). Despite the postmodern disruption that one might ascribe to the depredations of late-capitalist society, there remains something Woolfian in the range of consciousness disclosed in shifting identities and locations, and something Arnoldian in a later scene by the seaside, where the narrator notes how rain transforms the water's surface (93). Clearly this aesthetic is not exactly harmonious, but is organized around a reconciliation of woman and the world, with a lingering note of optimism. Second, in a novel around ten years later one sees a more fractious, dissonant apprehension of the world in which such reconciliations are absent. At the beginning of Ian McEwan's *Saturday* (2005), in a similar London Fitzrovian Regency Square to that featured in Winterson's novel, another excessiveness has entered the human world, but one turning towards a more anarchic and destructive violence. In a location identifiable as where Virginia Woolf once lived with her brother is the home of successful surgeon, Henry Perowne. His house overlooks a façade reconstructed after wartime Luftwaffe bombing, as McEwan makes clear, but behind this evocation of past violence and trauma is a submerged awareness of the very history of a city shattered by the war, and of the Woolfian aesthetic reveries that conflict extinguished. There is also a reassertion of certain masculine principles; at the least, an unembarrassed and confident investment in male middle-class identity. McEwan's protagonist awakes from his sleep nakedly finding himself in motion, in the middle of the night being drawn to his window, at a time just prior to the Iraq War. Thus, McEwan encapsulates and symbolizes the uncertain emergence of the present from the past in a narrative full of introspective self-absorption. Perowne's nakedness conveys mankind's vulnerability. Disturbing his reveries is a flaming object in descent, difficult to make out at first, but subsequently identified as a plane, evoking 9/11 eighteen months before when as McEwan writes, 'half the planet watched, and watched again the unseen captives driven through the sky to the slaughter, at which time there gathered round the innocent silhouette of any jet plane a novel association. Everyone agrees, airliners look different in the sky these days, predatory or doomed' (16). Perowne's notion of a penumbra of fear and uncertainty signifies a more general perspective, a post-millennial vulnerability and unease; one that displaces any nuanced idea of what Luckhurst imagines is the significance of the intermediacy of knowingness and unknowingness (33). The retrieval of facts or need to engage with verification procedures confound Perowne precisely because the possibilities of the city have been drawn into the maelstrom of larger, geopolitical events of which he becomes an unwillingly passive observer, the worst condition for this archetypal representative of professional middle-class engagement and knowingness. Worse still for Perowne who regards himself as socially significant he is confronted by brutish will-to-power, part of a recognizably contemporary culture where as Amis indicates in *Yellow Dog*, there is a superficially democratic cult of celebrity, a banalization of experience where even 'People who weren't famous behaved famous' (8).

The Traumatological Self: Matt Thorne *Cherry: A Novel* (2004)

Neither traumatological novels nor traumatological selves entirely abandon an antecedent sense of personal trauma. However, they adopt a very different narrative centre, one concerned comprehensively with both the disruptions of and the very specific (although sometimes imagined) threats to the social self (not always to the individual subject *per se*, and although that may be the case, increasingly the menace is broadly conceived). Such threats purvey materially and ideologically a sense of a larger sociological and historical condition that refuses a reduction to solipsism or self-obsession. Often this entails variously a combination of abjection, marginalization, abuse, violence, fear and so forth as a pathological general cause, although its narration may be far from grandiloquent and may rather be conveyed in a matter of fact fashion.

Hence, this realization may be expressed simply in as mundane fashion as the recognition of what is an almost sociological set of forces that the reader encounters at the beginning of Matt Thorne's *Cherry*:

A Novel (2004), a bizarre male fantasy of desire with grotesque consequences. The protagonist, Steve, a thirty-something teacher with a speech impediment (clearly a symbol of inner conflict and social as well as relationship failure), realizes, 'When all of this started (2003), I lived alone in a dangerous borough of London: My postcode prevented me from doing most things; my credit rating took care of the rest. Unlike the other teachers at my comprehensive, I saw nothing virtuous in this' (3). Here there is no direct sense of fear, of what Kai Erikson in 'Notes on Trauma and Community' describes as *individual trauma*, but rather more of a diffuse feeling, what Erikson identifies as *collective trauma* (187). The threat exists in the interstices of such an urban existence, a pathological obsession with the other.

The externalization of suppressed emotion and identity on the part of Thorne's protagonist is significant, and so commences an unlikely tale of a young, attractive woman, Cherry, sent as a sexual partner after a chance encounter and as part of an unfathomable Faustian bargain by a local businessman, Harry Hollinghurst, in an intertextual reworking of a Fowlesian God-Game. Or so the reader believes, until the final suggestion in Steve's prison cell that the whole Mephistophelian dynamics have been the product of Steve's pathological mind. He has been incarcerated because he has killed his best friend, Tom, and Tom's lover, Mary, because of his desire for Tom's wife, Judith, suggesting a displacing delusionality. Steve's concerns are articulated through imagining and thereby conjuring the whole mystery of Cherry and her disappearance, rather than confronting his inadequacy and his guilt. In inflicting an almost unaccountable set of events, and avoiding them, Steve's provisionality and self-delusions partake of what Seltzer describes:

> The basic uncertainty as to what counts as the 'real foundation' of trauma is bound up with what counts as trauma in the first place. For if trauma is, first, the wound, it is second, a wounding in the absence of a wound: trauma is in effect an effect in search of a cause. (8)

Steve's sense of being wounded himself, both by first his sexual isolation and second on behalf of Judith, allow him to narrate and believe in not only a spurious affair, but to act out a murderous intervention in his friends' lives. The traumatological incorporates the various kinds of logic of the trauma over and above any contracted interiority of selfhood, which as Seltzer explains includes the public pathological sphere, with its inherent uncertainties of 'a sort of crossing-point of the "psycho-social"' (4), and a 'mimetic compulsion' creating 'a sociality bound to pathology' (9).

Traumatological Violence and Fear: Martin Amis, Ian McEwan and Pat Barker

However one might contest theoretically the legitimacy of any literary periodization, the plain fact is that a new century is upon us, one already recognizably distinguishable from the old one in cultural, in aesthetic and in many other senses. As Amis says of the protagonist of *Yellow Dog*, Xan Meo, recovering in hospital from a beating, 'His condition felt like the twenty-first century: it was something you wanted to wake up from – snap out of. Now it was a dream within a dream. And both dreams were bad dreams' (37). This sense transcends what Luckhurst describes as the public displays of grief emanating from the deaths of ninety-five football fans at Hillsborough Stadium in April 1989, and the 'displays of exaggerated, hysterical mourning in English culture – a chain of events that included the death of James Bulger (1994), the massacre of Dunblane (1996), and the death of Diana (1997)' (34), and precisely transcends such feelings because of the psychic and cultural generality of the later, post-9/11 malaise. Traumatological culture actuates social engagement and immersion rather than either Luckhurst Habermasian 'empathetic identification' (35) or his 'traumatic exceptionality' (36). A pervasive traumatological aesthetic represents an edgy, conflicted, fearful world.

Certainly, the notion of the traumatic event serves to inform the underlying motifs in Amis's *Yellow Dog*, with its evocations of entrapment and disaster. Moreover, its focus on the mass media reflects certain key dynamics of the period. In the current age of digital television and global news and entertainment (where the two often seemed blurred) a series of global traumas, including 9/11 to which McEwan alludes explicitly, but additionally the Bali bombs, the Iraq War, the late-2004 Tsunami, the London bombings and the floods in New Orleans have together brutally asserted the material origins of experience, of ideas and conceptions, and the limits of a linguistic determination of historicity. Although narrated, these cannot be reduced to narrative form alone, but signify an externality beyond the proportions of singular selfhood. As ever, although ephemeral in its nature and scintillating in its possibilities, literature co-exists with such hard external realities; it offers a zone of mediation, reflection, and perhaps, as some assert, transcendence. In a text haunted by uncanny manifestations of disaster and conflict, by their strange iterations, McEwan's protagonist perceives in supernatural beliefs 'an excess of the subjective, the ordering of the world in line with your needs, an inability to contemplate your own unimportance' (17). In *Yellow Dog*, Amis has the charmless tabloid journalist, Clint Smoker, survey a symbol of the preceding period's gloomy and insistent orthodoxies: 'the room – the hotel – was postmodern, but darkly, unplayfully so. It seemed that the gunmetal furniture was trying to look like the refrigerator, the television, the safe' (163). Thus, at least symbolically, Amis designates the end of the postmodern, reducing it to a series of stylistic gestures and thereby foregrounding its failings, its paradoxical homogeneity. Post-9/11, many writers conceive that major world events have reshaped both aesthetic and cultural sensibilities. McEwan's narrative reflects upon the impact of the Twin Towers on the protagonist's 16-year-old son who begins to become aware of the international scene, and on Perowne, who has tried unsuccessfully to think of it as a historical aberration: 'No going back. The nineties are looking like an innocent decade, and who would have thought it at the time? Now we breathe a different air' (32). As Macleod comments, this is a 'novel about living in London in the aftermath of September 11 and the new forms of consciousness which have been created in the new world order' (45).

The single day of McEwan's novel, an explicitly Woolfian point of reference, is that of the protest against the Iraqi war, but more important for Perowne is his apparently glib response to a road-traffic accident occasioned by the march in London that leads to a physical assault on his family and the potential humiliation and rape of his daughter. Violence and threat abound. The rupture of consensus (and familiar expectations) is symbolized by the disruptive conjunction of events, personal relations in turmoil, the incommensurability of one's fate, the inability of individuals in predicting occurrences, and McEwan's visions of the grotesque in Baxter and his entourage. As we shall see, some combination of at least some of these elements reflect recent narratives of trauma, as novelists begin to explore personal, historical and cultural moments in the light of this conjunction of perspectives, responding to the events in New York in 2001 that Barker describes in *Double Vision* through the explicit recollections of her protagonist, foreign correspondent Stephen Sharkey.

> When he closed his eyes, Stephen's brain filled with images of shocked people covered in plaster dust. Grey dust blocking his nostrils, caking his eyelids. Gritty on the floor of the hotel lobby, trampled up the stairs and along the corridors to his room, where the television screen domesticated the roar and the tumult, the dust, the debris, the thud of bodies hitting the ground, reduced all this to silent images, played and replayed, and played again in a vain attempt to make the day's events credible: the visual equivalent of what you heard repetitively on the street: Christ, Holy shit, Oh my God. (96–7)

Ironically, on this day his telephone call home precipitates the end of his marriage, literally discovering his wife in bed with another man. Significantly, Stephen copes with his career, chiefly reporting on wars and conflict, until this point. However, subsequently in Afghanistan, he suffers a breakdown after the death of Ben, a war photographer, with whom Stephen has shared numerous assignments and the experience of New York on 9/11. He decides to write, retreating to a cottage owned by his doctor brother, Robert, coincidentally near to Kate, Ben's widow. Instead of dwelling upon his presence at Ben's shooting, rather Stephen returns to his memory of the conjunction in New York of the revelation of marital infidelity and Ben's compulsion, having showered off the dust of the event, to watch images of that very event on television. Both are drawn to the televisual representations, discussing the signification of what they are experiencing.

> 'I can't stop watching it.'
> 'No, nor me. Ridiculous, isn't it. When it's out there.' He sat down. 'Are you going back out?'
> 'Yes, in a few minutes. I just had to get the dust off.' [. . .]
> Ben said, 'Do *you* think the world just changed?'
> 'I think America will.'
> 'I think things have changed. I mean real change. That was designed to be a photo-opportunity, and what have I done? I've spent the whole bloody day photographing it. Along with everybody else. Because we can't escape from the need for a visual record. The appetite for spectacle. And they've used that against us, just as they've used our own technology against us.
> 'So what are you saying? We shouldn't cover it?'
> 'I don't know what I am saying. But I know something happened here – and it isn't just that the Americans found out that they're vulnerable too.' (100–1)

Barker uses their conversation to suggest that any transformation might be elusive, but that it remains an inherently profound one.

Barker's juxtaposition of past and present, a multi-chronic scheme, emphasizes the disruption of lives by other traumatic events, and yet suggests that nevertheless a new consciousness has been set in motion. Having made 9/11 a first-hand experience, such a survival of literal traumas recurs in the text in more familiar contexts. The novel commences with Ben's widow, sculptor Kate, suffering debilitating injuries in a car accident, and as she learns to walk she reflects that Ben's photographs of landscapes all possessed 'the same brooding darkness in them. They were supposed to be peaceful, these photographs, a break from the subjects he spent most of his life pursuing, but they weren't' (64). Stephen enters into his unlikely relationship with teenager, Justine and he learns to value love as a result of his affair. It is as if the world for everyone is reconfigured and any former optimism has been negated by recent events, but moreover each character is forced by external circumstances into a reappraisal of the past and simultaneously the present. The new trajectories and differently centred positivism that the central characters acquire is always fragile and threatened, not so much by any provisionality of meaning, but more by a sense of literal threat, the possibility of violence no longer safely contained. In the church Kate observes again the faces of Green Men that she had noticed at Ben's funeral, apparently symbols of renewal, but signifying something more malevolent. 'What faces: savage, angry, tormented, desperate, sly, desolate' (29).

A subplot is the apparent mystery of Peter, a former convict employed by Kate to help her in a large-scale sculptural project, and his obsession with her. The novel even offers a red herring of Peter's cross-dressing at night in Kate's workshop in her clothes. When Stephen's adolescent girlfriend, Justine, is attacked viciously by thieves who believe Robert and his wife, Beth, have left an empty house while on their reconciliatory holiday, initially it seems likely that Peter is one of the perpetrators. Justine's vulnerability and the fear of drowning to which Stephen admits when taking a boat trip with her at the end of the novel affirm the traumatological uncertainties central to the text. Just after the attack on Justine there is a significant scene, when in his study Justine's father cannot rid himself of a desire for revenge, despite both his profession as a clergyman, and his prayers. He looks at a symbolic print where 'William Penn is concluding his treaty with the Indians, sealed with an oath and never broken, but the struggle against violence has simply moved back into the individual human mind, and those eyes tell you that victory is far from certain' (270).

A historical sense of the continuity of violence underpins the traumatological, as if a post-9/11 malaise responds to a general underlying fear and foreboding. However, unlike in wartime, with its sense of the need to sustain normative forms of behaviour collectively, the social determination of the traumatological self appears more diffuse, being more like an uncertainty principle potentially shared by all, at least unconsciously. Bosnia is Barker's correlative of suffering, but it becomes evident to Stephen that the changing world has made the meaning of such events immanent and less remote. Stephen's dream-like recollection of a raped girl, her corpse among the rats, segues into the first meeting with Justine, sent with towels from his brother's

206 THE CONTEMPORARY BRITISH NOVEL

house. Only at the end with his fragile, unlikely love can Stephen face
the facts of Ben's death, the wasteful sacrifice for the right photo-
graphic shot, forfeiting life for an aesthetic obsession.

Considering Andrea Levy's *Small Island* (2004)

Andrea Levy's *Small Island* (2004) is concerned with large-scale disruption and the change in consciousness engendered by the traumatological aspects of the period around and during the Second World
War. It is about the challenges faced by individuals as their historical
certainties dissolve, and concrete threats impinge upon their lives, in a
world characterized by a backdrop of violence: the bombing of Britain
in the 1940s, and the battle in the Far East. Levy's immensely complex
novel revolves around several literal sites and psychic locations of
traumatic encounters and of loss, from a hurricane in the Caribbean
that reveals first the broken body of the white American headmaster
who runs the local school and through Hortense's indiscretion the
relationship of Michael Roberts with the dead man's American wife, to
wartime experiences of the London Blitz which has profound and
liberatory effects upon Queenie Bligh, who also has an evening of
passion with Michael before his posting. His first Caribbean affair, his
subsequent enlistment in the air force and his departure not only
frustrate Hortense's childish passion for him, but precipitate a crisis of
his family which later leads to his denial of his parents to Queenie. For
all the tenderness and comedy of the text, melancholic substrata
persist.

The various strands are interwoven around one that concerns Gilbert Joseph, another wartime pilot whose return to the Caribbean finds
him marrying the feisty Hortense, and returning first alone to Britain.
The country is war weary, a postcolonial environment suffering a
general sense of loss and unsettlement, a common thread for most of
the characters, all of whom are displaced by war, by the end of Empire
and whose lives are shaped according to various personal quests. The
text's synthesis of a sense of historical ambivalence and personal
incomprehension seems apt for as Caruth writes:

> Trauma consists not only in having confronted death but in
> *having survived, precisely, without knowing it.* What one returns to
> in the flashback is not the incomprehensibility of one's near
> death, but in the very incomprehensibility of one's own survival.
> Repetition, in other words, is not simply the attempt to grasp that
> one has almost died but, more fundamentally and enigmatically,
> the very attempt *to claim one's own survival.* (64)

This provides the informing concept explaining both the power and the effect of the analeptic structure of Levy's novel, the flashbacks very largely exploring this disjuncture, one that separates Hortense from the other characters in Britain, not having directly experienced the war which so determines the post-war consciousness. In the war Queenie deals with 'the bombed-out who'd had the cheek to live through the calamity of a world blown to bits' (278). For Macleod, 'Levy offered the most sustained focus to date upon migrant women's experience of postwar London often missing from London writing of the 1950s' (43), and he sees as positive the outcome of the relationship between Michael and Queenie, despite the fact she has to abandon the child for adoption by Gilbert and Hortense which Macleod interprets as Queenie's 'act of love and compassion', although he admits it remains 'both extremely moving and remarkably bleak' (44).

The novel's mood remains sombre. Traumatic moments of death and parting permeate all of the episodes of the novel. Arthur, Bernard's father, dies in a riot of GIs caused by Gilbert's initial refusal to be parted from Queenie in a wartime cinema. In India Bernard, imprisoned for losing his rifle, mourns for Maxi and seven other RAF comrades he is unable to save, and who are burnt alive apparently by Hindu insurgents as part of their campaign for freedom. Later in London in 1948, unable to bid Hortense farewell as she takes her child, for Queenie the infant disappears from her life, just as during the war Michael, an old man and a corner pub disappear instantly and troublingly when a German rocket explosion blows her off her feet while pursuing Michael with his forgotten battered leather wallet with its mementoes. Although Levy's novel was generally regarded as being positive it can be read as a very often pessimistic narrative, abjuring any final optimism, especially with the abandonment of the mixed-race child by Queenie essentially on racial grounds, unable to face her loss, and as Hortense realizes, the child's only legacy from her real mother is tears. Poignant personally for all involved, a touching scene, allegorically this may be intended to sustain a notion of the fractured fault-lines at the heart of our contemporary culture, and recent events hardly suggest conciliation. In this sense, Levy's choice of highly troubled, embattled times for much of her setting, is doubly significant.

Traumatological Families: Nadeem Aslam, Ali Smith and Toby Litt

The next group of novels analysed is concerned primarily with the multiple traumas that lie at the heart of the family, not simply in the sense of personal identity, but as part of a larger cultural cartography and interrogation. Charting the effects of migration and Islamic culture on women in the East End of London, Monica Ali literally ends *Brick Lane* (2003) on a note of freedom, where Asian women throw off the oppression of their patriarchal cultures.

> Nanzeen turned round. To get on the ice physically – it hardly seemed to matter. In her mind she was already there.
> She said, 'But you can't skate in a sari.'
> Razia was already lacing her boots. 'This is England,' she said. 'You can do whatever you like.' (492)

Ali's account of passion and an ill-matched marriage is a comedy of social observation very much concerned with individual failings. It remains optimistic, especially concerning the power and imagination of women, seen as a force for change. Without sounding too pessimistic, unfortunately this seems to exemplify an overly optimistic kind of humanism especially given the current political climate. Moreover, almost troublingly although powerfully, certain key writers from immigrant communities seem to be shifting toward a more pessimistic world-view, including a notable novel, Nadeem Aslam's *Maps for Lost Lovers* (2004), which is an immensely complex book full of observations, symbols and events that critique migrant culture and colonialism. Very much in contrast to Ali, in a highly symbolic novel, Aslam weaves a lyrical and descriptive narrative concerning chiefly the different perspectives of a Pakistani family living within a multicultural migrant community in an unnamed town in Britain. Shamas, the educated and liberally inclined father, a Muslim whose father was a Hindu orphan adopted while wandering during partition, works for the Council for Racial Equality and at weekends in the local park runs an esoteric bookshop inherited from a friend. Michael O'Connor in 'Writing Against Terror – Nadeem Aslam' records the novelist's Joycean influence, and to whom Aslam asserts his admiration of 'How beautifully *The Dead* takes seemingly minor details of everyday life and turn them into a howl about the despair of being alive' (n. pag.).

The novel is throughout a nuanced and fulsome account of the quotidian co-ordinates of alienation, ennui, fear, cultural perversity and ignorance in a migrant ethnically mixed community. According to O'Connor:

> Small details in *Maps for Lost Lovers* have violent consequences, such as a woman being seen in the company of the wrong man, or the criticism of elements within the community. There are no terrorist bombs, nor Al-Qaeda links in Aslam's novel. Nothing as sensational, but rather a mosaic of violence on a smaller, local level, of intimidation, and murder. The Pakistani community in

the novel live in a nameless, shapeless place, at once in England and yet not there. It's a bleak picture, particularly in the current climate. There is no integration in the novel, England, as it were, is absent. 'England is not absent from my novel – only the WHITE England is absent,' Aslam corrects, carefully. (n. pag.)

Aslam's strategies are not simply aesthetic, but ideological, and the fate and meaning of each life and its limitations intersects. At the novel's beginning Kiran, a Sikh calls to persuade Shamas to help her lift her bedridden father from the floor after a fall. Such helplessness is a recurrent underlying motif. A younger Kiran has wanted to marry Shamas's brother-in-law thirty years before, but in Karachi she is intercepted by a brother and an arranged marriage hastily organized for her impassioned Muslim lover. A year previously Shamas's wife Kaukab has attempted to prevent the two former lovers from meeting, despite her brother by then being a widower. On this unannounced visit Kiran asks after Shamas's son married to an English girl, a situation horrific to his mother and an enigma for his father.

> 'They *were* married, but are now divorced.' They've set off again, along the road through the cherry trees towards Kiran's house. 'I can't really remember the last time I saw the grandchild.'
>
> Seven years old, the little boy is 'half Pakistani and half ... er ... er ... er ... human' or so a child on his English mother's side is reported to have described him in baffled groping innocence.' (10)

Coincidentally, like Shamas, Kiran and her father are part of the human emigrant legacy of the frenzy and bloodshed at India's partition, of its ethnic cleansing, as such actions would later be referred. The dynamics of division recur, and the book's cycle takes the world from winter to winter as if to reinforce its pessimistic mood.

Set in what appears to Asian visitors to be a prosperous Britain (4–5), the plot revolves around the disappearance of his younger brother Jungu and Jungu's lover Chanda. Murder is suspected especially as Chanda's brothers, Chotta and Barra, disapprove of the relationship because under Muslim law she is not yet divorced. Ironically given his fate, in the racist, confrontational years of the 1970s Jungu's arrival had illuminated and lightened the family's burden (11). The knowledge that cannot be certified turns Shamas's narrative into a traumatic encounter, unable to grasp either the certainty or magnitude of Jungu's death. His constant return to the possibility represents what Caruth describes as 'the painful repetition of the flashback [that] can only be understood as the absolute inability of the mind to avoid an unpleasurable event that has not been given psychic meaning in any way' (59). Kaukab's responses are channelled by her narrow, even slavish adherence to an ill-informed notion of her faith, so much so that at times she emerges as almost monstrous, at others worthy of sympathy.

Another young Muslim woman has a Hindu lover; Shamas sees the pair frequently, although he cannot help sufficiently to change their fate whatever his liberal empathy. She is killed by a cleric attempting to drive out a spirit during an exorcism arranged for by her parents. 'The girl was taken into the cellar and the beatings lasted several days with the mother and father in the room directly above reading the Koran out loud' (185). As O'Connor concludes,

> The novel's title is misleading. Whereas maps lay out a clearer path, here, the obstacles of religious strictness and prejudice seem insurmountable. Not only does this rigidity prevent the narrative from progressing smoothly, it also highlights the isolation of the community in a dualistic world. Islam is depicted as a compassionless religion. Its hypocrisies over women's rights and the injustices of the 'organized crime of arranged marriages' are laid bare. (n. pag.)

Certainly Aslam details the indignities of the girl's abuse. Religiosity, its limitations, and its constraints on women are motifs throughout, and Aslam is highly critical of such religious orthodoxy. The novel ends by returning to the brothers at the scene, dismembering their sister, only to discover Jungu's body hidden by coloured clothes and a peacock's body. And finally Shamas reflects upon the fate of his lover, Suraya, trapped in a traditional frame of thought and behaviour, only released from this by a further deception.

> And now he hopes she *has* become pregnant by him during the summer, that her new husband – thinking he himself is the father – is leaving her in peace because of it.
> Shamas's child is already saving her, already lessening the amount of pain in this Dsht-e-Tanhaii called the planer earth. (367)

Ironically, Shamas soon dies, and the boy paid to pretend to be Jungu by Chanda's family, a task he escapes, reading of the death in the snow-covered streets of winter, senses calamity, a negation of the symbols of rebirth, engendering an archetypal, archaic symbol of sterility. In the movement from Ali's literary disposition to that of Aslam one senses a growing disquietude, a prevailing unease. The latter's novel matches the very kind of sensibility that Piotr Sztompka says, in 'The Trauma of Social Change: A Case of Postcommunist Societies', characterizes a more collective trauma, in that it can be:

> expressed as complex *social moods*, characterized by a number of collective emotions, orientations, and attitudes. First, there is a general climate of anxiety, insecurity, and uncertainty [...]. Second there is a prevailing syndrome of distrust, both toward people and institutions [...]. Third, there is a disorientation concerning collective identity. Fourth, there is widespread apathy, passivism, and helplessness. Fifth, there is pessimism concerning the future, matched with nostalgic images of the past. (166)

This approximates closely the framework of the characterization in Aslam's novel, emphasized by lyrical, allegorical and symbolic tendencies. The pastoral image of the park and certain nostalgic impulses prove insufficient to assuage the underlying traumatological elements that create conflict in a bleak suburban setting.

Two novels demonstrating another traumatological emphasis are Ali Smith's *The Accidental* (2006) and Toby Litt's *Ghost Story* (2004), both featuring the apparent perversity of female behaviour within white middle-class environments, foregrounding conflict and intimacy in the apparently narrow bounds of domesticity. *The Accidental* is prefaced by a number of epigraphs, including one from John Berger's *The Shape of a Pocket* (2001), made even more pertinent by events subsequent to Berger's novel. 'Between the experience of living a normal life at this moment on the planet and the public narratives being offered to give a sense to that life, the empty space, the gap, is enormous' (quoted in Smith, n. pag.). Smith frames and thus defers her main narrative, mystifying its status and validity, for as Sophie Ratcliffe writes in 'Life in Sonnet Form' the book 'begin[s] with a frame narrator, the mysterious Alhambra, who was conceived on a table in a cinema cafe in 1968' (19). On vacation in a rented home in Norfolk, 12-year-old Astrid Smart (prior to her parents' divorce she is Berenski) obsesses over video-recording among other things each dawn with her digital camera. Her family's lives are disrupted by a stranger; according to Ratcliffe, 'Amber arrives, establishes herself as a house-guest, and sets about simultaneously entrancing and disrupting the Smart family' (19). In the background is the turbulence of Britain at war in Iraq, with the news of the death of Saddam Hussein's sons. 'Magnus looks at the photos of the dead faces on the screen. They were tyrants = all sorts of torturing, raping, systematic or random killings' (147). These concerns contrast the stultifying stillness of the Norfolk countryside, and evoke in Marcus thoughts of the broken man his father has become, and his complicity in breaking the spirit of a fellow school-girl.

Initially Michael presumes the interloper is a friend of his wife, Astrid's mother, Eve, while Eve thinks she is one in a long line a young students from his university classes with whom Michael has affairs. Eve is in crisis concerning the latest in a series of wartime historical accounts she publishes for a living, each of which bizarrely imagines the lives wartime victims might have had had they lived (82). Marcus, Eve's son, is a recluse, suffering from guilt about editing the picture of a girl at his school who has committed suicide after the nude photograph was distributed. There is a sense of fragmentation extending beyond the personal, and even without Amber, as Ratcliffe says of this family from Islington, 'All seem disconnected from each other' (19). Amber's intrusion represents an attempt to undermine and challenge Eve's authority, the family's identity and the pattern of their lives, literally by smashing Astrid's video camera, by instructing her how to avoid supermarket security to shoplift, by seducing Marcus both in the attic and in the local church, and even flirting with Michael only to reject him. Her strange looks are also seen differently by various family members, indicating her chameleon status. For Michael, 'She looked like the dishevelled, flower-strewn girl in Botticell's Sping' (76). Even Eve's accent is enigmatic, regarded as Scandinavian by Michael (65), Irish or American by Astrid (31), and Scottish by Eve (91). With his student seductions, increasingly Michael seems anachronistic, ending up an object of self-parodying 'end-of-pier jokes about him [...]' (259), living up to his 'History Man' image, once again seducing a young female, and threatening his career. The world's new moralistic order impacts upon such self-destructive urges. Whatever the irony, subject to such tensions throughout the narrative the family inhabit the world each from a different position of vulnerability, under threat on many fronts. Suspended on half-paid leave, Michael's final illusion is of being freed by his suspension to climb mountains, buying books on the topic. In this he defies the common sense, logic and overall reality principle to which the narrative returns. 'There was no way on earth Michael Smart, at his age, could go up the side of a mountain' (264).

One evening joining Amber for a drive, Eve tells the story of her first chance encounter with Adam, her first husband; volubly Amber rejects Eve as boring, self-obsessed and predictable, inducing fear by driving immensely fast. Eve realizes soon that Amber has lied to her concerning her guilt at killing a young child in a road accident while driving, an incident Amber has invented. Amber is an amoral, sociopath; her qualities are clarified in this moment, emphasizing that her world is not provisional, but like Michael's based on elaborate deceit, hers being manipulative and comfortable with concrete evasions of the world. And yet perversely Amber may serve as a force for renewal;

both she and Michael in their duplicity represent yet one more, at least unconscious attack upon the prevailing postmodernist relativism. These events serve as a catalyst for Eve, but more so a kiss from Amber. 'Eve was moved beyond belief by the kiss. The place beyond belief was terrifying. There, everything was different, as if she had been gifted with a new kind of vision, [...] to reveal the spaces between what she usually saw and the way things were tacked temporarily together with thin thread across these spaces' (202). Eve takes the initiative, catching Amber by surprise by ejecting her, abandoning her family in the house apparently stripped clean by Amber and her associates.

Finally Eve travels to visit the New England home of her dead father, a rebirth where she gate-crashes the home of an American family, mimicking the abrupt interventions of Amber. The novel ends with the framing narrative, an admixture or collage of cultural, filmic and historical references to the meaning of the Alhambra, its Moorish, Arab, Berber, Muslim origins and circuitous influence on Western culture, with its aesthetic impulse toward otherness. The novel ends enigmatically, 'It's a derelict old cinema packed with inflammable filmstock. Got a light? See? Careful. I'm everything you ever dreamed' (306). Smith positions the traumatological within the realm of one's underlying fears and desires. The cardinal meaning of the novel lies in its use of the family paradigmatically, representing a social order challenged by contemporary mores and belief systems, hedged in by a culture that without renewal is under threat.

In 'Possessing Toby Litt's *Ghost Story*', Leigh Wilson, a contemporary literary academic critic, variously reveals her role as Litt's partner (110), the traumatic loss of pregnancies by the couple that underlie the novel and are featured in the first section 'Story', and she also argues for the power of experiential, first readerly understandings of fiction. Wilson contrasts Litt's notion of an 'enraptured reading' with a 'professionalized' one (110). As Lucy Dallas says in 'The Arc of Grief', 'The opening section, called simply "Story", is calculated to baffle. The author is chasing a hare through the British Library – metaphorically, and then literally' (23). Wilson concludes, concerning the 'Jamesian' qualities of the second section 'Ghost Story' identified by reviewers, that such an interpretation is 'not a misreading, but it mistakes the extent to which such devices are themselves an attempt to write a second reading to contain the pain of the first' (113). Leaving London, after the initial viewing and purchase of a house on the coast with her partner, Paddy, it is evident they are escaping the trauma of losing a baby during a miscarriage.

The seaside house seems alive, full of movement and noise, but soon Agatha is apparently haunted by their new home. She becomes reclusive, abjures any normal pattern of sleep or waking, and this withdrawal, as does her agoraphobia, seemingly in part a response to larger cultural, existential conditions. The fear is diffuse, inexact, but omnipresent, another symbol of the age. In his use of the house Litt utilizes in part the sensibilities outlined by Gaston Bachelard in *The Poetics of Space* (1994) where a house is not simply a literal or geometric object, but rather understood in part symbolically, 'But the complex of reality is never definitively resolved. The house itself, when it starts to live humanly, does not lose all its "objectivity"' (48). However, the warmth of intimacy of the new house becomes malevolent, and becomes akin to the house Bachelard describes 'Like the house of breath, the house of wind and voice is a value that hovers on the frontier between reality and unreality' (60).

This unease permeates Agatha's unconscious self, and she dreams of Max's abduction, of his death, and nevertheless on awakening she realizes she has orgasmed in her sleep. She is convinced that, 'She wasn't, as people sometimes said, afraid of the fear, so much as the fear of the fear – or the fear of the fear of the fear' (52). In this odd domestic crisis Agatha inhabits an utterly contemporary sense of displaced, decentred terror. Whereas her pregnancy with Max had 'given her physical confidence', she feels ravaged by the second pregnancy, evoking in Paddy a sense of guilt (76), and finally a morbidity overcomes her, fantasizing about Paddy's death (57). As Dallas concludes:

> Our sympathies are with him but our attention is on Agatha and the strange imperatives that govern her life: she cannot walk through the front door, she is compelled to listen to the house's noises for half an hour at a time. Litt tracks the inner journey of this intelligent, neurotic, distraught woman and brings the reader round to an understanding of her near-madness. (23)

Agatha refuses to relate to her first-born, Max. After the move she abandons him to her mother, until on her return she attempts to drown him in his bath. As Wilson indicates, as unlikely as the rescue by Paddy may seem aesthetically, Litt construes this as exactly what the reader requires (114–15), and thereby charts the cultural hankering for and doubts concerning redemption in post-9/11 culture.

The house's mysterious cellar for Agatha represents the unknown, the alien and her unconscious terror, undermining her. 'Agatha no longer felt convinced of her own persona: Agatha, Aggie, Mummy. The house she realised, was full and had been for days, nights, of different versions of her; sometimes she walked in upon herself at her absolute worst, keening almost inhumanly on the bathroom floor' (91). That the overall disquietude and Agatha's traumatological presence both derive from the domestic sphere, from the very fabric of the house, can be regarded as constituting not only something symbolic, but part of the novel's allegorical possibility. Thus it represents and articulates the depth and profundity of the malaise permeating Britain as part of a contested, changing contemporary Western culture traumatized by that very change, of which by the end Max becomes both a symbol and a paradigm. Agatha hallucinates that Paddy returns to save him, but in fact Agatha herself does so instinctively. As Paddy ruminates concerning their son, ' "He *has* changed," Paddy said, "and I don't think for the better. Whatever he is, it's our fault, yours and mine; we have to cope" ' (221). Agatha responds that they require redemption, and after they attend the funeral of Paddy's father, Paddy himself confronts the sense of 'terror' and yet simultaneously the excitement that Max will have to face in even the most mundane and yet exhilarating aspects of the world (224–5). And finally 'Aggie, too, felt for the first in a long time, exhilarated by the possible dangers of the world, and of her dangerous presence in it. The world would remain with her, but she would express herself – from now on – by joyous resistance and if not that by stubborn participation' (225).

Thoroughly British Dystopias: J. G. Ballard, Rupert Thomson and Will Self

This final section considers three dystopias, each of them a satirical depiction of contemporaneity, but each far too complex to outline fully: J. G. Ballard's *Kingdom Come* (2006), Rupert Thomson's *Divided Kingdom* (2005) and Will Self's *The Book of Dave: A Revelation of the Recent Past and the Distant Future* (2006). Ballard and Thomson's settings are the immediate future, whereas Self combines the present and far distant future. All are quintessentially British, displaced visions of the traumatological threat within aspects of the present. Moreover, all of these texts are concerned with the logic and economy of fundamentalism, of beliefs that constrain and narrow human possibilities through violence and coercion. The contemporary parallels that inform these fictions are self-evident.

Intriguingly Ballard, who might be considered Self's *éminence grise*, centres *Kingdom Come* on the experiences of the kind of archetypal psychiatrist so familiar in Self's work, Dr Maxted, who is based in Brooklands, a London suburb near the M25. Ballard explores the meaning of an emergent British fascism which is characterized by local sports clubs, of spectators rather than those participating in sport, St George's flags and in particular a local shopping centre, the huge

Metro-Centre, modelled on the Millennium Dome. Ballard's narrator, Richard Pearson, is a redundant advertising executive, thus professionally concerned with a contemporary consumerism which is established as the driving force of this new belief system, where its adherents previously according to Ursula LeGuin in 'Revolution in the Aisles', in this 'paradise of consumerism, have nothing to do but consume, and their consumerism is consummate' (16). This dystopia conjures casual mass violence, alienation, commodity fetishism and racial attacks as a fatal synthesis for a new emergent, recognizably post-Thatcher middle class. The exigencies of consumerism have further divided society, leaving individuals bored, vacant and vulnerable, but also dangerous, and always in a collective sense volatile and potentially violent. These are familiar Ballardian themes, but the malaise is much more collective and far more subliminal than in his previous texts; this mood or disposition is compared by certain of the novel's characters to the fascism of the 1930s. Ostensibly Pearson seeks an explanation for his father's death in a hail of bullets in the shopping centre, but he discovers locally a layer of pathology and hatred. He is present as a sense of ill-defined malaise helps engender a new virtual political populism without any policies, centred around a second-rate actor on the shopping centre's cable television channels.

> People are deliberately re-primitivizing themselves. They yearn for magic and unreason, which served them well in the past, and might help again. They're keen to enter a new Dark Age. The lights are on, but they're retreating into the inner darkness, into superstition and unreason. The future is going to be a struggle between vast systems of competing psychopathies. (105)

Pearson himself, as LeGuin says, 'has no access to work worth doing or any bond but sex; he is totally alienated' (16). Despite the novel's final return to an individual perspective and the apparent triumph of conventional forces, it retains a broadly traumatological tenor, concluding pessimistically 'One day there would be another Metro-Centre and another desperate and deranged dream' (280). Crucially Ballard captures something of the public character of the ideological interplay of almost subliminal opinions and almost hysterical events that seems increasingly to characterize the post-9/11 world, the blurred distinction of the private and the ideological realm, where conflict is personalized and irrationally impulsive.

In Thomson's *Divided Kingdom*, political events supersede personal predispositions or views. It opens with the apparent abduction of eight-year-old Mathew Micklewright, who will be renamed Thomas Parry, taken from his parental home, in a scene reminiscent of media images of recent episodes of ethnic cleansing and evoking those of the Holocaust. The novel's premise is that in an increasingly socially fractured and conflicted Britain (the setting is evident from the novel's map on the inside covers) the government divides the capital, the country and the population into four republics which quarter Britain according to the dictates of an apparently arbitrary system, and as Michael Sadler comments in 'A Sanguinary Tale':

> Each [area is] dedicated to a homogeneous citizenry corresponding to one of the four personality types adumbrated by the premodern theory of the humours. Individuals are given personality tests and forcibly transferred to the republic matching their type, be it choleric, phlegmatic, melancholic, or sanguine. This might seem arbitrary and bizarre – but we are meant to reflect that it is no more so than contemporary calls for division along cultural, political, or religious lines. (20)

The scheme is elaborate and ironic, but overall it serves to parody the fixations accorded to nationalist, fundamentalist, ethnic and other extreme products of a generation and as Sadler indicates it also 'tackles identity politics' (20). After 'The Rearrangement', as the separation of families is described, the sanguine whose dominant humour is blood are considered optimistic, even tempered and constructive, must reside in the Red Quarter, whose capital is Pneuma; the empathetic, passive and indecisive are categorized phlegmatic and inhabit the Blue Quarter, its capital named Aquaville; aggressive, impulsive people and those prone to excess whose dominant humour is yellow bile are considered choleric, and assigned to live in the Yellow Quarter whose capital is Thermopolis; and finally melacholics, dominated by black bile, characterized by introspection, pessimism, and an inclination towards intellectualism reside in the Green Quarter, whose capital is Cledge. By utilizing an arbitrary scheme to assign fundamental characteristics Thomson undermines the essentialism of nationalist, ethnic and other categorizations of a typology of interest that have so dominated late-twentieth-century thought, and have rebounded in other even more aggressive delineations by fundamentalists.

As a trusted government employee at the Ministry, Parry protects his adoptive father and sister, Victor and Marie, who become exempted from the testing of character and views. He is allowed to travel to Aquaville for a conference where he meets delegates from all of the quarters. He also encounters the Bathysphere, a bizarre club, for which he is given a card. He is instructed to choose a door. 'You're choosing without knowing what you're choosing. You're taking a chance. You're going into the unknown' (116). Clearly this is intended to convey the power of the mind and its suppressed knowledge, of the kind that all authoritarian and fundamentalist creeds seek to erase or control. He faces his forgotten, effaced past. First he sees one of the boys from the home to which he was taken on separation from his parents and where as children they had been inculcated with their new characters according to the dictates of 'The Rearrangement'. On his second visit he has a vivid vision of his mother from before his reallocation.

The conference delegates are transferred for a surprise trip to the Yellow Quarter, where after a bomb, Parry who is desperate to return to the Bathysphere, uses the confusion to disappear and attempt to return to the Blue Quarter, which he does circuitously, only to be arrested and reclassified by officials there. He is deported to the Green Quarter where he lives for a while, encountering eventually a record of his two parents, now dead. Thus he encounters all of the quarters, and his past, until finally living and travelling with the White People, mutes who communicate telepathically. He sees them hunted and slaughtered. Saved by Odell Burfoot, who has the ability to appear invisible like a shape-shifter, he returns home with her, only to discover the authorities have been monitoring him, gathering information and using his experiences. After Odell's boss, Adrian Croy, is arrested Parry decides to try to save her. And yet significantly he will have to adapt the system which persists, and therefore the novel ends enigmatically. As Sadler says the novel 'interrogates the scope and limits of human identity, the necessities and restrictions of social cohesion, the yearning for mystery and fear of the unknown' (20). The borders serve as an analogy for all belief systems and coercive regimes, at times reassuring and convincing, but finally constrictive and oppressive. Parry learns of their permeability and artificiality, given that they can only be historically constituted. The reader recognizes the authoritarian impulses that threaten the world currently in many guises.

Self's *The Book of Dave* is far too long (at almost 500 pages) and too complex to summarize fully, but essentially the text projects a future where the ranting of an early twenty-first century London cabdriver, Dave Rudman, during and after his divorce with the loss of his son, become the basis of a future religion. Dave has had his ravings printed onto metal sheets and they are retrieved centuries later from the site of his new wife's garden in Hampstead. During his madness, Dave believes he is instructed by his god. In this distant future global warming has caused the seas to rise and has marooned Hampstead, now known as the Isle of Ham, and England or Ing's capital is New London. On Ham the locals raise and slaughter motos, partly human beasts who are the result of twentieth-century genetic engineering. They can communicate in a childlike fashion, although often seemingly their comments are profound. Carl Dévúsh escapes to New London in a search for the father, Simon, who was sent there to be punished, and who has returned unbeknown to Carl in secret with the knowledge that the religion texts were recanted by Dave, which knowledge constitutes a heresy. Both Thomson and Self use the notion of a quest which allows an epiphany or revelation for the individual, but in both the social order is unaffected. In some ways Self's satire of the fundamentalist nature of religion is more direct and explicit than Thomson's. Dave is a sceptic, running into an old Muslim school-friend, Faisal, and is surprised first that he is running a restaurant rather than having qualified as a doctor, and second at his religiosity. Ironically as a future messiah, Dave is dismissive of the religious views of Faisal and other fundamentalist Christian characters like his aunt.

In the future the adherents to the new religion insist their holy text is the given, unalterable word, and the critique of current funda-mentalisms is self-evident. The two time sequences are interwoven: the future period, according to the new religion Dave has spawned, runs from 523 to 524 A.D. (After Dave); and Dave's vicissitudes and madness from December 2001 until October 2003, which allows Dave to recall the legacy of the Thatcherite past and its collapse. Self uses this to comment narratorially acerbically on the Thatcherite legacies, while Dave's ranting commentary is italicized.

> At the beginning of the year the cabbie had been clearing a minimum of seven hundred pounds every week. *A flat fucking news, no joke, mate, double-bloody-bubble fer Sundays ...* Then BCCI collapsed. *Gang of fucking coke heads, it never looked like a bank to me anyway, I remember ferrying those dodgy wallahs to their gaff on the Cromwell Road, all smirk an' no bloody tips ...* And the unemployment figures cranked up to three million. (202)

In the future, as Michael Caines writes in 'Nu Lundun', 'people who seek moral certainty and dogma will discover individual and collective understanding in a single surviving book – a book containing a sacred text, the "Knowledge" (or "Nolidj") that they must commit to memory ("4wud Kenzingtun Mal, ri Kenzingtun Chirch Stree, leff No-ing-ill, ri Pemrij Rod . . .")' (25). Self's bleak satirical comedy adapts the argot of contemporary cabdrivers to provide both the vocabulary and the rituals of these future fanatics who greet each other with the phrase 'Ware2 guv', and also torture apostates and non-believers on a giant wheel. For them souls are 'fares', and adolescent women 'opares'. The cohabitation of husband and wife is blasphemous, and they share childcare according to the ordained weekly ritual of the 'Changeover', all patterns and views derived from Dave's confessional text written mostly in a period when he was clearly insane. Ironically, as Caines says, 'the book was written [...] not as the founding text of a religion, but madly, as a message to his estranged son' (25).

Self's recurrent character, psychiatrist Zack Busner, discusses Dave's case, which as a fellow psychiatrist, Jane Bernal, explains has 'a set of doctrines and covenants as well' (280), and 'a bundle of proscriptions and injunctions that seem to be derived from the working life of London cabbies, a cock-eyed grasp on a mélange of fundamentalism, but mostly from Rudman's own vindictive misogynism.' (281) Under Busner's care he meets Phyllis, the mother of an inmate, and eventually Dave cures himself, although almost bathetically his demise is a result of earlier debts to sustain his work as a cabby that he later abandons escaping to rural Essex. In a curious way Dave becomes a martyr, although even Phyllis concludes his death a suicide. His legacy is the twisted world of his passing madness, where on Carl's return the authorities send the Supreme Driver to oversee the destruction of the motos and of Ham itself. Carl descends to face them. 'Carl took a deep breath. He needed no intercom to tell him this: that if it hadn't been Dave who so blighted the world, it would've been some other god – Jeebus or Joey or Ali – with his own savage edicts' (450). Carl's uncertain future typifies the traumatological aesthetic, its provisionality rather than being conceptual in fact derives from immediate, attribu-table threats, neither playful nor inchoate in any sense that matters.

Finally Self's text typifies certain features of the traumatological novel, which can be summarized as variously involving: a response to uncertainty; a notion of fluctuating historical conditions; a response to or an inclusion of the threat of social upheaval, and often the immi-nence of an apparently regressive epoch, which is either ideologically or ecologically unstable. The chaos that also centres such narratives may be individual or collective, but it is marked paradoxically by its tangibility, a distinctive meta-realism, a palpable sense of clear and present dangers.

Further Reading

Bachelard, Gaston *The Poetics of Space* [see bibliography].
Critical account of the domestic realm interpreted spatially and which set out philosophical and critical meanings of such spaces; it is a complex text, but it remains largely under-standable, and is excellent background for those prepared to theorize such spaces.

Cokal, Susann (2004) 'Expression in a diffuse landscape: contexts for Jeanette Winter-son's lyricism', *Style*, 38 (1), 16–37.
An essay which focuses well on style using effective close readings of the major works, including *Arts & Lies*; it is recommended for all levels of students.

Easthope, Antony (1999) *Englishness and National Culture*, London and New York: Routledge.

This is a sociological and cultural critique of the nature of Englishness, its culture, traditions and historical notion of itself. It offers itself as a sound background for literary scholars unaware of other traditions of critical intervention. The literary contexts featured are somewhat trite and self-evident.

Hadley, Elaine (2005) 'On a darkling plain: Victorian liberalism and the fantasy of agency', *Victorian Studies*, 48 (1), 92-102.
An accessible and considered article that considers the signification of Arnold's 'Dover Beach' in McEwan's *Saturday*, detailing the shared faith in the efficaciousness of the 'liberal cultivation of the self' as a self-evident good, and other general comparisons.

Hutter, Mark (2003) 'The World Trade Center: The Icon and Terrorism', in Will Wright and Steve Kaplan (eds) *The Image of the City in Literature, Media and Society*, Pueblo, CO: The Society for the Interdisciplinary Study of Social Imagery, Colorado State University-Pueblo, 67–73.
This is an intriguing essay on iconography and symbolic meaning of World Trade Center, and the socio-cultural effects of the attacks; however, it appears in an obscure publication of conference proceedings.

Parker, Emma (ed.) (2004) *Contemporary British Women Writers*, Cambridge: D. S. Brewer in association with the English Association.
This is a useful introductory collection of essays concerned with women writers, that is suitable for undergraduates.

Tew, Philip and Rod Mengham (eds) (2006) *British Fiction Today*, London and New York: Continuum.
This is an informative and well-researched series of sixteen essays that considers many of the novelists producing the most significant texts from the 1990s onward; it will be rewarding reading for all levels of students.

Wilson, Leigh 'Possessing Toby Litt's *Ghost Story*' [see bibliography].
A careful and inspired reading of Litt's novel, Leigh's essay considers how it can be assessed, as on first reading, in terms of affect, arguing for a reassertion of sensibility.

CHAPTER SEVEN

Epilogue: The Teaching and Study of the Contemporary British Novel

This end-piece, a summary of the major emphases in my own work, is addressed primarily to teachers and students of literature. Simply stated the book provides informative and thought-provoking material in the form of a number of interlinked ideas for teaching and learning for those concerned with recent British fiction. As I set out in my preface and critical introduction, 'Critiquing Contemporary Fiction', it is necessary to discuss key moments in literary and critical texts through the medium of a detailed theoretically informed interpretative analysis, so as to understand some idea of what we can make of the content of such fiction, as well as its many other attributes.

One important historical fact (set of observable and arguable circumstances) about contemporary British fiction is that it is being increasingly studied very widely in a range of institutions, perhaps most particularly in higher education, but there are dynamics and trajectories in such activities that have a habit of becoming embedded. Academics are not always brave enough in pursuing independent thought; the scope of recent critical orthodoxies suggests to my mind an analogy of beasts that prefer to hunt in packs. As this book suggests, for the students engaged upon such studies there remains something both relevant and challenging about interpreting works completed in recent years, ones which either reflect directly upon or react to current and recent cultural conditions that are part of a broader *Zeitgeist* than literary studies.

I find students are often enthused by taking apart a novel that appeared only a year or so previous to their scrutiny in class. As I demonstrate in both Chapter Four, 'The Past and the Present', and Chapter Five, 'Multiplicities and Hybridity', any contemporaneous quality of a work may well consist of perspectives and narrative nuances regarding gender, sexuality and class, rather than being present directly, or in a realist mode, in terms of its subject matter or setting. Hence, as I elucidate, what might seem otherwise to be a historical account reflects the mood or judgement of our own period, as with Pat Barker's *Regeneration* trilogy, or much of Jeanette Winterson's work including *The Passion*. Alternatively, as we have also seen in the preceding chapters the work of writers such as Martin Amis, Jenny Diski, Hanif Kureishi, Will Self and Zadie Smith are inflections of the social conditions of a modern urban, multicultural society that seems drawn mainly from one like our own. Such apparently realistically situated parallels seem irresistible. The events of 9/11 emphasized the real world features of the literary realms, and the influence of actual events. Students should recall that fiction has never existed in a vaccum.

This afterword might help you both read the book in an informed fashion and aid placement of its textual and historical evidence by defining and situating my arguments and analyses. As I explain in the critical introduction this study is selective because that is the nature of all aspects of human attention, ranging across the specifics of various fictional texts and certain broad contexts for the possibilities for their interpretation, especially drawing upon the critical arena Although the material is at times complex, I have tried to avoid being too arcane or too lost in the currency of negating ideas and possibilities. This strategy is undertaken, because as is made clear particularly in the preface and first chapter, recent critical contexts have influenced both university teaching and the intellectual output of academics, where previously a postmodern perspective in textual interpretation has predominated. This in itself has very much depended on deconstructive readings as I discuss in my readings of postmodern theory and examine closely in my questioning of postmodern critical readings of literature that I argue have characterized the dominant literary-critical discourse of recent years. In response, drawing upon a whole range of critical perspectives, this study seeks to empower readers, to enable them to say definite things about fiction, to allow them to redress the critical balance in reading, as I explain in detail in the initial phase, so that texts are capable of satisfying the criteria to which Gibson alludes in *Postmodernity, Ethics and the Novel: From Leavis to Levinas*. 'At some level or other, novels cannot but adumbrate a common sphere, what criticism calls a "world". A novel that dispensed with all the consistencies that make up a world – even supposing they are reducible to questions of naming – would no longer be a novel or readable' (103). I would add that the same reservation applies ultimately to criticism, which always finally in at least an understated fashion appeals to a 'reality principle' of some kind. As I clearly imply in all of my chapters, exegesis, or acts of textual criticism, should not simply be primarily involved in producing arcane avowals of the inability to know or define knowledge or experience. Chapters Four and Five draw on the fiction of Byatt, Fowles, Harris, Rushdie and Winterson in particular to demonstrate how texts that have been taken as representing the dissolution of meaning and universals can be read as more concerned with a social integration and concretion that expresses at least implicitly some wariness about relativistic readings and the threats of the loss of meaning. In a general sense one must ask oneself, as I illustrate textually, if words are as illusory or elusive as some suggest. If so, one is still faced with the question of how words are capable of recovering anyone's thoughts or actions, or whether they exist solely in a linguistic void or framework that is a straitjacket limiting one's capacities, or might one recognize that words and objects in fact relate to one another. Surely words are interconnected, admittedly in a highly complex fashion, to an alterity that remains pervasive in apparently theoretical readings drawing on high theory. Such things cannot be too oversimplified or one risks being accused of being critically and theoretically naive. This is something students need to bear in mind in their work, but it might reassure them that despite the apparently plangent certainty of many critics, one can comment nevertheless, as this book suggests, that the jury is out on these fundamental issues and principles. Where I myself appear too certain and enthusiastic, I apologize to my readers, but in my defence I calculate that there are some obtuse and crazy ideas to confront.

As I examine in the critical introduction very possibly postmodern readings represent ironic positions adopted toward knowing and reading; that is in the simplest sense why so many critics, in recent years, have used so many words and such assertive readings to declare that everything is subordinate to their interpretative intervention or ones they recognize, deferring any notion of the originary or primordial, refusing the material and the objective. Such a stance assumes an exact quality in writing and formal expression that over-determines rational and enlightenment thought so as in contrast to prioritize the plurality of reading. A counter-intuitive understanding to this is especially important so as to mediate excessive fragmentation of criticism and reinstate critical views of the possibilities of both representation and universal critical readings, a critique that is seen as being in opposition to the strategy of seeing broad groups of interest, such as defining swathes of individuals by gender, sexual orientation, ethnic grouping and generations. These are positions I counter very specifically as the backdrop to my reading of counter cultures in Chapters One and Two, and postmodern and postcolonial contexts in Chapters Four and Five. Overall the main emphases of this study, in terms of both its content and its methodology, are intended to raise issues that readers of fiction might use as a basis for situating the contemporary British novel. The 1970s was characterized by debates about the demise of the novel and death of the author. This engendered a notion of crisis, but as I seek to suggest in Chapter Two, 'The Fall and Rise of the Middle Classes', this did not prevent critics from seeing in middle-class literary renditions of intellectual culture a fiction of struggle and various political dimensions. As Gibson describes in his instructive critique, what followed was a period where the acts of literary criticism were 'politicized' (2) and subsequently according to Gibson one must confront the position whereby 'It [criticism] has no stable base in constants or universals' (3). In fact, apart from its class bias subtly inflected in both fiction and criticism, and institutionally inscribed, such politicization often meant in practice a determined effort to read texts in terms of gender, ethnicity, postcoloniality and radical issues, but ended in ghettoizing or marginalizing such creative efforts in thematic studies of these issues. Like so much critical practice it raises some awareness, but its appropriateness diminishes as cultural acceptance of such voices broadens, since their very separation as separable categories of voice and subjectivity maintains the dynamics of the too knowing categorizations of oppression. Hence, the aim of this study is to reflect current cultural practice and regard all manner of narratives as interlinked, particular writing by previously marginalized groups who can now be argued as crucial to an intellectual culture. Moreover, as I imply, there are limits to attempts at any supposed radicalizations which often reproduce, however transfigured, the marginalizing categories of gender, ethnicity and nationhood, a point especially under consideration in Chapter One, 'Contemporary Britishness: Who, What, Why and When?'

Subsequently, as we see from evidence considered in the critical introduction and the first three chapters, seduced by the deconstructive enterprise, the period from the 1980s appeared far from optimistic about fiction or the possibilities of its critical reception. Gibson's scepticism concerning the radical potential and practice of English is instructive (3) and is the kernel of the stance I adopt toward the self-declared radicality of deconstructive and postmodern thought in my readings of fiction. In a more localized sense, critical encounters with the genre continue in universities, colleges and schools. Clearly in great part this study will be read in order to initiate and support such acts of interpretation embarked upon very specifically for academic purposes, such as an essay, an oral assignment, or even the odd thesis. If criticism has to respond to the demands of teaching and learning, as I demonstrate, the boundaries that separate the apparent categories of 'serious' narrative and its more popular counterparts have become blurred in part because of the adoption of populist forms and a more 'democratic' argot and style that has permeated increasingly texts with 'high art' aspirations.

In fact curiously, despite his apparent adherence to deconstruction's efficacy, Gibson both echoes and breaches the parameters apparently established by this practice in a period when postmodern thinking largely dominated literary criticism, an emphasis that shifted readings away from interpreting social, symbolic and other parallels with lived experience, mystifying the quotidian. In such criticism, any counter-intuitive readings that appear to equate a text with these elements of reality are accused of naivety and risk being accused of claiming an understanding that subdues difference and 'heterogeneity'. Any concrete claim in this context is simply a totalizing movement. As a consequence for the student everything often appears fragmented and heterogeneous to the point that paradoxically both any and yet in contrast no singular opinion could be validated. This creates problems for comprehending or understanding texts in their broader contexts, even though such contextualization was often the stated aim of deconstructive readings, claiming an enhanced awareness of the plural nature of knowledge and narrative, of its constructedness. This is especially significant for literary studies students because each one not only has to respond to the text as a matter of language, but is inevitably also required to think of something persuasive and relevant to say about wider issues of subject matter and cultural relevance, drawing on a range of critical sources and a variety of secondary material. This has been the model followed in my preceding analyses of literary-critical issues, and the structure of my text is in part predicated on the socialization of multiplicities, and on processes Gibson interrogates when he wonders 'How far might hybridity be taken as a rule rather than an exception?' (197). As I outline in detail in the critical introduction and Chapter Five, unlike Gibson, I see this less as an inordinately signified challenge of the ego than an experientially constituted social condition to which narrative both responds and contributes. The work may make demands of us as Gibson predicates (194), but the material and perhaps even metaphysical ontology of the life-world has its own interplay and insistence that acts upon the reader and the text.

It seems to me almost a platitude to signify that the challenge of interpretation is an active, changing process, which even a passing familiarity with literary-critical history would suggest. Emerson indicated as much in the nineteenth century. That fashions in doing things change is self-evident. Take a more personal example. I no longer write exactly the kinds of things that I was required to produce as a student of literature in the 1970s, as did everyone else of my generation, when a descriptive, thematic account dominated and was a required outcome of appropriate study. It is the emphasis of reading the text that is suggestive, but more significantly the role one requires of the text in its relationships with other elements of the world and with our own understanding. Although among my peers he remains a critic I admire, for my taste Gibson tends too much toward, to use his own terminology, an 'awareness of moralities as myriad, groundless, incommensurable and interminable' (14), whilst undoubtedly he might well cast my position as that of a 'neo-humanist'. The concept of hybridity, social consciousness, of historical influence and shared identities which I explore as fictional and cultural themes in this study, I regard as being reached experientially, in what is an intersubjective encounter that has pre-conscious, intuitive elements. Ontology is that set of engagements in which we are embedded; no one thing is another. Fiction and narrative intersect, constitute, challenge and mirror that being through the medium of a linguistic and creative synthesis.

Increasingly the student of the contemporary scene is faced with a number of very specific problems that this study is designed to address. The first major problem is to specify what one means by the contemporary, which I take to be to identify which phase can be so described in a coherent fashion. One has to ask quite what themes and issues, events or activities can be taken as ongoing, relevant to current practice and so forth. As I specify in the critical introduction and the first chapter, 'Critiquing Contemporary Fiction' and 'Contemporary Britishness: Who, What, Why and When?', the phase from the mid-1970s offers a sufficiently discrete mode of new writing and response to historical conditions to be regarded as relevant to the present. To engage with this period requires situating fiction in a larger and changing conception of Britishness, about which opinions abound and about which much of this study is concerned. Moreover, as I point out, one illusion is that a changing culture in terms of shifting elements of gender, sexuality, ethnicity, youth, and social mobility has somehow erased or diminished the significance of understanding class. Clearly in the kind of literary and social cultures from which the contemporary has emerged, this is an absurdity, a position addressed particularly in Chapter Two, 'The Fall and Rise of the Middle Classes'.

Another problem in dealing with the contemporary in terms of fiction, is engaging with the established convention of emphasizing a reflexive tradition in literary studies as a field of activity, both in defining matters in terms of prior examples of writing (the great books model) or exemplary, classic critics in a chiefly English tradition (often Matthew Arnold, T. S. Eliot despite his North American intellectual origins, and F. R. Leavis); it is my conviction that this adherence to a supposedly 'high' critical tradition has been insufficiently offset by a full integration of social, historical and ontological conditions. This present book redresses something of the balance with its adoption of themes and methodological sources concerning fiction which stress both its objective and experiential possibilities, and those of criticism itself. The real historical world is a constant source of the narratological alongside intertextual influence. Lived experience both conditions us as readers, and produces fiction in the first place. From where else are the raw materials of narrative drawn; even intertextuality is a matter of drawing upon the mediated material and offers its recognition of the place and influence of fiction in the world (of readers, of criticism, and the academy). A third problem is constituted by the late twentieth-century critical emphasis (one might say bias) toward postmodern readings, that predominated until very recently, which distorts these preceding factors, apparently making it difficult for students to compare texts and periods of writing to their own lives and encounters. Life is appropriated to the textualizing process and the referent elided so that everything is simply a symbolic and linguistic interplay. This recurs as an issue in my interpretation, but is very specifically considered in the critical introduction, 'Critiquing Contemporary Fiction', and the fourth chapter, 'The Past and the Present', where the idea of the 'postmodern' British novel is situated in a re-reading of the narrative emphasis toward myth and history. The constructed nature of such engagements is mediated by an objective, correlating impulse, a humanistic concern with the effects of power upon people. As I indicate, despite deconstructive claims a sense of the rawness and relative unalterability (or persistence) of the world, the universe and larger forces persists, often displaced into single-issue politics, or environmental concerns, or new age belief systems. If novels are ontologically centred, our shared lives are finally our only source for comparison, knowledge and way of activating the narrative. Even the arcane ludic text draws on real-life games and their contextual significance. There is nothing more intersubjective (in its simplest sense necessarily communicated and shared between people) than the playful, but clearly it draws upon life. Of course, a fictional moment is not identical to (that is equates exactly to) a real-life moment (mimetic realism), but draws upon it in a whole variety of ways, some of which, like the aesthetic and intuitive, are at the limits of our knowledge, our self-knowledge, and therefore any claims for reflexivity (all reflexivity is a self-reflexive manoeuvre). As this study assumes as its subtext, it is simply a platitude that the world changes constantly, and is uncertain. So too is criticism, theory and literature, but all are bound by the constant necessity to say something (as people are by the requirement to act, since inaction is a form of action). Ultimately even in life, in the world no one moment or thing is another, but we assume some repetition and coherence (even as animals do) to proceed in the world. As contemporary fiction suggests, narrative may be seen as a fusion of memory, elaborations, rehearsals and negations of the real. It also involves a hybridity of cultures and identities, neither of which are fixed, but nor are they in absolute flux (how else could we know them?).

It is important to recognize that contemporary fiction may respond to the contemporary conditions of life and its emphases either culturally or aesthetically. If such parallels drawn from historicity are unsayable, nonsensical, or unsupportable, then so too is any critique of power which responds to material conditions and relations. This blunt logjam or impasse confronts the apparent subtleties and nuances of the radicalizing assumptions of deconstructive readings. If one adopts a more integrative dialectical view, the admixture of essences, events and intuition of the objective world, one can recover efforts of a reflection upon the state of the nation narrative and of direct reflection of changing social values as we have found in the writers featured in my critique of specific texts of this kind, for instance Jonathan Coe, Will Self, and Zadie Smith. The novel is explored in its generic continuity and contradictions, in its search for some concept of recuperating the past so as to invoke universal or consistent human values and responses that counter an intellectual culture obsessed with the postmodern in the work of A. S. Byatt, Angela Carter, and Jeanette Winterson. Contemporary narrative reflects actively upon the process of cultural hybridity and intermixture in the work of Martin Amis, Hanif Kureishi and Salman Rushdie among others. One may read in the reworking of the mythopoeic an insistence on emotional, historical and humanistic possibilities in the apparently untraditional fictional strategies of Jim Crace, Wilson Harris, and Adam Thorpe. Generally what is noticeable is a stylistic and formal hybridity, with many of the authors featured going beyond the major dynamics of the text and interfusing them with other gestures or elements as a kind of layering. If postmodern theory indicates anything it is that fiction cannot be contained, not even in the 'prison-house' or straitjacket of language. As Gibson describes in his instructive critique the hybridity of culture and understanding involves fluid processes; so too does fiction (even once printed, since interpretative modes and fashions change, and in reading can be argued to be drawing more potential from a text). Of course one element critics in oppositional camps share with myself is an enthusiasm for literature and the interpretative, critical act. It is this we are attempting to inculcate in students, and I think we all hope to see work produced that is thoughtful, perceptive and informed rather than slavishly adhere to a theoretical position that happens to mirror our own. It will give me great joy if in future my students oppose my views from a position of their own knowledge and do so persuasively. Student readers might bear that in mind throughout their studies. No worthwhile tutor is prescriptive, but offers a reading to aid comprehension. I hope I have done so in small part.

APPENDIX

Granta 'Best of Young British Novelists' lists

Granta 81: Best of Young British Novelists 2003
Edited and Introduced by Ian Jack
Monica Ali
Nicola Barker
Rachel Cusk
Peter Ho Davies
Susan Elderkin
Stephen Gill
Philip Hensher
A. L. Kennedy
Hari Kunzru
Toby Litt
David Mitchell
Andrew O'Hagan
David Peace
Dan Rhodes
Ben Rice
Rachel Seiffert
Zadie Smith
Adam Thirlwell
Alan Warner
Sarah Waters
Robert McLiam Wilson

Granta 43: Best of Young British Novelists 2 (1993)
Edited and Introduced by Bill Buford
Iain Banks
Anne Billson
Louis de Bernières
Tibor Fischer

Esther Freud
Alan Hollinghurst
Kazuo Ishiguro
A. L. Kennedy
Philip Kerr
Hanif Kureishi
Adam Lively
Adam Mars-Jones
Candia McWilliam
Lawrence Norfolk
Ben Okri
Caryl Phillips
Will Self
Nicholas Shakespeare
Helen Simpson
Jeanette Winterson

Granta 7: Best of Young British Novelists (1983)
Edited by Bill Buford
Martin Amis
Pat Barker
Julian Barnes
Ursula Bentley
William Boyd
Buchi Emecheta
Maggie Gee
Kazuo Ishiguro
Alan Judd
Ian McEwan
Adam Mars-Jones
Shiva Naipaul
Philip Norman
Christopher Priest
Salman Rushdie
Clive Sinclair
Graham Swift
Rose Tremain
A. N. Wilson

Bibliography

Note: *Where a first edition is not used, the year of original publication text is indicated in additional parentheses thus: [1996].*

Section One: Fiction Cited and Discussed
Ackroyd, Peter (1993) [1985] *Hawksmoor*, London and New York: Penguin.
Ackroyd, Peter (2001) [2000] *London: The Biography*, New York and London: Nan A. Talese.
Ali, Monica (2004) [2003] *Brick Lane*, London: Black Swan.
Amis, Kingsley (1992) [1954] *Lucky Jim*, Harmondsworth: Penguin.
Amis, Kingsley (1978) *Jake's Thing*, London: Hutchinson.
Amis, Martin (2000) [1984] *Money: A Suicide Note*, London and New York: Penguin.
Amis, Martin (1999) [1989] *London Fields*, London: Vintage.
Amis, Martin (1996) [1995] *The Information*, London: Flamingo.
Amis, Martin (2003) *Yellow Dog*, London: Jonathan Cape.
Aslam, Nadeem (2004) *Maps for Lost Lovers*, London: Faber & Faber.
Ballard, J. G. (1993) [1973] *Crash*, London: Flamingo
Ballard, J. G. (1974) 'Introduction', in J. G. Ballard, *Crash*, London: Flamingo, 5–9.
Ballard, J. G. (1993) [1975] *High-Rise*, London: Flamingo.
Ballard, J. G. (2000) [1979] *The Unlimited Dream Company*, London: Flamingo.
Ballard, J. G. (2006) *Kingdom Come*, London: Fourth Estate.
Banks, Iain (2002) *Dead Air*, London: Little, Brown.
Barker, Pat (1996) *The Regeneration Trilogy* [(1991) *Regeneration*; (1993) *The Eye in the Door*; (1995) *The Ghost Road*], London: Viking.
Barker, Pat (2004) [2003] *Double Vision*, London: Penguin.
Barnes, Julian (1981) [1980] *Metroland*, London: Robin Clark.
Barnes, Julian (1990) [1989] *A History of the World in 10½ Chapters*, London: Picador.
Berger, John (2001) *The Shape of a Pocket*, London: Bloomsbury.
Binding, Tim (2006) [2005] *Man Overboard*, London: Picador.
Bracewell, Michael (1988a) *Missing Margate*, in Michael Bracewell, Don Watson and Mark Edwards, *The Quick End*, London: Fourth Estate, 1–80.
Bracewell, Michael (1988b) *The Crypto-Amnesia Club*, London: Serpent's Tail.
Bracewell, Michael (1989) *Divine Concepts of Physical Beauty*, London: Secker & Warburg.
Bracewell, Michael (1992) *The Conclave*, London: Secker & Warburg.
Brackenbury, Rosalind (1979) *The Coelacanth*, Sussex: Harvester Press.
Bradbury, Malcolm (1977) [1975] *The History Man*, London: Arrow Books.
Burgess, Anthony (1972) [1962] *A Clockwork Orange*, London: Penguin.
Byatt, A. S. (1990) *Possession*, London: Chatto & Windus.
Byatt, A. S. (2001) [2000] *The Biographer's Tale*, London: Vintage.
Carter, Angela (1985) [1984] *Nights at the Circus*, London: Picador.
Carter, Angela (1992) [1991] *Wise Children*, London: Vintage.
Christie, Agatha (1948) [1926] *The Murder of Roger Ackroyd*, Harmondsworth: Penguin.

Christie, Agatha (1954) [1933] *Lord Edware Dies*, London: Fontana.
Christie, Agatha (1964) *A Caribbean Mystery*, London: The Book Club.
Coe, Jonathan (1991) [1990] *The Dwarves of Death*, London: Sceptre.
Coe, Jonathan (1995) [1994] *What a Carve Up!*, London and New York: Penguin.
Coe, Jonathan (1998) [1997] *The House of Sleep*, London and New York: Penguin.
Coe, Jonathan (2001) *The Rotters' Club*, London: Viking.
Conrad, Joseph (1983) [1902] *The Heart of Darkness*, London and New York: Penguin; introd. Paul O'Prey.
Crace, Jim (1986) *Continent*, London and New York: Heinemann.
Crace, Jim (1988) *The Gift of Stones*, London: Secker & Warburg.
Crace, Jim (1997) *Quarantine*, London and New York: Viking.
Crace, Jim (1999) *Being Dead*, London and New York: Viking.
Davies, Pete (1986) *The Last Election*, London: André Deutsch.
Diski, Jenny (1986) *Nothing Natural*, London: Methuen.
Diski, Jenny (1987) *Rainforest*, London: Methuen.
Diski, Jenny (1994) *Monkey's Uncle*, London: Phoenix.
Diski, Jenny (1996) *The Dream Mistress*, London: Weidenfeld & Nicolson.
Diski, Jenny (2000) *Only Human: A Divine Comedy*, London: Virago.
Drabble, Margaret (1965) *The Millstone*, London: Weidenfeld & Nicolson.
Drabble, Margaret (1973) [1972] *The Needle's Eye*, London and New York: Penguin.
Drabble, Margaret (1979) [1977] *The Ice Age*, Harmondsworth and New York: Penguin.
Drabble, Margaret (1980) *The Middle Ground*, London: Weidenfeld & Nicolson.
Drabble, Margaret (1988) [1987] *The Radiant Way*, London and New York: Penguin.
Ellmann, Lucy (1989) [1988] *Sweet Desserts*, London and New York: Penguin.
Ellmann, Lucy (1991) *Varying Degrees of Hopelessness*, London: Hamish Hamilton.
Elms, Robert (1988) *In Search of the Crack*, London and New York: Viking.
Fowles, John (1987) [1969] *The French Lieutenant's Woman*, London: Pan.
Freud, Esther (1999) [1992] *Hideous Kinky*, London and New York: Penguin.
Garland, Alex (2004) *The Coma*, London: Faber & Faber.
Golding, William (1954) *Lord of the Flies*, London: Faber & Faber.
Golding, William (1980) *Rites of Passage*, London: Faber & Faber.
Hardy, Thomas (1996) [1895] *Jude the Obscure*, London: Penguin.
Harris, Wilson (1998) [1960] *Palace of the Peacock*, London and Boston: Faber & Faber.
Harris, Wilson (1996) *Jonestown*, London and Boston: Faber & Faber.
Ishiguro, Kazuo (1990) [1989] *The Remains of the Day*, London and Boston: Faber & Faber.
Johnson, B. S. (1964) *Albert Angelo*, London: Constable.
Johnson, B. S. (1967) [1964] *Albert Angelo*, London: Panther.
Johnson, B. S. (2001) [1973] *Christie Malry's Own Double-Entry*, London: Picador; foreword John Lanchester.
Johnson, B. S. (1973) *Aren't You Rather Young to be Writing Your Memoirs?*, London: Hutchinson.
Johnson, B. S. (1975) *See the Old Lady Decently*, London: Hutchinson.
Joyce, Graham (2004) [2003] *The Facts of Life*, New York and London: Washington Square Press.
Joyce, James (1971) [1922] *Ulysses*, Harmondsworth: Penguin.
Kelman, James (1989) [1983] *Not Not While the Giro and Other Stories*, London: Minerva.
Kelman, James, (1985) [1984] *The Bus Conductor Hines*, London and Melbourne: J. M. Dent.
Kelman, James (2005) [2004] *You Have to be Careful in the Land of the Free*, London: Penguin.
Kelman, James, Agnes Owens and Alisdair Gray (1987) [1985] *Lean Tales*, London: Abacus.
Kennedy, A. L. (1993) [1990] *Night Geometry and the Garscadden Trains*, London: Phoenix.
Kureishi, Hanif (1990) *The Buddha of Suburbia*, London and Boston: Faber & Faber.

Kureishi, Hanif (1995) *The Black Album*, London and Boston: Faber & Faber.
Kureishi, Hanif (2001) *Gabriel's Gift*, London: Faber & Faber.
Lessing, Doris (1964) [1962] *The Golden Notebook*, Harmondsworth: Penguin.
Levy, Andrea (2004) *Small Island*, London: Hodder Headline.
Litt, Toby (2000) *Corpsing*, London and New York: Penguin.
Litt, Toby (2001) *deadkidsongs*, London: Hamish Hamilton.
Litt, Toby (2005) [2004] *Ghost Story*, London: Penguin.
Lodge, David (1978) [1975] *Changing Places*, Harmondsworth and New York: Penguin.
Lodge, David (1989) [1988] *Nice Work*, London and New York: Penguin.
Lodge, David (2001) *Thinks ...* , London: Secker & Warburg.
Lott, Tim (2000) [1999] *White City Blue*, London and New York: Penguin.
Lott, Tim (2002) *Rumours of a Hurricane*, London and New York: Viking.
Lott, Tim (2006) [2005] *The Seymour Tapes*, London and New York: Penguin.
McEwan, Ian (1988) [1987] *The Child in Time*, London: Picador.
McEwan, Ian (2002) [2001] *Atonement*, London: Vintage.
McEwan, Ian (2005) *Saturday*, London: Jonathan Cape.
Millar, Martin (1987) *Milk, Sulphate and Alby Starvation*, London: Fourth Estate.
Millar, Martin (1988) *Lux the Poet*, London: Fourth Estate.
Millar, Martin (1989) *Ruby and the Stone Age Diet*, London: Fourth Estate.
Miller, Miranda (1987) *Smiles and the Millennium*, London: Virago.
Moorcock, Michael (1989) [1988] *Mother London: A Novel*, London and New York: Penguin.
Murdoch, Iris (2002) [1954] *Under the Net*, London: Vintage.
Murdoch, Iris (1958) *The Bell*, London: Chatto & Windus.
Murdoch, Iris (1969) [1968] *The Nice and the Good*, Harmondsworth: Penguin.
Murdoch, Iris (1978) *The Sea, the Sea*, London: Chatto & Windus.
Norfolk, Lawrence (2000) *In the Shape of the Boar*, London: Weidenfeld & Nicolson.
Nye, Simon (1989) *Men Behaving Badly*, London and New York: Penguin.
Peace, David (2004) *GB84*, London: Faber & Faber.
Phillips, Caryl (1986) *A State of Independence*, London and Boston: Faber & Faber.
Phillips, Caryl (1991) *Cambridge*, London: Bloomsbury.
Phillips, Caryl (1997) *The Nature of Blood*, London and Boston: Faber & Faber.
Rushdie, Salman (1995) [1981] *Midnight's Children*, London: Vintage.
Rushdie, Salman (1998) [1988] *The Satanic Verses*, London: Vintage.
Salinger, J. D. (1951) *The Catcher in the Rye*, New York : Modern Library.
Self, Will (1996) *The Sweet Smell of Psychosis*, London: Bloomsbury.
Self, Will (1998) *Tough, Tough Toys for Tough, Tough Boys*, London: Bloomsbury.
Self, Will (2000) *How the Dead Live*, London: Bloomsbury.
Self, Will (2002) *Dorian: An Imitation*, London and New York: Viking.
Self, Will (2006) *The Book of Dave: A Revelation of the Recent Past and the Distant Future*,
    London and New York: Viking.
Selvon, Samuel (1966) *The Lonely Londoners*, London: Mayflower-Dell.
Sheridan, Richard (1986) *END OF '77*, London: Sceptre.
Sinclair, Iain (1998) [1987] *White Chappell, Scarlet Tracings*, London: Granta.
Sinclair, Iain (1997) *Lights Out for the Territory*, London: Granta.
Smith, Ali (2006) *The Accidental*, London and New York: Penguin.
Smith, Joan (1987) *A Masculine Ending*, London: Faber & Faber.
Smith, Joan (1988) *Why Aren't They Screaming?*, London: Faber & Faber.
Smith, Joan (1990) *Don't Leave Me This Way*, London: Faber & Faber.
Smith, Zadie (2001) [2000] *White Teeth*, London and New York: Penguin.
Storey, Jack Trevor (1963) *Live Now, Pay Later*, Harmondsworth: Penguin.
Swift, Graham (1983) *Waterland*, London: Heinemann.
Thomson, Rupert (1987) *Dreams of Leaving*, London: Bloomsbury.
Thomson, Rupert (2005) *Divided Kingdom*, London: Bloomsbury.
Thorne, Matt (2004) *Cherry: A Novel*, London: Weidenfeld & Nicolson.
Thorpe, Adam (1994) [1992] *Ulverton*, New York: Noonday Press, Farrar, Straus and
    Giroux.
Weldon, Fay (1993) [1989] *The Cloning of Joanna May*, London: Flamingo.

Welsh, Irvine (1997) [1993] *Trainspotting*, in *The Irvine Welsh Omnibus*: *'Trainspotting'*; *'The Acid House'*; *'marabou stork nightmares'*, London: Jonathan Cape/Secker & Warburg.
Welsh, Irvine (1995a) *The Acid House*, London: Jonathan Cape.
Welsh, Irvine (1995b) *marabou stork nightmares: a novel*, London: Jonathan Cape.
Wilson, Angus (1992) [1956] *Anglo-Saxon Attitudes*, London and New York: Penguin.
Wilson, Robert McLiam (2003) 'The Dreamed', in Ian Jack (ed.) *Granta 81: Best of Young British Novelists 2003*, London and New York: Granta, 301–22.
Winterson, Jeanette (1991) [1985] *Oranges Are Not the Only Fruit*, London: Vintage.
Winterson, Jeanette (1987) *The Passion*, London: Bloomsbury.
Winterson, Jeanette (1990) [1989] *Sexing the Cherry*, London: Vintage.
Winterson, Jeanette (1994) *Art and Lies*, London: Jonathan Cape.
Winterson, Jeanette (1996) [1992] *Written on the Body*, London: Vintage.
Winterson, Jeanette (1997) *Gut Symmetries*, London: Granta Books.
Woolf, Leonard (1914) *Wise Virgins: A Story of Words, Opinions, and a few Emotions*, London: Edward Arnold.
Woolf, Virginia (1922) *Jacob's Room*, London: Hogarth Press.
Woolf, Virginia (1925) *Mrs Dalloway*, London: Hogarth Press.
Woolf, Virginia (1927) *To the Lighthouse*, London: Hogarth Press.
Woolf, Virginia (1993) [1928] *Orlando*, London and New York: Penguin; Brenda Lyons (ed.); introd. Susan M. Gilbert.
Woolf, Virginia (1941) *Between the Acts*, London: Hogarth Press.

Section Two: Secondary Sources

Adorno, Theodor (1990) [1973] *Negative Dialectics*, London: Routledge & Kegan Paul; trans. E. B. Ashton.
Ahmad, Aijaz (1992) *In Theory: Classes, Nations, Literatures*, London and New York: Verso.
Alexander, Jeffrey C. (2004) 'Toward a Theory of Cultural Trauma', in Jeffrey C. Alexander, Ron Eyerman, Bernhard Giesen, Neil J. Smelser and Piotr Sztompka, *Cultural Trauma and Collective Identity*, Berkeley, Los Angeles and London: University of California Press, 1–30.
Arnold, Matthew (1994) [1869; rev. 1875] *Culture and Anarchy*, Cambridge: Cambridge University Press; introd. J. Dover Wilson.
Ashcroft, Bill, Gareth Griffiths and Helen Tiffin (2002) *The Empire Writes Back: Theory and Practice in Post-Colonial Literatures*, 2nd edition, London and New York: Routledge.
Bachelard, Gaston (1994) *The Poetics of Space*, Boston, MA: Beacon Press; trans. Maria Jolas.
Baker, Stephen (2003) 'Salman Rushdie: History, Self and the Fiction of Truth', in Richard Lane, Rod Menghan and Philip Tew (eds) *Contemporary British Fiction*, London and New York: Polity, 145–57.
Bataille, Georges (1991) [1976] *The Accursed Share: An Essay on General Economy*, Volume II: *The History of Eroticism* and Volume III: *Sovereignty*, New York: Zone Books; trans. Robert Hurley. Originally published in 1976 as *L'Histoire de l'érotisme* and *La Souveraineté* in *Ouevres Complètes* Vol. 8, Paris: Editions Gallimard.
Bataille, Georges (2001) *the unfinished system of nonknowledge*, Minneapolis and London: University of Minnesota Press; Stuart Kendall (ed.); trans. Michelle Kendall and Stuart Kendall.
Bauman, Zygmunt (1991) *Modernity and Ambivalence*, Ithaca: Cornell University Press.
Bell, Michael (1999) 'The Metaphysics of Modernism: Aesthetic Myth and the Myth of the Aesthetic', in David Fuller and Patricia Waugh (eds) *The Arts and Sciences of Criticism*, Oxford and New York: Oxford University Press, 238–56.
Benjamin, Walter (1992) [1955] *Illuminations*, London: Fontana; Hannah Arendt (ed.); trans. Harry Zohn.
Bennett, Jill (2003) '*Tenebrae* after September 11, Art, Empathy, and the Global Politics of Belonging', in Jill Bennett and Rosanne Kennedy (eds) *World Memory: Personal Trajectories in Global Time*, Basingstoke and New York: Palgrave Macmillan, 177–94.

Bennett, Jill and Rosanne Kennedy (2003) (eds) *World Memory: Personal Trajectories in Global Time*, Basingstoke and New York: Palgrave Macmillan.

Berger, Peter L. and Thomas Luckmann (1971) [1966] *The Social Construction of Reality*, Harmondsworth and New York: Penguin.

Bergonzi, Bernard (1970) *The Situation of the Novel*, London: Macmillan.

Bergson, Henri (1913) *An Introduction to Metaphysics*, London: Macmillan; trans. T. E. Hulme.

Berman, Marshall (1983) [1982] *All That Is Sold Melts Into Air: The Experience of Modernity*, London and New York: Verso.

Bhabha, Homi K. (ed.) (1990) *Nation and Narration*, London and New York: Routledge.

Bhabha, Homi K. (1994) *The Location of Culture*, London and New York: Routledge.

Bhaskar, Roy (1993) *Dialectic: The Pulse of Freedom*, London and New York: Verso.

Bhaskar, Roy (2002) *Reflections on Meta-Reality: Transcendence, Emancipation and Everyday Life*, New Delhi and London: Sage.

Blincoe, Nicholas and Matt Thorne (2001a) 'Introduction: The Pledge', in Nicholas Blincoe and Matt Thorne (eds) *All Hail the New Puritans*, London: Fourth Estate, vii–xvii.

Blincoe, Nicholas (2001b) 'Short Guide to Games Theory', in Nicholas Blincoe and Matt Thorne (eds) *All Hail the New Puritans*, London: Fourth Estate, 34–50.

Blincoe, Nicholas and Matt Thorne (eds) (2001c) *All Hail the New Puritans*, London: Fourth Estate.

Bock, Hedwig and Albert Wertheim (eds) (1986a) *Essays on Contemporary Post-Colonial Fiction*, Munich: Max Hueber.

Bock, Hedwig and Albert Wertheim (1986b) *Essays on the Contemporary British Novel*, Munich: Max Hueber.

Bourdieu, Pierre (1996) [1992] *The Rules of Art: Genesis and Structure of the Literary Field*, Cambridge: Polity; trans. Susan Emanuel.

Bourdieu, Pierre (1993) *The Field of Cultural Production: Essays on Art and Literature*, Cambridge: Polity; trans. Randal Johnson.

Bradbury, Malcolm (ed.) (1977a) *The Novel Today: Contemporary Writers on Modern Fiction*, Manchester: Manchester University Press.

Bradbury, Malcolm (1977b) 'Introduction', in Malcolm Bradbury (ed.) *The Novel Today: Contemporary Writers on Modern Fiction*, Manchester: Manchester University Press, 7–21.

Brah, Avtar and Annie E. Coombes (eds) (2000) *Hybridity and its Discontents: Politics, Science, Culture*, London and New York: Routledge.

Brannigan, John (2003) *Orwell to the Present: Literature in England 1945–2000*, Basingstoke and New York: Palgrave Macmillan.

Brathwaite, Edward (1971) *The Development of Creole Society in Jamaica 1770–1820*, Oxford: Clarendon Press.

Brathwaite, Edward (1974) *Contradictory Omens: Cultural Diversity in the Caribbean*, Mona, Jamaica: Savacou Publications [Monograph no. 1].

Briggs, Asa (1991) *A Social History of England*, London: Penguin.

Buchanan, Brad (2003) 'Caryl Phillips: Colonialism, Cultural Hybridity and Racial Difference', in Richard Lane, Rod Menghan and Philip Tew (eds) *Contemporary British Fiction*, London and New York: Polity, 183–7.

Buford, Bill (ed.) (1993a) *Granta 43: Best of Young British Novelists 2*, London: Granta.

Buford, Bill (1993b) 'Editorial', in Bill Buford (ed.) *Granta 43: Best of Young British Novelists 2*, London: Granta, 9–16.

Butler, Christopher (1994) *Early Modernism: Literature, Music and Painting in Europe, 1900–1916*, Oxford: Clarendon Press.

Caines, Michael (2006) 'Nu Lundun', *TLS*, June, 25.

Cairncross, Alec (1985) *Years of Recovery: British Economic Policy*, London: Methuen.

Callaghan, John (1993) 'In Search of Eldorado: Labour's Colonial Economic Policy', in Jim, Fyrth (ed.) *Labour's High Noon: The Government and the Economy 1945–51*, London: Lawrence & Wishart, 115–34.

Carter, Angela (1979) *The Sadeian Woman: An Exercise in Cultural History*, London: Virago.

Caruth, Cathy (1996) *Unclaimed Experience: Trauma, Narrative, and History*, Baltimore and London: Johns Hopkins University Press.

Cassirer, Ernst (1944) *An Essay on Man: An Introduction to a Philosophy of Human Culture*, New Haven: Yale University Press.

Cassirer, Ernst (1961) *The Logic of the Humanities*, New Haven: Yale University Press; trans. Clarence Smith Howe.

Cassirer, Ernst (1955a) *The Philosophy of Symbolic Forms, Volume 1: Language*, New Haven and London: Yale University Press.

Cassirer, Ernst (1955b) *The Philosophy of Symbolic Forms, Volume 2: Mythical Thought*, New Haven and London: Yale University Press; trans. Ralph Manheim.

Cassirer, Ernst (1957) *The Philosophy of Symbolic Forms, Volume 3: The Phenomenology of Knowledge*, New Haven and London: Yale University Press; trans. Ralph Manheim.

Cassirer, Ernst (1996) *The Philosophy of Symbolic Forms, Volume 4: The Metaphysics of Symbolic Forms*, New Haven and London: Yale University Press; John Michael Krois and Donald Phillip Verene (eds); trans. John Michael Krois.

Childs, Peter (1997) 'Place and Environment', in Mike Storry and Peter Childs (eds) *British Cultural Identities*, London and New York: Routledge, 46.

The CIA World Factbook 2001 at http://www.cia.gov/publications/factbook/

Comfort, Alex (1948) *The Novel & Our Time*, London: Phoenix House.

Connor, Steven (1996) *The English Novel in History 1950–1995*, London: Routledge.

Crossley, Nick (1996) *Intersubjectivity: The Fabric of Social Becoming*, London and Thousand Oaks, CA: Sage.

Currie, Mark (ed.) (1995) *Metafiction*, London and New York: Longman.

Dallas, Lucy (2004) 'The Arc of Grief', *TLS*, 22 October, 23.

Dällenbach, Lucien (1989) [1977] *The Mirror in the Text*, Chicago: University of Chicago Press; Cambridge: Polity; trans. Jeremy Whiteley, with Emma Hughes.

Davey, Kevin (1999) *English Imaginaries: Six Studies in Anglo-British Modernity*, London: Lawrence & Wishart.

Debord, Guy (1995) [1967] *The Society of the Spectacle*, London: Zone Books; trans. Donald Nicholson-Smith.

Deleuze, Gilles (1993) *Essays Critical and Clinical*, London and New York: Verso; trans. Daniel W. Smith and Michael A. Greco.

Diedrick, James (2003) 'The Fiction of Martin Amis: Patriarchy and its Discontents', in Richard Lane, Rod Menghan and Philip Tew (eds) *Contemporary British Fiction*, London and New York: Polity, 239–55.

Douglass, Ana and Thomas A. Vogler (2003) 'Introduction', in Ana Douglass and Thomas A. Vogler (eds) *Witness and Memory: The Discourse of Trauma*, New York and London, 1–53.

Eagleton, Terry (1998) 'Postcolonialism and "Postcolonialism"', *Interventions: International Journal of Postcolonial Studies*, 1 (1) October, 24–6.

Eliade, Mircea (1963) *Myth and Reality*, New York and London: Harper & Row; trans. Willard R. Trask.

Emery, Mary Lou (1997) ' "Space Sounds" in Wilson Harris's Recent Fiction', *The Review of Contemporary Fiction*, 17 (2), 98–103.

Erickson, John (1998) *Islam and Postcolonial Narrative*, Cambridge and New York: Cambridge University Press.

Erikson, Kai (1995) 'Notes on Trauma and Community', in Cathy Caruth (ed.) *Trauma: Explorations in Memory*, Baltimore and London: Johns Hopkins University Press, 183–99.

Fanon, Frantz (1967) [1963] *The Wretched of the Earth*, Harmondsworth: Penguin; introd. Jean-Paul Sartre; trans. Constance Farrington.

Fokkema, Aleid (1991) *Postmodern Characters*, Amsterdam and Atlanta, GA: Editions Rodopi B. V.

Fornäs, Johan (1995) *Cultural Theory and Late Modernity*, London and Thousand Oaks, CA: Sage.

Fraser, Robert (2000) *Lifting the Sentence: A Poetics of Postcolonial Fiction*, Manchester and New York: Manchester University Press.

Fyrth, Jim (ed.) (1993) *Labour's High Noon: The Government and the Economy 1945–51*, London: Lawrence & Wishart.

Gandhi, Leela (1998) *Postcolonial Theory: A Critical Introduction*, Edinburgh: Edinburgh University Press.

Gąsiorek, Andrej (1995) *Post-War British Fiction: Realism and After*, London: Arnold.

George, Rosemary Marangoly (1996) *The Politics of Home: Postcolonial Relocations and Twentieth-Century Fiction*, Cambridge and New York: Cambridge University Press.

Gibson, Andrew (1999) *Postmodernity, Ethics and the Novel: From Leavis to Levinas*, London and New York: Routledge.

Gray, John (2003) *Al Qaeda and What it Means to be Modern*, London: Faber & Faber.

Habermas, Jürgen (1990) *The Philosophical Discourse of Modernity: Twelve Lectures*, Cambridge: Polity Press; trans. Frederick Lawrence

Hakraharty, Dipesh (2000) *Provincializing Europe: Postcolonial Thought and Historical Difference*, Princeton and Oxford: Princeton University Press.

Halliday, Fred (2002) *Two Hours that Shook the World: September 11, 2001: Causes and Consequences*, London: Saqi Books.

Hallward, Peter (2001) *Absolutely Postcolonial: Writing Between the Singular and the Specific*, Manchester and New York: Manchester University Press.

Haywood, Ian (1997) *Working-class Fiction from Chartism to 'Trainspotting'*, Plymouth: Northcote House in association with the British Council.

Head, Dominic (2002) *The Cambridge Introduction to Modern British Fiction, 1950–2000*, Cambridge and New York: Cambridge University Press.

Head, Dominic (2003) 'Zadie Smith's *White Teeth*: Multiculturalism for the Millennium', in Richard Lane, Rod Menghan and Philip Tew (eds) *Contemporary British Fiction*, London and New York: Polity, 106–19.

Higdon, David Leon (1984) *Shadows of the Past in Contemporary British Fiction*, London: Macmillan.

Holmes, Frederick M. (1997) *The Historical Imagination: Postmodernism and the Treatment of the Past in Contemporary British Fiction*, Victoria, BC: University of Victoria [ELS Monograph Series no. 73].

Huggan, Graham (2001) *The Postcolonial Exotic: Marketing the Margins*, London and New York: Routledge.

Hutcheon, Linda (1988) *A Poetics of Postmodernism: History, Theory, Fiction*, London and New York: Routledge.

Hutcheon, Linda (1989) *The Politics of Postmodernism*, London and New York: Routledge.

Hutcheon, Linda (1994) *Irony's Edge: The Theory and Politics of Irony*, London and New York: Routledge.

Hutton, Will (1997) *The State to Come*, London: Vintage.

Jack, Ian (ed.) (2003a) *Granta 81: Best of Young British Novelists 2003*, London and New York: Granta.

Jack, Ian (2003b) 'Introduction', in Ian Jack (ed.) *Granta 81: Best of Young British Novelists 2003*, London and New York: Granta, 9–14.

Johnson, B. S. (1973) *Aren't You Rather Young to be Writing Your Memoirs?* London: Hutchison.

Keenan, Brian (1993) [1992] *An Evil Cradling*, London: Hutchison.

King, Roger (1979) 'The Middle Class in Revolt?', in Roger King and Neill Nugent (eds) *Respectable Rebels: Middle Class Campaigns in Britain in the 1970s*, London: Hodder & Stoughton, 1–22.

King, Roger and Neill Nugent (eds) (1979) *Respectable Rebels: Middle Class Campaigns in Britain in the 1970s*, London: Hodder & Stoughton.

Lakoff, George and Mark Johnson (1980) *Metaphors We Live By*, Chicago: University of Chicago Press.

Lamarque, Peter (1996) *Fictional Points of View*, Ithaca and London: Cornell University Press.

Lane, Richard Rod Mengham and Philip Tew (eds) (2003a) *Contemporary British Fiction*, Cambridge: Polity Press.

Lane, Richard and Philip Tew (2003b) 'Introduction: Cultural Hybridity', in Richard Lane, Rod Mengham and Philip Tew (eds) Contemporary British Fiction, Cambridge: Polity Press, 143–4.

Lee, Alison (1990) Realism and Power: Postmodern British Fiction, London: Routledge.

Lee, A. Robert (ed.) (1995a) Other Britain, Other British: Contemporary Multicultural Fiction, London: Pluto Press.

Lee, A. Robert (1995b) 'Changing the Script: Sex, Lies and Videotapes in Hanif Kureishi, David Dabydeen and Mike Phillips', in A. Robert Lee (ed.) Other Britain, Other British: Contemporary Multicultural Fiction, London: Pluto Press, 69–89

Lefebvre, Henri (1991) [1974] The Production of Space, Oxford and Cambridge, MA: Blackwell; trans. Donald Nicholson-Smith.

LeGuin, Ursula (2006) 'Revolution in the Aisles', The Guardian, Saturday Review, 9 September, 16.

Leys, Ruth (2000) Trauma: A Genealogy, Chicago and London: University of Chicago Press.

López, José and Garry Potter (eds) (2001) After Postmodernism: An Introduction to Critical Realism, London and New York: Athlone.

Lovatt, David (1980) Unemployment and Class Conflict in Britain During the 1970s, London: University College London, Bartlett School of Architecture & Planning [Town planning discussion paper no. 35].

Luckhurst, Roger (1997) 'The Angle Between Two Walls': The Fiction of J. G. Ballard, Liverpool: Liverpool University Press.

Luckhurst, Roger (2003) 'Traumaculture', in Joe Booker and Roger Luckhurst (eds) New Formations: A Journal of Contemporary Culture/Theory/Politics: Remembering the 1990s, 50 Autumn, 28–47.

Lynch, Kevin (1960) The Image of the City, Cambridge, MA and London: MIT Press.

Lynch, Kevin (1972) What Time Is This Place? Cambridge, MA and London: MIT Press.

Mac Cormac, Earl R. (1985) A Cognitive Theory of Metaphor, Cambridge, MA and London: MIT Press.

McDonough, Frank (1997) 'Class and Politics', in Mike Storry and Peter Childs (eds) British Cultural Identities, London and New York: Routledge, 201–39.

McEwan, Neil (1981) The Survival of the Novel: British Fiction in the Later Twentieth Century, London: Macmillan.

McHale, Brian (1987) Postmodernist Fiction, New York and London: Methuen.

Macherey, Pierre (1995) [1990] The Object of Literature, Cambridge and New York: Cambridge University Press; trans. David Macey.

Macleod, John (2005) 'Revisiting Postcolonial London', The European English Messenger, 14 (2) Autumn, 39–46.

Marcuse, Herbert (1964) One-Dimensional Man: Studies in the Ideology of Advanced Industrial Society, London: Routledge & Kegan Paul.

Marcuse, Herbert (1968) Negations: Essays in Critical Theory, London: Allen Lane; partial trans. Jeremy J. Shapiro.

Marwick, Arthur (1991) Culture in Britain since 1945, Oxford and Cambridge, MA: Basil Blackwell.

Mengham, Rod (1999a) 'Introduction', in Rod Mengham (ed.) An Introduction to Contemporary Fiction: International Writing in English since 1970, Cambridge: Polity Press, 1–11.

Mengham, Rod (ed.) (1999b) An Introduction to Contemporary Fiction: International Writing in English since 1970, Cambridge: Polity Press.

Mengham, Rod (2003) 'General Introduction: Contemporary British Fiction', in Richard Lane, Rod Menghan and Philip Tew (eds) Contemporary British Fiction, London and New York: Polity, 1–7.

Middlemas, Keith (1991) Power, Competition and the State: Volume 3 The End of the Postwar Era: Britain Since 1974, Basingstoke: Macmillan.

Middleton Myer, Kim (2003) 'Jeanette Winterson's Evolving Subject: "Difficulty into Dream"', in Richard Lane, Rod Menghan and Philip Tew (eds) Contemporary British Fiction, London and New York: Polity, 210–25.

Miller, J. Hillis (1990) *Tropes, Parables, Performatives: Essays on Twentieth-Century Literature*, New York and London: Harvester Wheatsheaf.

Milne, Drew (2003) 'The Fiction of James Kelman and Irvine Welsh: Accents, Speech and Writing', in Richard Lane, Rod Menghan and Philip Tew (eds) *Contemporary British Fiction*, London and New York: Polity, 158–73.

Moore-Gilbert, Bart (2001) *Hanif Kureishi*, Manchester and New York: Manchester University Press.

Moretti, Franco (1983) *Signs Taken for Wonders: Essays in the Sociology of Literary Forms*, London: Verso; trans. Susan Fischer, David Forgacs and David Miller.

Mulhern, Francis (1990) 'English Reading', in Homi K. Bhabha (ed.) *Nation and Narration*, London and New York: Routledge, 250–64

Murdoch, Iris (1977) [1961] 'Against Dryness: A Polemical Sketch', in Malcolm Bradbury (ed.) (1977) *The Novel Today: Contemporary Writers on Modern Fiction*, Manchester: Manchester University Press, 23–31.

Murray, Stuart (1997) 'Postcoloniality/Modernity: Wilson Harris and Postcolonial Theory', *The Review of Contemporary Fiction*, 17 (2), 53–8.

Neagu, Adriana and Sean Matthews 'Peter Ackroyd', at British Council website http://www.contemporarywriters.com/authors

Neal, Arthur G. (2005) *National Trauma and Collective Memory: Extraordinary Events in the American Experience*, 2nd edition, Armonk, New York and London: M. E. Sharpe.

Norris, Christopher (1982) *Deconstruction: Theory and Practice*, London and New York: Routledge.

Nugent, Neill (1979) 'The National Association for Freedom', in Roger King and Neill Nugent (eds) *Respectable Rebels: Middle Class Campaigns in Britain in the 1970s*, London: Hodder & Stoughton, 76–100.

O'Connor, Michael (2005) 'Writing Against Terror – Nadeem Aslam', *Three Monkeys Online*, July, www.threemonkeysonline.com/article_nadeem_aslam_interview.htm [accessed 22 August 2006, n. pag.].

Orwell, George (1970) [1968; 1941] 'The Lion and the Unicorn: Socialism and the English Genius - "Part 1: England Your England"', in Sonia Orwell and Ian Angus (eds) *The Collected Essays, Journalism and Letters of George Orwell*, Volume II 'My Country Right or Left 1940–1943*, London: Penguin, 74–99.

Pajaczakowska, Claire (1997) 'The Ecstatic Solace of Culture: Self, Not-self and Other; a Psychoanalytic View', in Juliet Steyn (ed.) *Other Than Identity: The Subject, Politics and Art*, Manchester and New York: Manchester University Press, 101–12.

Parrinder, Patrick (1991) *Authors and Authority. English and American Criticism 1750–1990*, London: Macmillan.

Peterson, Nancy J. (2001) *Against Amnesia: Contemporary Women Writers and the Crises of Historical Memory*, Philadelphia : University of Pennsylvania Press.

Pols, Edward (1982) *The Acts of Our Being: A Reflection on Agency and Responsibility*, Amherst: University of Massachusetts Press.

Pols, Edward (1992) *Radical Realism: Direct Knowing in Science and Philosophy*, Ithaca and London: Cornell University Press.

Pols, Edward (1998) *Mind Regained*, Ithaca and London: Cornell University Press.

Ratcliffe, Sophie (2005) 'Life in Sonnet Form', *TLS*, 20 May, 19–20.

Ricoeur, Paul (1969) [1967] *The Symbolism of Evil*, Boston: Beacon Press; trans. Emerson Buchanan.

Riddell, Peter (1989) *The Thatcher Decade: How Britain Has Changed During the 1980s*, Oxford and Cambridge, MA: Blackwell.

Rimmon-Kenan, Shlomith (1983) *Narrative Fiction: Contemporary Poetics*, London and New York: Routledge.

Rushdie, Salman (1992) [1991] *Imaginary Homelands: Essays and Criticism, 1981–1991* (rev. edn 1992), London: Granta.

Sadler, Michael (2005) 'A Sanguinary Tale', *TLS*, 15 April, 20.

San Juan Jr, E. (1998) *Beyond Postcolonial Theory*, London: Macmillan.

Sanga, Jaina C. (2001) *Salman Rushdie's Postcolonial Metaphors: Migration, Translation,*

Hybridity, Blasphemy, and Globalization, Westport, CT: Greenwood.

Sauerberg, Lars Ole (1991) *Fact into Fiction: Documentary Realism in the Contemporary Novel*, New York: St Martin's Press.

Scarborough, Milton (1994) *Myth and Modernity: Postcritical Reflections*, Albany, NY: State University of New York Press.

Schwarz, Daniel R. (1997) *Reconfiguring Modernism: Explorations in the Relationship between Modern Art and Modern Literature*, London: Macmillan; New York: St Martin's Press.

Self, Will (1995) *Junk Mail*, London: Bloomsbury.

Self, Will (2000) *Sore Sites*, London: Ellipsis.

Self, Will and David Gamble (2000) *Perfidious Man*, London and New York: Viking.

Seltzer, Mark (1997) 'Wound Culture: Trauma in the Pathological Public Sphere', *October*, 80 (Spring), 3–26.

Sheppard, Richard (2000) *Modernism – Dada – Postmodernism*, Evanston, IL: Northwestern University Press.

Smyth, Edmund J. (1991a) *Postmodernism and Contemporary Fiction*, London: B. T. Batsford.

Smyth, Edmund J. (1991b) 'The Nouveau Roman: Modernity and Postmodernity', in Edmund J. Smyth (ed.) *Postmodernism and Contemporary Fiction*, London: B. T. Batsford, 54–73.

Sommer, Doris (1990) 'Irresistible Romance: Foundational Fictions of Latin America', in Homi K. Bhabha (ed.) *Nation and Narration*, London and New York: Routledge, 71–98.

Spivak, Gayatri Chakravorty (1999) *A Critique of Postcolonial Reason: Toward a Vanishing History of the Present*, Cambridge, MA and London: Harvard University Press.

Stevenson, Randall (2004) 'Big Sister', *TLS*, 19 March, 21.

Steyn, Juliet (ed.) *Other Than Identity: The Subject, Politics and Art*, Manchester and New York: Manchester University Press.

Stonehill, Brian (1988) *The Self-Conscious Novel: Artifice in Fiction from Joyce to Pynchon*, Philadelphia: University of Pennsylvania Press.

Storry, Mike and Peter Childs (eds) (1997) *British Cultural Identities*, London and New York: Routledge.

Sztompka, Piotr (2004) 'The Trauma of Social Change: A Case of Postcommunist Societies', in Jeffrey C. Alexander, Ron Eyerman, Bernhard Giesen, Neil J. Smelser, and Piotr Sztompka, *Cultural Trauma and Collective Identity*, Berkeley, Los Angeles and London: University of California Press, 155–95.

Taylor, D. J. (1989) *A Vain Conceit: British Fiction in the 1980s*, London: Bloomsbury.

Tew, Philip (2001a) *B. S. Johnson: A Critical Reading*, Manchester and New York: Manchester University Press.

Tew, Philip (2001b) 'Reconsidering Literary Interpretation', in José López and Garry Potter (eds) *After Postmodernism: An Introduction to Critical Realism*, London and New York: Athlone, 196–205.

Thieme, John (2001) *Postcolonial Con-Texts: Writing Back to the Canon*, London and New York: Continuum.

Thiong'o, Ngũgĩ Wa (1986) *Decolonizing the Mind: The Politics of Language in African Literature*, London: Currey.

Valdés, Mario J. (1987) *Phenomenological Hermeneutics and the Study of Literature*, Toronto: University of Toronto Press.

Valdés, Mario J. and Owen Miller (eds) (1985) *Identity of the Literary Text*, Toronto, Buffalo and London: University of Toronto Press.

Wells, Lynn (2003) *Allegories of Telling: Self-Referential Narrative in Contemporary British Fiction*, Amsterdam and New York: Editions Rodopi B. V.

Wheeler, Wendy (1999) *A New Modernity? Change in Science, Literature and Politics*, London: Lawrence & Wishart.

Wilson, Angus (1983) [1961] 'The View from the 1950s', in Angus Wilson, *Diversity and Depth in Fiction: Selected Critical Writings of Angus Wilson*, London: Secker & Warburg, 120–39; ed. Kerry McSweeney .

Wilson, Angus (1983) [1967] 'Evil in the English Novel', in Angus Wilson, *Diversity and Depth in Fiction: Selected Critical Writings of Angus Wilson*, London: Secker & Warburg, 3–24; ed. Kerry McSweeney.

Wilson, Angus (1983) *Diversity and Depth in Fiction: Selected Critical Writings of Angus Wilson*, London: Secker & Warburg; ed. Kerry McSweeney.

Wilson, Leigh (2006) 'Possessing Toby Litt's *Ghost Story*', in Philip Tew and Rod Mengham (eds) *British Fiction Today*, London: Continuum, 105–16.

Young, Robert J. C. (1995) *Colonial Desire: Hybridity in Theory, Culture and Race*, London and New York: Routledge.

Index